Case Study Research

Principles and Practices

Case Study Research: Principles and Practices provides a general understanding of the case study method as well as specific tools for its successful implementation. These tools are applicable in a variety of fields, including anthropology, business and management, communications, economics, education, medicine, political science, psychology, social work, and sociology. Topics include: a survey of case study approaches; a methodologically tractable definition of "case study"; strategies for case selection, including random sampling and other algorithmic approaches; quantitative and qualitative modes of case study analysis; and problems of internal and external validity. The new edition of this core textbook is designed to be accessible to readers who are new to the subject and is thoroughly revised and updated, incorporating recent research.

John Gerring is Professor of Government at University of Texas at Austin. He is the author of *Party Ideologies in America, 1828–1996* (Cambridge, 1998), *A Centripetal Theory of Democratic Governance* (Cambridge, 2008), *Concepts and Method: Giovanni Sartori and His Legacy* (with David Collier, 2009), *Social Science Methodology: A Unified Framework*, 2nd edition (Cambridge, 2012), and *Applied Social Science Methodology: An Introductory Guide* (with Dino Christenson, Cambridge, 2017), along with numerous articles.

Strategies for Social Inquiry

Case Study Research Principles and Practices

Editors

Colin Elman, *Maxwell School of Syracuse University*
John Gerring, *University of Texas at Austin*
James Mahoney, *Northwestern University*

Editorial Board

This book series presents texts on a wide range of issues bearing upon the practice of social inquiry. Strategies are construed broadly to embrace the full spectrum of approaches to analysis, as well as relevant issues in philosophy of social science.

Published Titles

John Gerring, *Social Science Methodology: A Unified Framework*, 2nd edition
Michael Coppedge, *Democratization and Research Methods*
Thad Dunning, *Natural Experiments in the Social Sciences: A Design-Based Approach*
Carsten Q. Schneider and Claudius Wagemann, *Set-Theoretic Methods for the Social Sciences: A Guide to Qualitative Comparative Analysis*
Nicholas Weller and Jeb Barnes, *Finding Pathways: Mixed-Method Research for Studying Causal Mechanisms*
Andrew Bennett and Jeffrey T. Checkel, *Process Tracing: From Metaphor to Analytic Tool*
Diana Kapiszewski, Lauren M. MacLean, and Benjamin L. Read, *Field Research in Political Science: Practices and Principles*
Peter Spiegler, *Behind the Model: A Constructive Critique of Economic Modeling*

James Mahoney and Kathleen Thelen, *Advances in Comparative-Historical Analysis*

Jason Seawright, *Multi-Method Social Science: Combining Qualitative and Quantitative Tools*

Case Study Research

Principles and Practices

Second Edition

John Gerring
University of Texas at Austin

CAMBRIDGE
UNIVERSITY PRESS

CAMBRIDGE
UNIVERSITY PRESS

University Printing House, Cambridge CB2 8BS, United Kingdom

One Liberty Plaza, 20th Floor, New York, NY 10006, USA

477 Williamstown Road, Port Melbourne, VIC 3207, Australia

4843/24, 2nd Floor, Ansari Road, Daryaganj, Delhi – 110002, India

79 Anson Road, #06–04/06, Singapore 079906

Cambridge University Press is part of the University of Cambridge.

It furthers the University's mission by disseminating knowledge in the pursuit of education, learning, and research at the highest international levels of excellence.

www.cambridge.org
Information on this title: www.cambridge.org/9781107181267
DOI: 10.1017/9781316848593

First published 2017

Printed in the United States of America by Sheridan Books, Inc.

A catalogue record for this publication is available from the British Library.

Library of Congress Cataloging-in-Publication Data
Names: Gerring, John, 1962– author.
Title: Case study research : principles and practices / John Gerring.
Description: Second edition. | Cambridge, United Kingdom ; New York, NY : Cambridge University Press, 2017. | Series: Strategies for social inquiry
Identifiers: LCCN 2016025901 | ISBN 9781107181267 (Hardback)
Subjects: LCSH: Social sciences–Research–Methodology. | Case method. | BISAC: POLITICAL SCIENCE / General.
Classification: LCC H62 .G47 2017 | DDC 001.4/33–dc23 LC record available at https://lccn.loc.gov/2016025901

ISBN 978-1-107-18126-7 Hardback
ISBN 978-1-316-63250-5 Paperback

Truth, naked and cold, had been turned away from every door in the village. Her nakedness frightened the people. When Parable found her, she was huddled in a corner, shivering and hungry. Taking pity on her, Parable gathered her up and took her home. There, she dressed Truth in Story, warmed her, and sent her out again. Clothed in Story, Truth knocked again at the villagers' doors and was readily welcomed into the people's houses. They invited her to eat at their table and to warm herself by the fire.

Jewish Teaching Story

People foolishly imagine that the broad generalities of social phenomena afford an excellent opportunity to penetrate further into the human soul; they ought, on the contrary, to realise that it is by plumbing the depths of a single personality that they might have a chance of understanding those phenomena.

Marcel Proust (1992: 450; quoted in Ginzburg 2007: 256)

Historical knowledge and generalization (i.e., classificatory and nomothetic) knowledge ... differ merely in the relative emphasis they put upon the one or the other of the two essential and complementary directions of scientific research: in both cases we find a movement from concrete reality to abstract concepts and from abstract concepts back to concrete reality – a ceaseless pulsation which keeps science alive and forging ahead.

Florian Znaniecki (1934: 25)

Immersion in the particular proved, as usual, essential for the catching of anything general.

Albert Hirschman (1967: 3)

The examination, surrounded by all its documentary techniques, makes each individual a "case": a case which at one and the same time constitutes an object for a branch of knowledge and a hold for a branch of power. The case is no longer, as in casuistry or jurisprudence, a set of circumstances defining an act and capable of modifying the application of a rule; it is the individual as he may be described, judged, measured, compared with others, in his very individuality; and it is also the individual who has to be trained or corrected, classified, normalized, excluded, etc.

Michel Foucault (1977:191; quoted in Forrester 1996: 12)

Contents

Figures

Tables

Preface

There are two ways to learn about a subject. One may study many examples at once, focusing on a few selected dimensions of the phenomena. Or, one may study a particular example, or several examples, in greater depth.

I shall refer to the first as a large-C approach, characterized by a large number of cases (denoted C) and a correspondingly narrow focus of attention. I shall refer to the second as a small-C or *case study* approach, characterized by one or several cases and a correspondingly broad focus of attention.[1]

While both are concerned with the same general subject they follow different paths to this goal. But they are not equally regarded. At the heart of social science lies a fundamental conflict between extensive and intensive modes of analysis.

By the standard of praxis, the case study method is flourishing (see Chapter 1). At the same time, case studies continue to be viewed with extreme circumspection. A work that focuses its attention on a single example of a broader phenomenon is apt to be described as a "mere" case study, and is often identified with loosely framed ideas, non-generalizable theories, biased case selection, undisciplined research designs, weak empirical leverage (too many variables and too few cases), subjective conclusions, and non-replicability.

This is a historic reversal of the case study's origins. When the term "case study" first entered scientific usage at the turn of the twentieth

---

[1] I reserve "N" to refer to the number of observations in a study, which is quite different from the number of cases (C) – a crucial distinction, as it turns out (see Chapter 8).

century, it represented an attempt to think more systematically about evidence and inference. Narratives about X were to be understood as "cases," signifying their connection to a broader set of phenomena and the possibility of developing a general theory of X. In this manner, it was thought that knowledge would cumulate and general theories would be formulated and systematically tested.

By the 1920s, however, the term had become suspect. In one of the first attempts to contrast case study and non-case study approaches to social science, Stuart Rice (1928: Chapter 4) associated the former with "history" and the latter with "statistics" and "science" – a telling contrast.[2] A few years later, Willard Waller (1934: 296–7) described the case study approach as an essentially *artistic* process.

Men who can produce good case studies, accurate and convincing pictures of people and institutions, are essentially artists; they may not be learned men, and sometimes they are not even intelligent men, but they have imagination and know how to use words to convey truth.

The product of a good case study is *insight*, and insight is

the unknown quantity which has eluded students of scientific method. That is why the really great men of sociology had no "method." They had a method; it was the search for insight. They went "by guess and by God," but they found out things (Waller 1934: 296–7).

Several decades later, Julian Simon (1969: 267, quoted in Platt 1992: 18) opines,

The specific method of the case study depends upon the mother wit, common sense and imagination of the person doing the case study. The investigator makes up his procedure as he goes along.

Practitioners of this method are prone to invoking its name in vain – as an all-purpose excuse, a license to do whatever a researcher

---

[2] See also Lazarsfeld and Robinson (1940), Sarbin (1943, 1944).

wishes to do with his or her particular topic. Zeev Maoz (2002: 164–5) noted recently,

There is a nearly complete lack of documentation of the approach to data collection, data management, and data analysis and inference in case study research. In contrast to other research strategies in political research where authors devote considerable time and effort to document the technical aspects of their research, one often gets the impression that the use of case study absolves the author from any kind of methodological considerations. Case studies have become in many cases a synonym for freeform research where everything goes and the author does not feel compelled to spell out how he or she intends to do the research, why a specific case or set of cases has been selected, which data are used and which are omitted, how data are processed and analyzed, and how inferences were derived from the story presented. Yet, at the end of the story, we often find sweeping generalizations and "lessons" derived from this case.

To say that one is conducting a case study sometimes seems to imply that normal methodological rules do not apply; that one has entered a different methodological or epistemological (perhaps even ontological) zone. Here, the term functions as an ambiguous designation covering a multitude of "inferential felonies."[3]

In the field of psychology, a gulf separates "scientists" engaged in large-*C* research and "practitioners" engaged in clinical research,

---

[3] Achen and Snidal (1989: 160). See also Geddes (1990, 2003), Goldthorpe (1997), King *et al.* (1994), Lieberson (1985: 107–15, 1992, 1994), Lijphart (1971: 683–4), Odell (2004), Sekhon (2004), Smelser (1973: 45, 57). In psychology, Kratochwill (1978: 4–5) writes: "Case study methodology was typically characterized by numerous sources of uncontrolled variation, inadequate description of independent/dependent variables, was generally difficult to replicate. While this made case study methodology of little scientific value, it helped to generate hypotheses for subsequent research." See also Hersen and Barlow (1976: Chapter 1), Meehl (1954). It should be underlined that these writers, while critical of the case study format, are not necessarily opposed to case studies per se; that is to say, they should not be classified as *opponents* of the case study.

usually focused on one or several cases.[4] In the fields of political science and sociology, case study researchers are acknowledged to be on the soft side of increasingly hard disciplines. And across fields, the case study orientations of cultural anthropology, education, law, social work, and various other fields relegate them to the non-rigorous, non-systematic, non-scientific, non-positivist end of the academic spectrum.

Even among its defenders, there is confusion over the virtues and vices of this ambiguous research design. Practitioners continue to ply their trade but have difficulty articulating what it is they are doing, methodologically speaking. The case study survives in a curious methodological limbo.

This leads to a paradox. Although much of what we know about the empirical world has been generated by case studies and case studies continue to constitute a significant proportion of work generated by the social science disciplines (see Chapter 1), the case study *method* is unappreciated, perhaps even under siege.

How can we make sense of the profound disjuncture between the acknowledged contributions of this genre and its maligned status? If case studies are methodologically flawed, why do they persist? Should they be rehabilitated, or suppressed? How fruitful *is* this style of research? And, finally, in what respects can current practices be improved?

Situating this book

This book aims to provide a general understanding of the case study as well as the tools and techniques necessary for its successful

---

[4] Hersen and Barlow (1976: 21) write that in the 1960s, when this split developed, "clinical procedures were largely judged as unproven, the prevailing naturalistic research was unacceptable to most scientists concerned with precise definition of variables, cause-effect relationships. On the other hand, the elegantly designed, scientifically rigorous group comparison design was seen as impractical, incapable of dealing with the complexities, idiosyncrasies of individuals by most clinicians."

implementation. The subtitle reflects my dual concern with general principles as well as specific practices. To assist the reader, a number of differences between this work and others on the same general topic should be signaled at the outset.

First, this book does not attempt to vindicate or vilify the case study method. There is much to be said "for" and "against" it. I think the genre is best served by a clear-eyed depiction of the pros and cons so that researchers can understand the benefits, as well as the limitations, of adopting a case study format. If the tone of the book is occasionally defensive, it is only because I wish to dispel certain misperceptions that (in my opinion) serve to downgrade the contributions of case studies to the work of social science.

Second, this book adopts what might be called (if one can stomach the term) a "positivist" approach to case study research. That is, I hope to show that case studies can be employed in a rigorous, systematic, replicable, and theoretically informed fashion – one that is fully consistent with, and complementary to, work conducted with a large sample of cases (large-C research).

Third, the book gives special attention to the role of case studies in facilitating causal analysis. This is because the descriptive aspects of case studies are difficult to distinguish from methods of data collection, e.g., surveys, interviews, ethnographies, archival research, and so forth. These topics are not unique to case study research, are well covered by other texts, and are not especially problematic from a methodological point of view. What is problematic – at least in the eyes of many methodologists – is the attempt to reach causal inferences from case study evidence. Accordingly, we focus our attention on this vexed subject. Even so, we should not lose sight of the fact that many of the most influential case studies are descriptive in nature. I hope, therefore, to encompass both sub-genres in the chapters that follow.

Fourth, rather than focusing on a single field or sub-field of the social sciences, I take a broad, cross-disciplinary view of the topic. My conviction is that the methodological issues entailed by the case study method are general rather than field-specific. Moreover, by examining basic methodological issues in widely varying empirical contexts we sometimes gain insights into these issues that are not apparent from a narrower perspective. Examples discussed in this book are drawn from all fields of the social sciences, and occasionally from the natural sciences and humanities. To be sure, the discussion betrays a pronounced tilt towards my own discipline, political science. However, the arguments should be equally applicable to other fields in the social sciences.

Fifth, this volume does not intend to provide a comprehensive review of methodological issues pertaining to social science research.[5] My intention, rather, is to home in on those issues that pertain specifically to case study research. Issues that apply equally to small- and large-C analysis are given short shrift. Thus, I do not have much to say about the process of data collection, the discovery of new ideas (the formulation of theories), the nature of causal inference, research ethics, or issues of epistemology or philosophy of science. Likewise, techniques drawn from the field of statistics and econometrics – *regression, matching, cluster analysis,* and so forth – are not fully explained or developed. To do so would require a very different sort of book. Readers who wish to know more about these and other topics touched upon in the text may consult cited references or general introductions to social science methodology and statistics.[6]

---

[5] Some case study textbooks seem to cover the subject of social research in its entirety – conceptualization, measurement, research design, analysis, along with reflections on epistemology and philosophy of science. As such, they function as introductory methods texts with a special focus on qualitative research methods (e.g., Berg and Lune 2011; Hancke 2009; Somekh and Lewin 2005; Yin 2009).

[6] General introductions to social science methodology include Gerring (2012b) and King *et al.* (1994) – pitched to graduate students – and Gerring and Christenson (2017), which is designed for an undergraduate or master's level audience. Introductory statistics texts are legion. Readers primarily concerned with causal inference might consider Angrist and Pischke (2009) or their shorter, pithier text (Angrist and Pischke 2015).

Even with respect to issues pertaining directly to case study research, the present volume cannot hope to be entirely comprehensive. Fortunately, there is now a sizeable literature on these topics. Readers looking for more in-depth treatment of various subjects are advised to follow the trail of citations in the text or meander through the voluminous references at the end of the book.

Finally, it should be emphasized that the text is designed to make the material accessible to readers who are new to the subject. Notation is minimal (see Key symbols and terms). Debates with the literature are minimized, or relegated to footnotes. Key terms are defined in the text, and may be located by consulting page references in the Index. At the end of each chapter, a concluding section summarizes the main points that have been presented.

I hope that the book is useful for those who are embarking for the first time in a social science field as well as those who have completed many voyages.

Outline

Part I of the book establishes our subject. Chapter 1 surveys the field of case study research across the social sciences. Chapter 2 proposes definitions for "case study" and associated terms. A great deal flows from these definitions so the chapter should not be passed over quickly.

Part II deals with case selection – the choice of cases to analyze intensively. Chapter 3 sets forth a summary of strategies. This serves to introduce readers to a wide variety of work conducted in a case study mode and more specifically, to illustrate the diversity of methods that may be employed to select cases for intensive analysis. Chapter 4 focuses on the selection of cases for purposes of description and Chapter 5 on the selection of cases for the purpose of causal inference. Chapter 6 discusses the application of random sampling and other algorithmic approaches to case selection, as well as the viability of medium-C samples.

Part III deals with methods of analysis – what to do with cases once they are chosen. Chapter 7 establishes a typology of research designs, distinguishing among case studies, large-C studies, and multimethod studies. Chapter 8 distinguishes quantitative and qualitative modes of analysis, focusing primarily on the latter.

Part IV deals with the problem of validity. Chapter 9 focuses on internal validity and Chapter 10 on external validity.

The book concludes, in Chapter 11, with a series of comparisons and contrasts between small-C and large-C research in order to understand their distinctive affinities. I argue that the many of the perceived weaknesses of the case study are overcome if case studies are complemented by large-C studies of the same general topic. Multimethod work – whether incorporated in the same study or in different studies – often provides a reasonable solution to situations where case studies sit uneasily on their own.

Acknowledgements

This book evolved from a series of papers (Gerring 2004b, 2006a, 2006b, 2007b, 2017; Gerring and Cojocaru 2016; Gerring and McDermott 2007; Gerring and Thomas 2005; Seawright and Gerring 2008). I am grateful to my collaborators and also to the publishers of these papers for permission to adapt these works for use in the present volume.

Drafts of the first edition were presented at Bremen University in 2004, sponsored by the Transformations of the State Collaborative Research Center (CRC); at the Third Congress of the Working Group on Approaches and Methods in Comparative Politics, Liège, Belgium; at the annual meetings of the Institute for Qualitative Research (IQRM); and at the annual meetings of the American Political Science Association. I am thankful for comments and suggestions from participants at these gatherings.

For detailed feedback on the first edition, I owe thanks to Andy Bennett, Melani Cammett, Kanchan Chandra, Renske Doorenspleet, Colin Elman, Gary Goertz, Shareen Hertel, Ronggui Huang, Staci Kaiser, Bernhard Kittel, Ned Lebow, Jack Levy, Evan Lieberman, Jim Mahoney, Ellen Mastenbroek, Devra Moehler, Howard Reiter, Kirsten Rodine, Ingo Rohlfing, Richard Snyder, Peter Starke, Craig Thomas, Lily Tsai, and David Woodruff. For clarification on various subjects, I am in debt to Bear Braumoeller, Patrick Johnston, Jason Seawright, Jas Sekhon, and Peter Spiegler.

The impetus for a second edition, nearly a decade after the first, came partly in response to the ongoing trajectory of work on case study methodology and related topics. Important recent works include Beach and Pedersen (2013), Bennett and Checkel (2015), Blatter and

Haverland (2012), Fearon and Laitin (2008, 2014, 2015), Glynn and Ichino (2015, 2016), Goertz (2017), Herron and Quinn (2016), Humphreys and Jacobs (2015), Levy (2008a, 2008b), Lieberman (2015), Mahoney (2012), Mahoney and Thelen (2015), Nielsen (2016), Rohlfing (2012), Schneider and Rohlfing (2013, 2016), Seawright (2016a, 2016b), Soifer (2015), Waldner (2012, 2015a, 2015b, 2016), and Weller and Barnes (2014).

Readers of the second edition will find a book that is re-written from scratch, with a revised summary of case-selection methods, an expanded section focused on case analysis, and a somewhat revised notation.

A preliminary draft of the revised manuscript was presented at the Authors' Workshop at the Institute for Qualitative and Multimethod Research, Syracuse University, June, 2015. I want to thank members of that workshop and others who have read various versions of the manuscript. This includes Colin Elman, Danny Hidalgo, Nahomi Ichino, Kendra Koivu, Markus Kreuzer, Jack Levy, Jim Mahoney, Gerry Munck, Hillel Soifer, and Nick Weller. For clarification and feedback on specific issues, I am grateful to Jim Fearon, Adam Glynn, and David Laitin. Carl Gershenson, along with several reviewers for the Press, gave the manuscript a thorough read and contributed greatly to its present shape. I am grateful to Gary Goertz for sharing his book manuscript – which will be published concurrently (Goertz 2017) – and for feedback on the text. Thanks to John Haslam from Cambridge University Press, who shepherded the book through review and production.

My final acknowledgement is to the generations of scholars who have written on this topic – whose ideas I appropriate, misrepresent, or warp beyond recognition. (In academic venues, the first is recognized as a citation, the second is known as a reinterpretation, and the third is called original research.) Specialists will appreciate the extent to which this book is a compendium of ideas extending back to an earlier generation of methodological work on the case study method by the likes of Donald Campbell, David Collier, Harry Eckstein, Alexander

George, Barney Glaser and Anselm Strauss, Arend Lijphart, Adam Przeworski and Henry Teune, and Neil Smelser – not to mention prior work by logicians and philosophers such as J.S. Mill and Cohen and Nagel. My debts are apparent in the crowded footnotes and lengthy set of references.

Key symbols and terms

Phenomena

D Descriptive features

M Mechanism connecting X and Y

X Causal factor of theoretical interest – usually a single factor but occasionally a vector of related factors

Y Outcome

Z Vector of background factors which may affect X and Y and thus serve as confounders

Causal argument

$X \rightarrow Y$ Apparent or estimated causal effect of a change in X on Y

H_X Hypothesis about $X \rightarrow Y$

$P(H_X)$ The probability of H_X being true

Research design

K Variables

N Observation(s): the lowest-level units in an analysis, which may or may not be of theoretical interest

C Case(s): a spatially and temporally delimited phenomenon of theoretical interest

T Time-periods $(T_1, T_2, T_3, \ldots, T_N)$

Sample   All the observations in an analysis, regardless of how they are chosen

Population   Cases/observations of theoretical interest, generally much larger than the sample.

Case selection

Algorithmic	By algorithm, e.g., descriptive statistics, regression, matching, QCA
Non-algorithmic	In an informal, qualitative fashion

Analysis

Small-C/ case study	One or several cases, each of which is analyzed intensively in order to shed light on a larger population
Medium-C	Hybrid – several dozen cases each of which is analyzed intensively
Large-C	Sizeable sample of cases, analyzed with a quantitative algorithm
Multimethod	Small- and large-C analyses combined in a single study or research stream
Cross-case	Cross-sectional, across cases
Within-case	Within a case, either longitudinally (through time) or at a lower level of analysis
Quantitative	Formal analysis based on matrix observations – generally with a large sample
Qualitative	Informal analysis based on non-comparable observations – generally with a small sample

Part I

Case studies

1 Surveys

There is a case study tradition of research within all the social science disciplines, as well as in adjacent fields in the natural sciences (e.g., medicine) and the humanities (e.g., history). To be sure, this tradition is more prominently on display in some fields than in others. Nonetheless, it is essential to survey our subject – very broadly defined – as it intersects with history, psychology, social work, applied linguistics, medicine, cultural anthropology, sociology, the study of science (sociology of science, history of science, and philosophy of science), education, political science, comparative-historical research, law, and economics (business, management, and organizational research).[1]

We begin with a discursive intellectual history of these disciplines. This is followed by several bibliometric analyses focused on Google Books and Web of Science, and, finally, by a compilation of key exemplars of the case study tradition.

1.1 Intellectual histories

The case study approach to knowledge begins with the oldest discipline, *history*, which evolved from oral and written chronicles of the sort produced by Homer, Herodotus, and Thucydides. Drawing on the specific features of the case at hand these chronicles imparted general

---

[1] Glimpses of the history can be found in Adcock (2008), Bromley (1986: Chapter 1), Brooke (1970), Dufour and Fortin (1992), Feagin *et al.* (1991), Forrester (1996), Hamel (1993), Healy (1923), Platt (1992, 2007), Scholz and Tietje (2002: Chapter 3), and the compendium provided in David (2005).

lessons pertaining to politics, society, human nature, or the gods. In this manner, they abstracted from the particular to the general. Contemporary histories, while focused mostly on explaining particular outcomes and events, provide the building blocks for our general knowledge of the world. In this respect, they function as case studies.[2]

The clinical approach to *psychology* and *social work* rests on an in-depth exploration of specific individuals, regarded as cases. Sigmund Freud's case histories (e.g., "Anna O") were formative in establishing this tradition of investigation and reportage. Other case-based researchers in the psychodynamic tradition include Erik Erikson, Erich Fromm, Karen Horney, Carl Jung, Melanie Klein, and D.W. Winnicott.[3] There is also a long-established tradition of behavioral research in psychology, stretching back to B.F. Skinner in the early twentieth century, that focuses on individual subjects.[4]

In *applied linguistics*, cases of interest are usually composed of language learners, e.g., children or immigrants. Issues of interest include "lexis, syntax, morphology, phonology, discourse-level features, pragmatics, narrative structure, reading and writing processes, content-based language learning, social and linguistic identities, attitudes and motivation, learning strategies, and anxiety" (Duff 2007: 35).

In *medicine*, the case history (also known as medical history or anamnesis) extends back to the origins of scientific study. Today, a patient's case history generally records demographic information, personal information (e.g.: occupation, living arrangements), symptoms, history of any present illnesses, general medical history, medical history of the patient's family, medications, and specific allergies. Published

---

[2] See the five-volume compendium, *Oxford History of Historical Writing*.

[3] For psychology, see Bolgar (1965), Brown and Lloyd (2001), Corsini (2004), Fishman (1999), McLeod (2010), O'Neill (1968), Radley and Chamberlain (2012), Robinson (2001), Sealey (2011), Wedding and Corsini (2013). For social work, see Gilgun (1994), LeCroy (2014), Sheffield (1920), Stake (1995).

[4] Benjamin (2006), Bromley (1986), Gast and Ledford (2009), Kaarbo and Beasley (1999), Oltmanns *et al.* (2014).

case studies often focus on patients whose frailties – or resilience – are not well accounted for by medical science. These anomalies are vigilantly recorded for further study. Examples may be found in the *Journal of Medical Case Reports* and "Case Records from the Massachusetts General Hospital," a regular feature in the *New England Journal of Medicine.*[5] Epidemiologists, meanwhile, construct case histories for every epidemic, while medical historians do the same for outbreaks in the past.[6]

In *cultural anthropology*, research has traditionally focused on groups (e.g., tribes, villages, communities) or rituals (e.g., coming-of-age rituals). Forerunners of modern anthropology rested on accounts by missionaries, military expeditions, and colonists. By the end of the nineteenth century, anthropologists were conducting original fieldwork, generally targeted at "primitive" peoples throughout the world. Leading exemplars include all the founding fathers of ethnography and of the discipline that became known as cultural anthropology – Gregory Bateson, Franz Boas, Mary Douglas, E.E. Evans-Pritchard, Bronislaw Malinowski, Margaret Mead, Gerhard Friedrich Mueller, and Edward Sapir.[7]

In *sociology*, a tradition of work known as urban sociology adapted ethnographic tools developed by anthropologists to study urban areas, focusing especially on families, ethnic groups, immigrants, gangs, and poor neighborhoods. A leading role in this movement was played by the sociology department at the University of Chicago, which included

---

[5] Ankeny (2011, 2012, 2014), Aronson and Hauben (2006), Hunter (1991). The Oxford Case Histories series includes titles such as Neurological Case Histories, Oxford Case Histories in Cardiology, Oxford Case Histories in Gastroenterology and Hepatology, Oxford Case Histories in Neurosurgery, Oxford Case Histories in Respiratory Medicine, Oxford Case Histories in Rheumatology, and Oxford Case Histories in TIA and Stroke.

[6] Jenicek (2001), Keen and Packwood (1995), Mays and Pope (1995), Vandenbroucke (2001), Zimmer and Burke (2009).

[7] Bernard (2001), Eggan (1954), Eriksen and Nielsen (2001), Gluckman (1961), Mitchell (1983), Moore (2010), Rosenblatt (1981), Small (2009). Case studies in forensic anthropology are surveyed in Steadman (2002).

(at various times) Herbert Blumer, Ernest Burgess, Everett Hughes, George Herbert Mead, Robert Park, Robert Redfield, William Thomas, and Louis Wirth, along with their students – Howard Becker, Erving Goffman, and Anselm Strauss. Many of the first research sites to deploy this fieldwork approach were located in Chicago – hence the moniker, "Chicago school." From there, the tradition expanded to other cities in the United States and, eventually, to the rest of the world.[8]

In the study of science – i.e., *sociology of science, history of science,* and *philosophy of science* – cases are often comprised of key anomalies, discoveries, or disagreements among scientists (Burian 2001; Kuhn 1962/1970).

In the field of *education*, case studies have focused on modules, programs, classrooms, schools, and universities (e.g., Bassey 1999; Cousin 2005; Crossley and Vulliamy 1984; Delamont 1992; Hancock and Algozzine 2011; Simons 2009; Thomas 2011).

In *political science*, the tradition of case study research remains highly influential (Blatter and Haverland 2012; Rohlfing 2012). In international relations, case studies often focus on conflicts (including wars), crises, and international agreements.[9] In comparative politics, the units of interest are typically nations, regions, or localities, though studies may also focus on political parties, interest groups, or events such as coups or elections (Collier 1993; Nissen 1998). In public administration, case studies often focus on particular agencies, programs, or decisions (Bailey 1992; Bock 1962; Jensen and Rodgers 2001).

---

[8] Influential early works include Smith and White (1921), Thomas and Znaniecki (1918), Wirth (1928), and Whyte (1943/1955). For secondary accounts, see Bulmer (1984), Hammersley (1989). See also Platt (1992), which focuses more broadly on the development of sociology through the early to mid-twentieth century. For work in environmental science, see Scholz and Tietje (2002).

[9] Bennett and Elman (2007), Elman and Elman (2001), George and Bennett (2005: Appendix), Harvey and Brecher (2002), Levy (2008a), Goertz and Levy (2007), Maoz *et al.* (2004), Sprinz and Wolinsky-Nahmias (2004), Tetlock and Belkin (1996). International political economy is surveyed in Odell (2004); Lawrence *et al.* (2005).

In urban politics, studies generally focus on municipalities and machines (Nicholson-Crotty and Meier 2002).

In *comparative-historical* research, a field that encompasses both sociology and political science, the cases of interest are macro-level units such as states, religions, or societies. Alexis de Tocqueville, Emile Durkheim, Karl Marx, and Max Weber are regarded as founders of this influential cross-disciplinary genre. In the postwar years, influential studies were produced by Seymour Martin Lipset, Barrington Moore, Theda Skocpol, and Charles Tilly (Lange 2012; Mahoney and Rueschemeyer 2003; Mahoney and Thelen 2015).

In the *legal profession*, jurists examine the facts of a case to determine what previous cases are most-similar to it, and hence what precedents might apply. What is it a case of? Naturally, there may be multiple ways of interpreting a case, especially a complex one, and multiple precedents may apply. This is largely what legal argumentation is about, as articulated in legal briefs and judicial decisions. In its essentials, legal reasoning is very similar to what one might call case-classification in other fields. The difference is that the canny jurist only occasionally strives to establish new ground – creating new theory of the law. While scientists strive for theoretical novelty, jurists strive to maintain precedent. Innovation is disguised in the garb of the status quo (Carter and Burke 2015).

In *business, economics, management,* and *organization theory,* case studies of firms, organizations, sectors, and networks (clusters) remain central to the adjoining fields of marketing and business, as well as to the development of new institutional economics, as evidenced in work by Alfred Chandler, Ronald Coase, N.S.B. Grass, Avner Greif, Michael Porter, and Oliver Williamson.[10] Likewise, case studies of countries and

---

[10] Alston (2008), Benbasat *et al.* (1987), Bonoma (1985), Dul and Hak (2007), Eisenhardt (1989), Ellram (1996), Grass and Larson (1939), Hartley (1994), Jones and Zeitlin (2010), Piekkari *et al.* (2009), Woodside and Wilson (2003), Woodside (2010).

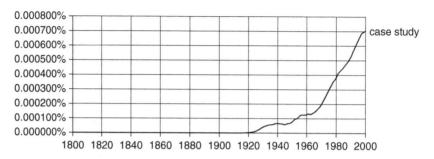

Figure 1.1   Frequency of "case study" in Google Books
Source: https://books.google.com/ngrams/graph?content=case+study&year_start=1800&
year_end=2000&corpus=15&smoothing=3&share=&direct_url=t1%3B%2Ccase%20study%
3B%2Cc0

regions remain a staple of economic history as practiced by Stanley
Engerman, Alexander Gerschenkron, Charles Kindleberger, Douglass
North, Kenneth Sokoloff, and others (Cipolla 1991; Kindleberger 1990;
Mokyr 2003). More recently, macro-economic work by Dani Rodrik
(2003) has focused on the conjunctural quality of growth, requiring
attention to country-specific trajectories. Work on the relationship
between trade policy and growth often integrates in-depth case analysis
with cross-national regression evidence (Srinivasan and Bhagwati 1999;
Stiglitz 2002, 2005; Vreeland 2003).

1.2   Bibliometrics

To survey our topic in a more systematic fashion, several bibliometric
analyses are undertaken. First, I search for mentions of "case study" in
the Google Books archive, which includes millions of books published
from 1500 to the present. Usage of this key term shows a striking
upward trend beginning in the 1920s and accelerating in the postwar
decades, as shown in Figure 1.1.

A second, more differentiated analysis is undertaken based on Web of Science. This collection of periodicals extends back to 1965 and includes over 300,000 articles published in journals across the social sciences. The latter is divided into four broadly defined disciplines: *anthropology*, including physical and cultural anthropology as well as archaeology (54 journals, with citations to a pool of 217,415 articles and books); *economics*, including business and management (214 journals, with citations to a pool of 683,034 articles and books); *political science*, including international affairs and public administration (202 journals, with citations to a pool of 559,294 articles and books); and *sociology*, including demography, cultural studies, gender studies, ethnic studies, and racial studies (286 journals, with citations to a pool of 312,060 articles and books).

To determine the most influential work, I cull the 100 most-cited publications – articles or books – in each of these disciplinary areas. Thus, in anthropology I identify the 100 most cited publications from the Web of Science pool, which includes 217,415 articles and books. These publications are then coded into one of four categories: *small-C (case study), large-C, mixed-method* (including both small- and large-C analyses), and *other*. The latter is a residual category, including studies that are non-empirical (theoretical or methodological) or have no clear units of analysis. Results are contained in Table 1.1.

Among the 100 most-cited studies in these four disciplinary areas, the residual category is by far the most common, suggesting that especially influential social science studies are generally not empirical in the usual sense. Next in citations are large-C studies, constituting nearly one-fifth of the total. Case studies rank third in this typology, mustering 7.5% of all studies surveyed.

There is considerable variation in the prevalence of case studies across disciplines, with anthropology and political science showing more enthusiasm than economics and sociology. Mixed-method studies barely register in this analysis except for in political science, where 5% are so classified.

Table 1.1 Most-cited studies in Web of Science

	AN	EC	PS	SO	Total	Mean
Small-C	14	1	11	4	*30*	*7.50*
Mixed	1	0	5	1	*7*	*1.75*
Large-C	17	15	21	19	*72*	*18.00*
Other	68	84	63	76	*291*	*72.75*
TOTAL	100	100	100	100	*400*	*100.00*

Notes: Most-cited studies in four disciplines, 1965–2014, as reported by Web of Science. AN = anthropology (cultural and physical), archaeology. EC = economics, business, management. PS = political science, international affairs, public administration. SO = sociology, demography, cultural studies, gender studies, ethnic studies, racial studies.

Using the benchmark of journal citations, the case study format holds up well when contrasted with its large-C cousin, at least for some disciplines. Leaving aside studies classified as "other," case studies and mixed-method studies, considered together, are almost as numerous as large-C studies in anthropology and political science (though not in economics and sociology). It is worth noting that the "large-C" category is enormously heterogeneous, including all manner of experimental and observational data analysis. Even so, this omnibus category is only slightly more numerous than case studies/mixed-method studies within anthropology and political science.[11]

Bibliometric analyses focused on political science journals find a similar set of results. Herron and Quinn (2016) report that "case study" (and analogs) generates more hits among the very top political science journals than techniques associated with large-C analysis such as "probit," "instrumental variable," and "field experiment" (though not the all-purpose term "regression").

---

[11] Note also that this sampling procedure may subtly discriminate against case study work. If article writers are more familiar with articles than with books, as we suspect, they are more likely to cite articles than books. Given that the book format is generally preferred by case study researchers, the Web of Science citation count may under-represent the influence of case study research in the social sciences today.

1.3 Exemplars

To define a methodological subject, one needs to have a sense not only of what is typical, but also of what is exemplary. What is it that we have in mind when we describe a study as a "case study"? What are the ideal-types?

An extensive compilation of case studies is provided in Table 1.2. Although lengthy ($N = 148$), this is but a tiny sample of the case studies produced in the social sciences. Nonetheless, it helps to clarify the topic at hand, illustrating the variety and scope of this much-practiced genre.

This table contains a good deal of information on various dimensions of case study research. As such, it will be referred to repeatedly throughout the book. That is, each topic addressed in the book will select examples from the table.

Since it is not a random sample, it is important to clarify how this list of exemplars was constructed, and what sorts of biases it might reflect.

Some exemplars are quite recent and others hark back to the turn of the twentieth century, coincident with the professionalization of the core disciplines – anthropology, economics, history, political science, and sociology. I include studies that focus on one or several units (*small-C*) as well as studies that incorporate several dozen units (*medium-C*) – so long as each case is studied intensively. I also include studies that combine small- and large-*C* analyses (*multimethod*).

In selecting studies, I privilege those with demonstrable influence in a field or sub-field; those that have become touchstones in methodological discussions of the case study method; and those that provide diversity in topic, method of case selection, method of analysis, theory, or disciplinary background. Diversity implies non-redundancy: if several studies are very similar, only one is likely to be included.

Inclusion on this list does not mean that I endorse the writer's findings or even their methodological choices. It means only that a work serves as a good example of something. The purpose of an exemplar is

Table 1.2 Exemplars

| Study | Field | Cites | SELECTION Algo. | Non-algo | CASES Phenomena | C | QUANT Cross-case | Within-case | SOURCES Ethnography | Interview | Survey | Primary | Secondary |
1	2	3	4	5	6	7	8	9	10	11	12	13	14
Abadie and Gardeazabal (2003) *Costs of Conflict*	EC	867		●	Spanish regions	1/17		●					●
Acemoglu et al. (2003) *African Success Story*	EC	638		●	Economic development	1		●				●	●
Adamson (2001) *Democratization*	PS	53		●	Foreign policies	1							●
Alesina et al. (2001) *Why Doesn't US Have Welfare State?*	EC	824		●	Welfare state	1	●						●
Allen (1965) *Nazi Seizure of Power*	HI	397		●	Towns	1		●	●			●	●
Allison and Zelikow (1999) *Essence of Decision*	PS	9,113		●	Foreign crises	1			●	●		●	
Almond and Verba (1963) *Civic Culture*	PS	12,679		●	Political cultures	5		●			●		●
Alperovitz (1996) *Decision to Use Atomic Bomb*	PS	409		●	Nuclear deploy.	1				●			●
Alston et al. (1996) *Property Rights*	EC	390		●	Brazilian states	2				●	●	●	
Amenta (1991) *Theories of Welfare State; American Experience*	SO	40		●	Welfare states	1							●
Anderson (1974) *Lineages of Absolutist State*	HI	2,508		●	Nation-building	10						●	●
Aymard (1982) *From Feudalism to Capitalism in Italy*	HI	22		●	Capitalism	1						●	

Citation	Field	N		Unit	k							
Banfield (1958) *Moral Basis of Backward Society*	PS	3,882	•	Villages	1						•	•
Becker (1961) *Boys in White*	SO	3,142	•	Medical schools	1			•			•	•
Belich (2010) *Exploding Wests*	HI	5	•	Colonialism	7						•	•
Bendix (1978) *Kings or People*	SO	664	•	Nation-building	5						•	
Benedict (1934) *Patterns of Culture*	AN	5,571	•	Cultures	3				•		•	
Bennett et al. (1994) *Burden-Sharing in the Persian Gulf War*	PS	90	•	Alliances	1			•	•		•	•
Bunce (1981) *Do New Leaders Make a Difference?*	PS	114	•	Succession	2			•		•		•
Caldwell (1986) *Routes to Low Mortality*	DE	1,022	•	Mortality	3				•			•
Campbell (1968/1988) *Connecticut Crackdown*	PY	384	•	Speeding laws	1				•		•	•
Chandler (1962) *Strategy and Structure*	EC	1,427	•	Firms	4			•		•		•
Childs et al. (2005) *Tibetan Fertility Transitions*	DE	19	•	Demog transitions	3				•		•	•
Coase (1959) *Federal Communications Commission*	EC	1,410	•	Agencies	1						•	
Collier and Collier (1991) *Shaping the Political Arena*	PS	2,171	•	State–labor relations	8	•						
Collier and Sambanis (2005a, b) *Understanding Civil War*	PS	430	•	Civil wars	21	•		•				•
Cornell (2002) *Autonomy as a Source of Conflict*	PS	256	•	Ethnic groups	9				•		•	
Curtiss (1977) *Psycholinguistic Study of "Wild Child"*	PY	933	•	Human development	1				•			

Table 1.2 (cont.)

Study	Field	Cites	SELECTION		CASES		QUANT		SOURCES				
			Algo.	Non-algo	Phenomena	C	Cross-case	Within-case	Ethnography	Interview	Survey	Primary	Secondary
1	2	3	4	5	6	7	8	9	10	11	12	13	14
Dafoe and Kelsey (2014) Observing the Capitalist Peace	PS	2	●		Nation dyads	6	●						●
Dahl (1961) Who Governs?	PS	5,810		●	Cities	1			●	●		●	
David (1985) Clio and the Economics of QWERTY	EC	6,473		●	Path dependence	1						●	
Dobbin (1994) Forging Industrial Policy	SO	745		●	Industrial policies	3						●	
Downing (1992) Military Revolution and Political Change	PS	398		●	Statebuilding	7						●	
Dreze and Sen (1989) China and India	EC	2,936		●	Economic development	2						●	●
Duneier (1999) Sidewalks	AN	997		●	Sidewalks	1			●	●			
Dunlavy (1994) Politics and Industrialization	HI	125		●	Industrial policies	2						●	
Dunning (2008) Crude Democracy	PS	395		●	Democratization	5		●		●	●	●	●
Epstein (1964) A Comparative Study of Canadian Parties	PS	113		●	Party systems	2						●	
Evans (1995) Embedded Autonomy	SO	5,281		●	Economic development	3				●		●	●
Fairfield (2013, 2015) Going Where Money Is	PS	7		●	Tax reform proposals	32				●		●	
Fearon and Laitin (2008, 2014, 2015) Random Narratives	PS	85	●		Civil wars	25	●					●	●
Fenno (1977, 1978) Home Style	PS	2,141		●	MPs and districts	17			●			●	

Reference	Disc.	N		Unit	Count
Fiorina (1977) Congress	PS	1,866	•	US leg. districts	2
Friedman and Schwartz (1963) Monetary History of US	EC	6,208	•	Monetary policy	1
Geertz (1963) Peddlers and Princes	AN	977	•	Towns	2
Geertz (1978) Bazaar Economy	AN	892	•	Communities	1
George and Smoke (1974) Deterrence in US Foreign Policy	PS	894	•	Crises	11
Goldstone (1991) Revolution and Rebellion	SO	994	•	Revolutions	4
Gouldner (1954) Patterns of Industrial Bureaucracy	SO	3,075	•	Factories	1
Gourevitch (1986) Politics in Hard Times	PS	1,112	•	Economic crises	5
Haber (2010) Politics, Banking, and Economic Development	HI	3	•	Banking systems	3
Handlin (1941) Boston's Immigrants	HI	488	•	Cities	1
Harding et al. (2002) Study of Rampage School Shootings	SO	77	•	School shootings	2
Heclo (1974) Modern Social Policies in Britain and Sweden	PS	1,920	•	Social policies	2
Homans (1951) Human Group	SO	4,633	•	Groups	5
Howard (2003) Weakness Civil Society in Post-Communist	PS	1,284	•	Civil society	2
Hsieh and Romer (2001) Was Federal Reserve Fettered?	EC	19	•	Monetary expansions	1

Table 1.2 (cont.)

Study	Field	Cites	SELECTION Algo.	Non-algo	CASES Phenomena	C	QUANT Cross-case	Within-case	SOURCES Ethnography	Interview	Survey	Primary	Secondary
1	2	3	4	5	6	7	8	9	10	11	12	13	14
Hunter (1953) *Community Power Structure*	SO	2,393		•	Cities	1			•				
Immergut (1992) *Health Politics*	PS	1,008		•	Health policy	3				•		•	
Johnson (1983) *MITI and the Japanese Miracle*	PS	3,185		•	Industrial policies	1				•		•	
Kalyvas (1996) *Christian Democracy in Europe*	PS	556		•	Christian demo parties	6						•	•
Kanter (1977) *Men and Women of the Corporation*	SO	11,950		•	Corporations	1			•				
Karl (1997) *Paradox of Plenty*	PS	1,892		•	Economic development	5/1				•		•	
Kaufman (1960) *Forest Ranger*	PS	1,073		•	Agencies	1				•			
Kemp (1986) *Urban Spatial Conflict*	SO	5		•	Local ethnic conflict	1		•			•	•	
Key (1949) *Southern Politics in State and Nation*	PS	3,238		•	US	11	•	•		•	•		•
Khong (1992) *Analogies at War*	PS	564		•	Crises	4				•		•	
Kindleberger (1996) *World Economic Primacy*	EC	213		•	Economic development	8	•						•
Kitschelt (1986) *Political Opportunity Structures and Protest*	PS	1,760		•	Social movements	4						•	•
Kocher and Monteiro (2015) *What's in a Line?*	PS	0		•	Devolution	1		•				•	•
Kohli (2004) *State-Directed Development*	PS	723		•	Industrial policies	4						•	•
Kuehn (2013) *Game Theory Models and Process Tracing*	PS	3	•		Civil-military rel.	2						•	•

Work	Discipline	Citations	Topic	N
Lane (1962) *Political Ideology*	PS	695	Workers	18
Lange (2009) *Lineages of Despotism and Development*	SO	69	Economic development	4/11
Le Roy Ladurie (1978) *Montaillou*	HI	384	Peasant cultures	1
Lerner (1958) *Passing of Traditional Society*	PS	4,912	Societies	1
Levi (1988) *Of Rule and Revenue*	PS	1,821	Fiscal policy	4
Lewis (1959) *Five Families*	AN	1,026	Families	5
Lieberman (2003) *Politics of Taxation Brazil, South Africa*	PS	172	Fiscal policy	2
Lijphart (1968) *Politics of Accommodation*	PS	2,026	Ethnic conflict	1
Linz and Stepan (1978a, 1978b) *Breakdown Demo. Regimes*	PS	1,765	Dem: breakdowns	11
Lipset et al. (1956) *Union Democracy*	SO	1,211	Union democracy	1
Luebbert (1991) *Liberalism, Fascism, or Social Democracy*	PS	356	Regime-types	15
Lutfey and Freese (2005) *SES and Health in Routine Clinic*	SO	144	Clinics	2
Lynd and Lynd (1929) *Middletown*	SO	2,199	Cities	1
Madrigal et al. (2011) *Community-Based Orgs*	EC	20	Water agencies	4
Mahoney (2002) *Legacies of Liberalism*	PS	337	Regime-types	5

Table 1.2 (*cont.*)

Study (1)	Field (2)	Cites (3)	SELECTION		CASES		QUANT		SOURCES				
			Algo. (4)	Non-algo (5)	Phenomena (6)	C (7)	Cross-case (8)	Within-case (9)	Ethnography (10)	Interview (11)	Survey (12)	Primary (13)	Secondary (14)
Mansfield and Snyder (2005) *Electing to Fight*	PS	627		•	Conflicts	10	•					•	
Martin (1992) *Coercive Cooperation*	PS	700		•	Sanctions	4	•					•	•
Martin (2008) *Permanent Tax Revolt*	SO	121		•	Tax revolts	1	•			•	•	•	•
McAdam (1982) *Political Process and Black Insurgency*	SO	4,534		•	Social movements	1				•		•	•
Michels (1911) *Political Parties*	SO	4,231		•	Parties	2						•	
Miguel (2004) *Tribe or Nation: Kenya v. Tanzania*	EC	326		•	Nation-building	2		•			•	•	•
Mondak (1995) *Newspapers and Political Awareness*	PS	95		•	Cities	2		•			•	•	
Moore (1966) *Social Origins of Dictatorship and Democracy*	SO	6,573		•	Regime-types	8						•	•
North and Weingast (1989) *Constitutions and Commitment*	EC	3,462		•	Limited govt	1						•	•
Ostrom (1990) *Governing the Commons*	PS	20,073		•	Common pool res.	~14		•	•			•	•
Pearce (2002) *Integrating Survey and Ethnographic Methods*	SO	47	•		Fertility	28	•		•	•	•	•	
Peters and Waterman (1982) *In Search of Excellence*	EC	17,443		•	Firms	43				•		•	•

Reference	Discipline	N	Unit of analysis	N
Pincus (2011) *1688: First Modern Revolution*	HI	247	Revolutions	1
Pinfari (2012) *Peace Negotiations and Time*	PS	5	Negotiations	4
Porter (1990) *Competitive Advantage of Nations*	EC	31,857	Economic development	10
Posner (2004) *Political Salience of Cultural Difference*	PS	376	Ethnic groups	4
Putnam et al. (1993) *Making Democracy Work*	PS	29,712	Italian regions	20
Raaflaub et al. (2007) *Origins of Democracy*	HI	98	Democratization	1
Ray (1993) *Wars between Democracies*	PS	157	Wars	5
Reilly (2000/2001) *Democracy, Ethnic Fragmentation*	PS	80	Regime-types	1
Richards (2011) *Cultural Explanations of War*	AN	8	Wars	2
Romer and Romer (2010) *Effects of Tax Changes*	EC	800	Fiscal policy	1
Rosenbaum and Silber (2001) *Matching*	PH	50	Patients	76
Rosenberg (1991) *Hollow Hope*	PS	2,761	Legal cases	2
Ross (2004, 2013) *Natural Resources Influence Civil War*	PS	566	Civil wars	13
Rueschemeyer et al. (1992) *Capitalist Development*	SO	2,727	Regime-types	22
Sagan (1993) *Limits of Safety*	PS	876	Nuclear accidents	4

Table 1.2 (cont.)

| Study | Field | Cites | SELECTION Algo. | Non-algo | CASES Phenomena | C | QUANT Cross-case | Within-case | SOURCES Ethnography | Interview | Survey | Primary | Secondary |
1	2	3	4	5	6	7	8	9	10	11	12	13	14
Sahlins (1958) *Social Stratification in Polynesia*	AN	726		•	Societies	17			•			•	
Schattschneider (1935) *Politics, Pressures and the Tariff*	PS	740		•	Tariff bills	1		•		•		•	
Scheper-Hughes (1992) *Death w/out Weeping*	AN	2,494		•	Poor communities	1			•				•
Schmidt (1983) *Interaction, Acculturation, Acquisition*	LI	515		•	2nd-lang. learners	1			•	•			
Schultz (2001) *Democracy and Coercive Diplomacy*	PS	590		•	Crises	4	•					•	
Scott (1998) *Seeing Like a State*	PS	8,634		•	Policy failures	6			•			•	•
Selznick (1949) *TVA and the Grass Roots*	SO	3,260		•	Agencies	1				•		•	
Shaw (1930) *The Jack Roller*	SO	654		•	Delinquents	1				•			
Shefter (1977) *Party and Patronage*	PS	237		•	Party systems	3/2						•	
Simmons (1994) *Who Adjusts?*	PS	348		•	Econ. policy crises	3	•					•	•
Skendaj (2014) *International Insulation from Politics*	PS	2		•	Agencies	4				•	•		
Skocpol (1979) *States and Social Revolutions*	SO	5,227		•	Revolutions	3/6			•	•		•	
Snow (1849) *Communication of Cholera*	PH	1,369		•	City blocks	N/A						•	
Snyder and Borghard (2011) *Cost of Empty Threats*	PS	78		•	Crises	4					•	•	•

Reference	Discipline	N		Unit	Count
Sombart (1906) *Why No Socialism in United States?*	SO	356	•	Socialism	1
Tannenwald (1999, 2007) *Nuclear Taboo*	PS	480	•	Nuclear-Use occasions	4
Taylor (1911) *Principles of Scientific Management*	EC	13,344	•	Industrial plants	3
Teorell (2010) *Determinants of Democratization*	PS	153	•	Regime-types	14
Thompson (1963) *Making of English Working Class*	HI	9,584	•	Class formation	1
Tilly (1964) *The Vendée*	SO	274	•	Counter-revs	1
Tsai (2007) *Accountability without Democracy*	PS	227	•	Village governance	4
Uphoff (1992) *Learning from Gal Oya*	PS	467	•	Irrigation projects	1
Useem and Goldstone (2002) *Riot and Reform US Prisons*	SO	32	•	Prisons	2
Vaughan (1996) *Challenger Launch Decision*	SO	15	•	Space launches	1
Veenendaal (2015) *Microstates*	PS	11	•	Democracy	4
Wade (1997) *How Infrastructure Agencies Motivate Staff*	PS	71	•	Irrigation agencies	2
Walter (2002) *Committing to Peace*	PS	821	•	Civil wars	2
Warner and Lunt (1941) *Yankee City*	AN	239	•	Cities	1
Weber (1979) *Peasants into Frenchmen*	HI	3,367	•	Nation-building	1

Table 1.2 (*cont.*)

Study	Field	Cites	SELECTION		CASES		QUANT		SOURCES				
			Algo.	Non-algo	Phenomena	C	Cross-case	Within-case	Ethnography	Interview	Survey	Primary	Secondary
1	2	3	4	5	6	7	8	9	10	11	12	13	14
Weinstein (2007) *Inside Rebellion*	PS	771		•	Rebel groups	4	•	•	•	•	•		•
Whyte (1943) *Street Corner Society*	SO	5,501		•	Gangs	3			•				•
Wilson (1889) *The State*	PS	268		•	Constitutions	10						•	
Wood (2000) *Forging Democracy from Below*	PS	353		•	Regime-types	2			•			•	
Ziblatt (2004, 2008) *Rethinking Origins of Federalism*	PS	36		•	Centralization	2						•	
SUMMARY													
Mean		2,262				5.2							
Median		679				2							
Total (N=148)		334,906	9	140		773	20	27	35	48	23	100	64
Total (%)			6	94.5			13.5	18.2	23.6	32.4	15.5	67.5	43.2

Note: Headings are explained in the text.

to illustrate a specific methodological issue, not to portray cutting-edge research in a field. More specifically, placement in this table should not be interpreted to mean that a study has strong claims to internal or external validity. These matters are difficult to evaluate and would require extensive discussion (see Part III). In any case, the contribution of a case study to knowledge of a subject is often exploratory (e.g., the elaboration of a new theory) rather than confirmatory (to test an extant hypothesis). As such, rock-solid claims to validity may not be their most important feature.

Column 1 lists the author(s), publication date, and title of a study, or set of closely related studies, e.g., an article and book version of the same analysis. (If several studies are listed, citation counts in Column 3 record those for the most cited work.)

Column 2 lists the main author's primary disciplinary field, categorized as follows: anthropology (AN, $N = 9$), demography (DE, $N = 2$), economics, business, and management (EC, $N = 18$), history (HI, $N = 13$), linguistics (LI, $N = 1$), political science (PS, $N = 72$), public health (PH, $N = 1$), psychology (PY, $N = 2$), and sociology (SO, $N = 30$). The reader will perceive that all social science disciplines are represented, though by no means equally. This skewed distribution reflects the prominence of case studies in different fields, but also, more crucially, my uneven acquaintance with the various fields of social science.

Column 3 provides a crude signal of scholarly influence – the number of hits a study obtains in Google Scholar. Bear in mind that some studies are older than others, and thus benefit from a longer time period over which to accrue citations. It is clear nonetheless that our assemblage includes some extremely influential studies, including several that have helped to establish new research paradigms. The average (mean) number of citations for studies in our sample is over 2,000.

Columns 4–5 note whether case selection was carried out by application of an algorithm (a "quantitative" approach) or an informal method (a "qualitative" approach). The latter approach dominates, constituting nearly 95% of the total sample. However, the use of algorithms appears to be increasing in prevalence: all examples were produced in the last decade or so. For further discussion of this issue, see Chapter 6.

Columns 6–7 describe the cases under intensive study – the phenomena of theoretical interest and the number of cases (*C*). Most case studies focus on a small number of cases. The median in our sample is two and the mean is just over five. If there are additional "shadow" cases that can be easily identified, these are listed after the slash. (Typically, shadow cases enter the narrative in an ad hoc manner and are therefore not easy to count.)

Columns 8–9 record whether a quantitative cross-case or within-case analysis is performed in the study. (I assume that informal, qualitative styles of cross-case and within-case analyses are applied in *any* case study analysis, so this is not featured in Table 1.2.) If quantitative cross-case analysis is applied, the resulting study may be classified as *multi-method* since it involves both large- and small-*C* analysis (see Chapter 7). This is still a relatively rare research design, constituting 14% of the sample, though much more common among recent studies. Quantitative *within-case* analysis is somewhat more common, characterizing nearly one-fifth of the sample.

The final columns (10–14) note the sources that the case study draws on, classified as *ethnography*/participant-observation (~23%), unstructured *interview* (~32%), *survey* (~16%), *primary* (~68%), or *secondary* (~43%). These categories are not mutually exclusive; indeed, most studies employ more than one data source.

Summary statistics for each column – including *mean, median, total,* and *total (percentage)* – are listed at the bottom of the table, where appropriate. However, readers should bear in mind that this is a non-random sample drawn from an undefined population. One should, therefore, be careful about forming generalizations based on these statistics.

1.4   Summary

This chapter has surveyed the genre known as *case study research*. Our survey included a discursive analysis of the major social science disciplines along with bibliometric analyses of Google Books and Web of Science. Rising to prominence in the early twentieth century, case study research designs are today ubiquitous. Among our sample of most-cited studies in Web of Science, small- and medium-C studies and multimethod studies are roughly half as numerous as large-C studies (see Table 1.1). That is to say, one-third of the empirical studies that are widely influential in the social sciences (as judged by citation counts) exploit a case study format. The rest are classified as large-C in the sense of relying exclusively or primarily on a great many units, each of which is analyzed in a schematic fashion through some quantitative algorithm.

I also introduced a compilation of "exemplary" works, listed in Table 1.2. These studies will be referred to repeatedly in the chapters to come. They constitute our empirical material, one might say, and also serve to define our subject in an ostensive fashion, providing a segue to the next chapter where we shall define our subject in a formal manner.

Definitions

Thus far, I have used the term "case study" loosely, in conformance with everyday speech. Case studies are fairly ubiquitous if one defines the subject in this catch-all fashion, as has been seen. However, people have many things in mind when they use this term.[1] Indeed, the concept is a definitional morass. Confusion is compounded by the existence of a large number of near-synonyms – single unit, single subject, single case, $N = 1$, case-based, case-control, case history, case method, case record, case work, within-case, clinical, and so forth.

The surfeit of meaning attached to the case study is partly responsible for its methodological disorganization. Proponents and opponents of the case study marshal a wide range of arguments but do not seem any closer to agreement than when this debate was first broached many decades ago. Perhaps this is not surprising, given that they are often talking about different things.[2]

[1] Various definitions are introduced and discussed in Blatter and Haverland (2012: 18–19), Flyvbjerg (2011), Platt (2007), Ragin and Becker (1992), and Swanborn (2010: Chapter 1).

[2] Platt (1992: 48) notes that "much case study theorizing has been conceptually confused, because too many different themes have been packed into the idea 'case study.'" Elsewhere in this perceptive article, Platt (1992: 37) comments: "the diversity of the themes which have been associated with the term, and the vagueness of some of the discussion, causes some difficulty . . . In practice, 'case study method' in its heyday [in the interwar years] seems to have meant some permutation of the following components: life history data collected by any means, personal documents, unstructured interview data of any kind, the close study of one or a small number of cases whether or not any attempt was made to generalize from them, any attempt at holistic study, and non-quantitative data analysis. These components have neither a necessary logical nor a regular empirical connection with each other."

For purposes of methodological discussion, it is essential to adopt a lexicon where terms are clearly and consistently delineated. Of course, it could be that topics associated with the case study meld into one another inconveniently, belying whatever distinctions one might wish to impose. I shall endeavor to show that this sort of confusion need not arise if we are careful with our language.

2.1   Case

In the present study, a *case* connotes a spatially and temporally delimited phenomenon of theoretical significance.

Cases may be comprised of states or state-like entities (e.g., empires, nation-states, regions, municipalities), organizations (e.g., firms, non-governmental organizations, political parties, schools), social groups (defined by, e.g., ethnicity, race, age, class, gender, or sexuality), events (e.g., foreign policy crisis, revolution, democratic transition, decision-point), or individuals (e.g., a biography, case history).

However a case is defined, it must comprise the phenomena that an argument attempts to describe or explain. In a study about nation-states, cases are comprised of nation-states. In a study that attempts to explain the behavior of individuals, cases are comprised of individuals. And so forth.

As it happens, the spatial boundaries of a case are usually easier to define than its temporal boundaries. We usually know (more or less) where a country's borders lie. But we may have difficulty specifying the date when that country began its existence. Often, temporal boundaries are arbitrarily assigned. This is particularly important when cases consist of discrete events – crises, revolutions, legislative acts, and so forth – within a single unit. Cases are thus equivalent to *units*, with the added implication that a case has a temporal boundary.

Occasionally, the temporal boundaries of a case are more obvious than its spatial boundaries. This is true when the phenomena under study are eventful, but the unit undergoing the event is amorphous. For example, if one is studying terrorist attacks, it may not be clear how the spatial unit of analysis should be understood, but the events themselves may be well bounded.

2.2 Case study

A *case study* is an intensive study of a single case or a small number of cases which draws on observational data and promises to shed light on a larger population of cases. "Case study" and "small-*C* study" are used synonymously, as the small number of cases defines the genre known as case study research. Several clarifications and implications stemming from this definition may be briefly noted.

A case study is highly *focused*, meaning that considerable time is spent by the researcher analyzing, and subsequently presenting, the chosen case, or cases, and the case is viewed as providing important evidence for the argument. Proper nouns are employed (e.g., "Russia," "World War I," "Stalin"). Narratives that touch briefly on many cases – as is common in works of synthesis produced by writers such as Jared Diamond, Samuel Finer, Samuel Huntington, Paul Kennedy, Michael Mann, William McNeill, Karl Polanyi, Immanuel Wallerstein, or Max Weber[3] – do not qualify as case studies because each case enters the narrative only fleetingly.

As the number of cases increases, the attention devoted to each must decrease (assuming the length of a study is fixed). Most well-known case studies incorporate one or several cases and are thus small-*C*, as demonstrated in Table 1.2. At the point where emphasis shifts from individual cases to a sample, the study may be described as large-*C*. (Medium-*C* samples – of several dozen – constitute a tenuous midway

---

[3] Diamond (1992), Finer (1997), Huntington (1968), Kennedy (1989), Mann (1986), McNeill (1963), Polanyi (1944/1957), Wallerstein (1974), Weber (1904–5/1958).

point, as discussed in Chapter 6.) Evidently, this is a continuum. The fewer cases there are, and the more intensively they are studied, the more a work merits the appellation *case study*. The greater the number of cases, and the more superficially they are studied, the more a work merits the appellation large-C. The number of cases in a study – C – is thus a matter of degrees. Even so, the small-/large-C contrast proves to be an essential distinction, and much follows from it. (Indeed, this entire book follows from it.)

The causal factor in case study research (if the goal of the research is indeed causal) is not intentionally manipulated by the researcher, and in this sense is *observational* (non-experimental). Note that where it is possible to manipulate a treatment, it is also usually possible to enlist a large number of cases, generating a cross-case format that minimizes stochastic threats to inference. Although experiments are occasionally conducted on a single case or a small number of cases, especially in the field of psychology, issues of research design and analysis are distinct from those that arise in observational settings (Davidson and Costello 1969; Kazdin 1982; Kennedy 2005). Thus, for reasons of practice and practicality it makes sense for us to define case study research as an observational form of analysis. That said, case studies may utilize data that exhibit characteristics of an experiment, i.e., where "nature" assigns a treatment in a random or as-if random fashion. I argue that any case study oriented toward causal inference is helpfully understood according to an experimental template (Chapter 5).

One may presume that a variety of styles of (observational) evidence are employed in a case study, lending it an *holistic* flavor. Note that in order to describe or explain a small number of cases, it is desirable – one might even say necessary – to enlist a wide range of evidence. If the goal is causal inference, one cannot measure X and Y across one or several cases and infer a causal relationship from covariational evidence alone. Case study evidence is also generally drawn from different levels of analysis, a form of *multilevel inference*. Typically, researchers compare the chosen case to others (a cross-case comparison), follow at least one case through time, and explore *within-case* observations at a lower level of analysis (e.g., individuals within an organization). Typically, some of this evidence is qualitative and some quantitative, as discussed in Chapter 8.

The goal of a case study is partly to explain the case(s) under investigation and also, at the same time, to shed light on a larger class of cases (a population). In order to qualify as a case study, it must be possible to put the study into a larger context – even if that was not the intention of the author. This is tricky, given that virtually any topic may be considered from a more general perspective. A study of the French Revolution may also be regarded as a case study of revolution. Nonetheless, this move to generalize is what distinguishes a *study of Y* from a *case study of Y*. A general study of France that tells us a great deal about that country – e.g., Theodore Zeldin's (1973–7) multivolume history – is not a case study. It becomes a case study only if there is an element of that study that can be generalized. By contrast, Eugen Weber's (1979) study of French history, *Peasants into Frenchmen*, is often viewed as a case study of nation formation. The studied unit is the same, but the topic is more susceptible to generalization. This is why Weber's study, but not Zeldin's, would normally be classified as a case study.

Finally, it follows from our definition that there is likely to be considerable uncertainty about how well the case, or cases, under study represents a larger population. This is because the cases are few, the population of interest is generally large, and the phenomena of interest are heterogeneous. While a chemist studying a single H_2O molecule may feel comfortable in assuming that the behavior of that molecule is identical to other H_2O molecules, in social science settings one rarely finds phenomena of such consistency. Consequently, to assert that a case is representative of a larger population of cases is to assert something that is plausible but also subject to doubt – not only about the representativeness of the case, but also about the boundaries of the larger population (for further discussion see Chapter 10).

2.3   Additional terms

A few additional terms may now be formally defined.

An *argument* refers to the central point of a study – what it is attempting to demonstrate or prove. The argument may be articulated in a formal *theory* and may also be disaggregated into specific *propositions* or *hypotheses*. (These terms are sometimes used interchangeably in the text when their methodological functions overlap.)

An *observation* (denoted N) defines the unit of analysis in a particular analysis. Unlike a case, it need not embody units of theoretical interest. Consider the classic "modernization" theory about the relationship of economic development to democracy: richer, more modern countries are more likely to attain a democratic regime type (Lipset 1959). Since the theory concerns nation-states, cases must be composed of nation-states. By contrast, observations could be composed of any phenomena so long as they form the units of analysis in some sort of study (qualitative or quantitative). This is why the distinction between cases (C) and observations (N) is so critical, and why I am scrupulous in the notation used throughout this book (see also Chapter 8).

A case may generate a single observation. This would be true, for example, in a cross-sectional analysis of a large sample of cases. Here, $C = N$. In a case study, however, the case under study always provides more than one observation. Thus, $C<N$. These may be constructed by observing the case *longitudinally* (through time) or by taking account of *within-case* observations at a lower level of analysis. Both types of evidence are *case-based*.

Note that small-C and large-C studies usually operate at different levels of analysis. The case study is typically focused on longitudinal and within-case variation; if there is a cross-case component, it is usually secondary in importance to the case-based evidence. The large-C study is typically focused on cross-case variation, and perhaps also longitudinal variation. If there is also within-case evidence, it is secondary in importance.

Sometimes, the distinction between cases (C) and observations (N) is ambiguous. For example, Daniel Posner's (2004) study of the politicization of ethnic identity in southern Africa includes a survey of individuals – members of the Chewa and Tumbukka ethnic groups in Malawi and Zambia. This provides fodder for a regression analysis with individuals as the units of analysis ($N = 180$). However, the treatment of theoretical interest (relative group size) is at the group level. Likewise, individuals within each group share many characteristics (clustering); they affect each other (violating the assumption of non-interference); and they are liable to a similar set of confounders. The research design is thus analogous to a clustered experiment with four clusters. For these reasons, I classify Posner's study and others like it (e.g., Childs 2005; Miguel 2004; Mondak 1995) as small-C studies where *groups* are defined as cases – rather than as large-C studies where *individuals* are regarded as cases. For Posner (2004), $C = 4$ and $N = 180$. As always, it pays to look closely at the details of a research design and not just at the number of observations in a statistical table.

A single observation may be understood as containing several dimensions, each of which may be measured (across disparate observations) as a *variable* – assuming the observation is of a matrix sort (as discussed in Chapter 8). Granted, features of theoretical interest are not always easy to measure in a systematic fashion, but they are at least potentially measurable.

Variables may assume any sort of scale – nominal, ordinal, interval, or ratio. Nominal variables may recognize multiple categories (Christian, Jewish, Hindu, Muslim) or dichotomous categories ("dummy" variables).

Where an argument is causal, we distinguish between an *outcome* variable (Y, also known as dependent variable), a *causal factor* (or condition) of theoretical interest (X), and *background factors* of no theoretical interest, which may affect X and Y and may therefore serve as confounders (Z).

A *sample* consists of whatever cases or observations are subjected to analysis. They are the immediate subject of a large- or small-C study. My use of the term does not imply random sampling (a technique for selecting cases), though it does not exclude this option either, as discussed in Part II.

The sample of cases rests within a *population* of cases to which a given proposition refers. The population of an inference is thus equivalent to the breadth or scope of an argument.

For those familiar with the matrix format of a dataset, it may be helpful to conceptualize observations as rows, variables as columns, and cases as either groups of observations or individual observations. Two possibilities are illustrated in the following figures: a case study with two cases (Figure 2.1) and a large-C study with multiple cross-sectional cases (Figure 2.2).

Note that all of these terms are definable only by reference to a particular proposition and a corresponding research design. A country may function as a case, an observation, or a population. It all depends upon what one is arguing. In a typical time-series cross-country regression analysis, cases are countries and observations are country-years (e.g., Przeworski *et al.* 2000). However, shifts in the level of analysis of a proposition necessarily change the referential meaning of all terms in the semantic field. If one moves down one level of analysis, the new population lies within the old population, the new sample within the old sample, and so forth. Population, case, and observation are nested within each other. Since most social science research occurs at several levels of analysis, these terms are often in flux. Nonetheless, they have distinct meanings within the context of a single proposition.

Consider a survey-based analysis of respondents within a single country under several scenarios. Under the first scenario, the proposition of interest pertains to individual-level behavior. It is about how individuals behave. As such, cases are defined as individuals, and this is properly classified as a *large-C* study. Now, let us suppose that the

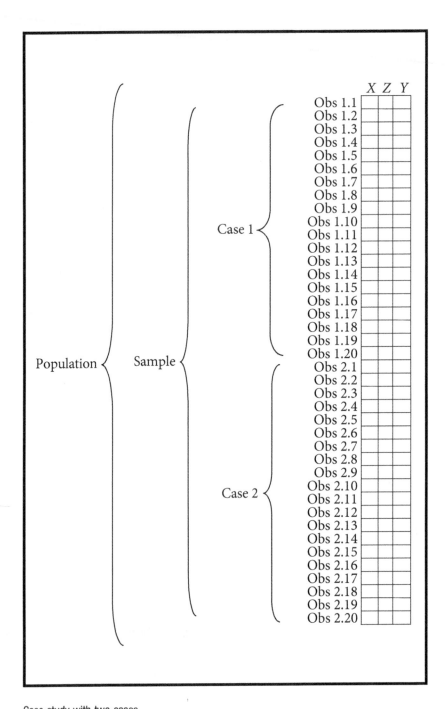

Figure 2.1   Case study with two cases

Notes: Population = 1; Sample = 1; Cases (*C*) = 2; Observations (*N*) = 40; Variables (*K*) = 3.

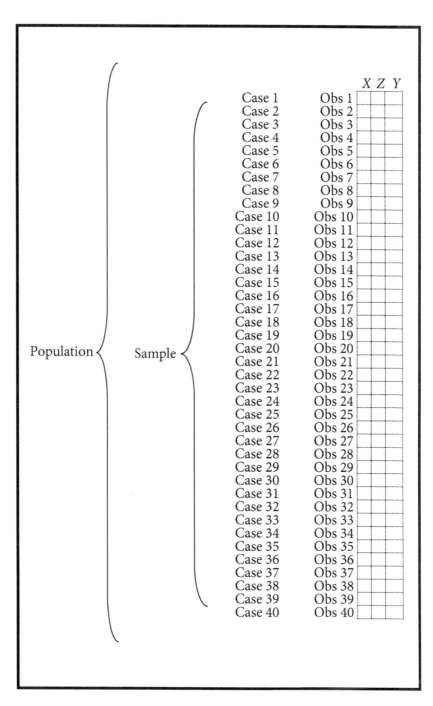

Figure 2.2   Large-C study with 40 cases/observations

Notes: Population = 1; Sample = 1; Cases (C) = 40; Observations (N) = 40; Variables (K) = 3.

researcher wishes to use this same survey-level data drawn from a single country to elucidate an inference pertaining to countries, rather than individuals. Under this scenario, each poll respondent constitutes a within-case observation. If there is only one country, or a few countries, under investigation – and the inference, as before, pertains to multiple countries – then this study is properly classified as a small-C study or *case study*. If many countries are under study (with or without individual-level data), then it is properly classified as a *large-C* study.

2.4   Summary

This chapter is devoted to defining terms – an especially important exercise in this setting where there is no settled meaning for many key concepts. To review, a *case* (C) is a spatially and temporally delimited phenomenon of theoretical interest. A *case study*, or *small-C* study, is an intensive study of a single case or a small number of cases which also promises to shed light on a larger population of cases. An *argument* refers to the central point of a study – what it is attempting to demonstrate or prove. The argument may be articulated in a formal *theory* and may also be disaggregated into specific *propositions* or *hypotheses*. An *observation* (N) is the most basic element of any empirical endeavor. A single case may be understood as containing several dimensions, each of which may be measured (across disparate observations) as a *variable* or factor. Where an argument is causal, we distinguish between an *outcome* variable (Y), a *causal factor* of theoretical interest (X), and *background factors* of no theoretical interest, which may affect X and Y and may therefore serve as confounders (Z). A *sample* consists of whatever cases are analyzed. The sample of cases rests within a *population* of cases to which a given proposition refers, defining its breadth or scope.

Part II

Selecting cases

3 Overview of case selection

Part I of the book surveyed and defined our subject matter. In this section of the book, I discuss various ways in which a single case, or a small number of cases, may be selected for intensive analysis. This chapter lays out an overview of case-selection strategies, while subsequent chapters elaborate on these strategies.

A typology, plus several omnibus criteria, is presented in the first section of the chapter. This is followed by some important clarifications relating to the goals, limitations, and ambiguities of the framework. Finally, I discuss the problem of validation – how to tell whether one or another strategy is most useful for the chosen task.

3.1 Strategies and criteria

Many typologies of case selection have been proposed over the years, and a good deal of progress can be discerned in successive work on this subject.[1] Even so, extant typologies are not always explicit about rules

---

[1] Mill (1843/1872) proposed the method of difference (also known as most-similar method) and the method of agreement (also known as most-different method), along with several others that have not gained traction. Lijphart (1971: 691) proposes six case study types: a-theoretical, interpretative, hypothesis-generating, theory-confirming, theory-infirming, and deviant. Eckstein (1975) identifies five species: configurative-idiographic, disciplined-configurative, heuristic, plausibility probes, and crucial-case. Skocpol and Somers (1980) identify three logics of comparative history: macro-causal analysis, parallel demonstration of theory, and contrast of contexts. Gerring (2007a) and Seawright and Gerring (2008) identify nine techniques: typical, diverse, extreme, deviant, influential, crucial, pathway, most-similar, and most-different. Levy (2008a) identifies five case study research designs:

for case selection that define each type in the typology,[2] and often conflate disparate strategies of case selection.[3] In these respects, I hope to improve upon past efforts (including my own).

Sections I and II of Table 3.1 follow the logic of a typology, where each category is mutually exclusive, and, collectively, the set of categories is exhaustive. The organizing feature of this typology is the goal that a case study is intended to achieve. Case studies serve a wide variety of functions and these functions rightly structure the process of selecting cases.

The most fundamental question is whether a case study aims for *descriptive* or *causal* inference. If the aim is causal, case studies may be further sub-divided according to their specific function – *exploratory*, *estimating*, or *diagnostic*. An exploratory case study is intended to identify a hypothesis, denoted H_x. An estimating case study is intended to estimate the causal effect of one factor on the outcome of interest, denoted $X \rightarrow Y$. A diagnostic case study is intended to assess whether a hypothesis (broadly understood) is true, which may involve an examination of measurement error, scope conditions, causal heterogeneity, confounders, and mechanisms. For each general aim or specific function, there are several potentially viable approaches to case selection, indicated in Column 1.

comparable, most and least likely, deviant, and process tracing. Rohlfing (2012: Chapter 3) identifies five case types – typical, diverse, most-likely, least-likely, and deviant – which are applied differently according to the purpose of the case study. Blatter and Haverland (2012: 24–6) identify three explanatory approaches – covariational, process tracing, and congruence analysis – each of which offers a variety of case-selection strategies. Additional typologies are laid out in Thomas and Myers (2015: 59). Occasionally, studies of case selection resist the typological exercise (e.g., Goertz 2017).

[2] For example, case studies described as a-theoretical, configurative, idiographic, disciplined-configurative, heuristic, or plausibility probe (Eckstein 1975; George and Bennett 2005: 75; Lijphart 1971) do not have well-defined methods for identifying relevant cases.

[3] Consider the three incarnations of most-similar analysis, as discussed below.

Table 3.1 Case-selection strategies and criteria

Goals/Strategies	C	K	Criteria
I. DESCRIPTIVE (to describe)			
Typical	1+	D	Mean, mode, or median of D
Diverse	2+	D	Typical sub-types
II. CAUSAL (to explain Y)			
1. Exploratory (to identify H_X)			
Extreme	1+	X *or* Y	Maximize variation in X or Y
Index	1+	Y	First instance of ΔY
Deviant	1+	$Z\ Y$	Poorly explained by Z
Most-similar	2+	$Z\ Y$	Similar on Z, different on Y
Most-different	2+	$Z\ Y$	Different on Z, similar on Y
Diverse	2+	$Z\ Y$	All possible configurations of Z (assumption: $X \in Z$)
2. Estimating (to estimate H_X)			
Longitudinal	1+	$X\ Z$	X changes, Z constant or biased against H_X
Most-similar	2+	$X\ Z$	Similar on Z, different on X
3. Diagnostic (to assess H_X)			
Influential	1+	$X\ Z\ Y$	Greatest impact on $P(H_X)$
Pathway	1+	$X\ Z\ Y$	$X \to Y$ strong, Z constant or biased against H_X
Most-similar	2+	$X\ Z\ Y$	Similar on Z, different on X and Y
III. OMNIBUS (broadly applicable)			
Intrinsic importance			Theoretical or practical significance
Case independence			X and Y unaffected by values for other cases
Within-case evidence			Suitability of case-based evidence
Logistics			Accessibility of evidence for a case
Representativeness			Generalizability

Notes: C = number of cases. K = factors relevant for case selection. D = descriptive features (other than those to be described in a case study). H_X = causal hypothesis of interest. $P(H_X)$ = the probability of H_X. X = causal factor(s) of theoretical interest. $X \to Y$ = apparent or estimated causal effect, which may be strong (high in magnitude) or weak. Y = outcome of interest. Z = vector of background factors that may affect X and/or Y.

Column 2 specifies the number of cases (C) in the case study. It will be seen that case studies enlist a minimum of one or two cases, with no clearly defined ceiling. This issue was discussed briefly in Chapter 2 and will be taken up again in Chapter 6.

Column 3 clarifies which dimensions (factors) of a case are relevant for case selection, i.e., descriptive features (D), the causal factor of theoretical interest (X), background factors of no theoretical interest (Z), and/or the outcome (Y). Generally, X and Y are regarded as single variables while Z is regarded as a vector. However, there are some exceptions, as noted in the following chapters.

Column 4 specifies the criteria used to select a case, or cases, from a universe of possible cases. These criteria will be elaborated in Chapters 4 and 5.

The third section of Table 3.1 departs from typological theorizing so as to recognize several "omnibus" goals of case selection – goals that apply broadly (though not quite universally) to case studies. We should not lose sight of the fact that case selection also has some generic features. These include: *intrinsic importance, case independence, within-case evidence, logistics,* and *representativeness,* as described in the following sections.

Intrinsic importance

The selection of cases is often influenced by the perceived importance of a case. Some cases – such as world wars, genocides, key inventions, revolutions – matter more than others because they have an obvious world historical significance. Others matter because they are important for a specific group of readers. I presume that every social group or organization is interested in its own history, and this may justify the choice of cases.

If this is the primary, or only, concern, the resulting study may be described as *idiographic* (Eckstein 1975; Levy 2008a; Lijphart 1971). Such studies appear to disavow any claims to generality and are thus not case studies by our definition (see Chapter 2). Nonetheless, cases chosen for idiographic reasons may result in insights that have broader applicability – and, as such, qualify as case studies.

It follows that the selection of a case, by itself, does not determine its future status as a case study. Indeed, there are plenty of examples of historical studies – usually selected by reason of their intrinsic importance – that come to be regarded, much later, as case studies of a more general phenomenon.

Likewise, even if the researcher aims for generalizable truths from the outset, s/he may also wish to say something about the case(s) under intensive investigation. (This tension – between the idiographic and nomothetic moments of a case study – is explored in Chapter 10.) From this perspective, it matters whether the case has some intrinsic importance to readers.

Independence

If a case study is designed to shed light on a causal question, the chosen cases should, ideally, be *independent* of each other and of other cases in the population. This is implicit in our definition of a case as a relatively bounded unit (Chapter 2). If cases are not bounded – if they affect each other with respect to the outcomes of concern – they are not providing independent evidence. This may be referred to as Galton's problem, interference, or a violation of SUTVA. (The exception would be a situation where interaction across cases happens to be the subject of investigation, as it would in a study of diffusion.)

Within-case evidence

If a case is to add to our knowledge of a subject, it must provide new evidence – evidence that is presumably not available – or not easily available or not in as precise or reliable form – for a larger sample. If sources are unreliable, scarce, or for one reason or another inaccessible, the case is of little value. Usually, this new evidence exists at a lower level of analysis, which we refer to as *within-case*. Within-case evidence is often the main value-added offered by a case study relative to a large-C analysis that has been, or might be, undertaken.

While the typology in Table 3.1 highlights case-level characteristics, it is notably silent on within-case characteristics. Yet, these may be the most important elements of all. Any case chosen for in-depth analysis must afford enough data, of the right kind, to address the question of interest at a lower level of analysis. This is not simply a question of data availability, but also – more crucially – of the suitability of that evidence for the researcher's purposes. If the aim of the case study is to shed light on causal relationships, then within-case evidence ought to exist that promises to shed light on those relationships. The evidence itself might be qualitative or quantitative. It might consist of pattern-matching – matching predictions emanating from a theory to facts of the case. It might consist of a quasi-experimental design with units that lie below the level of the case. (For further discussion, see Part III.)

Logistics

The availability of within-case evidence is partly a product of the case itself and partly a product of the researcher's personal attributes – his or her linguistic competences, connections, and previous acquaintance with a region, time period, or topic. I assume that these *logistical* features are taken into account – implicitly if not explicitly – in any case-selection process.

Sometimes, a logistically driven selection of cases is referred to as *convenience sampling*, though researchers may be loath to admit that they have chosen one case over another simply because it is easier to study. Nonetheless, if a researcher has special access to Site *A*, but not Site *B*, one should be grateful if s/he chooses *A* over *B* (so long as other criteria are not sacrificed). And we must acknowledge the fact that many authors find their cases through some serendipitous process that could scarcely be predicted or replicated, rather than the reverse. Darwin did not select the Galapagos Islands from a universe of potential cases.[4]

The same is true for many large-C studies, one must assume – though here it is the site that is chosen for logistical reasons rather than the case. Consider Ben Olken's (2007) renowned field experiment

---

[4] Gerry Munck, personal communication (2015).

on corruption, which was conducted in Indonesia. Olken's decision to choose Indonesia as a site of investigation is not explicitly explained or defended, though one may surmise that it had much to do with logistical factors such as the existence of World Bank sponsored infrastructure projects in that country and the cooperation Olken was able to obtain from the Indonesian government. (Such cooperation is rare, especially with respect to a subject as sensitive as corruption and in a country generally assumed to be riddled with corruption.) No one finds this "convenience" sample particularly troubling as it is assumed that site-selection does not bear on internal validity.

What differentiates logistically driven case study research from large-C research is that the relationships of interest are often known to the researcher beforehand, allowing her to cherry-pick cases that prove her theory. This is more than a convenience sample. It is a theory-affirming sample.

If, however, the outcome under study is not known to the researcher, or if it plays no part in the selection of cases, then the application of logistical criteria to case selection should be no more troubling in case study research than it is in large-C research.

Representativeness

In order for a case to be something broader than itself – a "case study" – the chosen case must be representative of a larger population in whatever ways are relevant for the larger argument.

If an argument is descriptive, then representativeness pertains only to features highlighted by the theory (denoted as D in Table 3.1). It is possible, in principle, to represent the descriptive features of a population with a single case if there is very little variation in that feature, i.e., if all cases in the population are the same with respect to the feature(s) of interest. This is unusual in social science settings. Consequently, the most one can usually achieve with a single case is to represent the central tendency of a distribution – its mean, median, or mode. This is the explicit goal of a *typical* case.

If the argument is causal, representativeness usually refers to the expected value of an outcome given its status on the causal variable of interest. Specifically, $E(Y|X)$ for the chosen case(s) should be the same as for cases in the broader population. This may be referred to as *causal comparability* or *unit homogeneity* (Glynn and Ichino 2016; Holland 1986; King *et al.* 1994).

Even if the case-selection technique does not prioritize representativeness, this criterion is present nonetheless. Note that deviant cases perform their function – identifying new causes of Y – only if they are representative of a larger population. (If the result of a deviant case study is to develop an idiosyncratic explanation – pertaining only to the chosen case – it is not very useful.) Likewise, influential cases are likely to be dismissed – as lying outside the population of the hypothesis – if they are too idiosyncratic. (A necessary condition may be disproven by a single case only if, for example, that case is judged to be part of the population of interest. Otherwise, scholars will rightly deal with the apparent exception by adopting tighter scope conditions.)

Granted, one can never know for sure whether a sample is representative of a population, especially with respect to causal properties. Representativeness is a matter of probability. Some samples are more likely to be representative than others, an issue taken up at greater length in Chapters 6 and 10.

3.2   Clarifications

Several features of Table 3.1 deserve clarification before we continue. These are not just academic niceties intended to protect the author's standing. They are in fact quite essential to the enterprise and should be read carefully, lest the exercise be misconstrued and misused.

1. The purpose of the typology summarized in Table 3.1 is primarily *descriptive* – to describe how cases are chosen. But it also contains

some *prescriptive* elements. Once a researcher has defined the goal a case study is intended to serve, I argue that there are a limited set of strategies available – as identified in Table 3.1. Among these strategies, I discuss (in succeeding chapters) the assumptions that undergird their employment, which may help researchers choose among them.

However, the final decision about which strategy to employ rests on upon contextual factors, i.e., the research question or hypothesis and the empirical lay of the land – matters that it would be vain to speculate upon. Suppose the research goal is to estimate a causal effect of X on Y. If a case offers comparisons before and after an intervention that do not confound, one might decide to employ a longitudinal design. If there are also well-matched comparison cases available, one might prefer the most-similar design. Since I cannot prejudge these contextual factors, I cannot specify, a priori, which of several case-selection strategies might be most useful in a given context. All I can do is to lay out the possible options.

2. Table 3.1 is intended to encompass the case-selection practices commonly used within the social sciences. It does not extend to selection procedures that are highly idiosyncratic, even though they might be justifiable in rare circumstances. Nor does it extend to cases that provide brief points of comparison for the case(s) of primary interest, i.e., *shadow* cases.[5]

---

[5] One type of shadow case seems especially important, and perhaps under-utilized, and therefore worthy of a short digression. If a hypothesis, H_x, suggests that X has a positive effect on Y, it is natural to focus on cases where X changes (a "treatment" case) and perhaps also on cases where X does not but where background factors (Z) are similar (a "control" case). This establishes the most-similar form of comparison, which we have discussed in exploratory, estimating, and diagnostic settings. Another sort of comparison arises between the control case and additional cases that exhibit similar values for X and Z. These cases serve a "placebo" function: since there is no exposure to the treatment, one would not expect a positive outcome for Y. If $Y = 1$, the hypothesis is called into question; if $Y = 0$, it is corroborated (Glynn and Ichino 2015). I regard the placebo case as a shadow case because it seems less important than

3. The list of possible strategies is lengthy and perhaps somewhat daunting, especially to those who are new to this subject. While it might be pleasing to be able to reduce the complexity of this subject to a small number of core strategies, this sort of reductionism would cause greater confusion downstream by conflating goals or techniques that are, in important respects, distinct. For example, there are three versions of the most-similar design – exploratory (selecting on ZY), estimating (selecting on XZ), and diagnostic (selecting on XZY). Each serves quite different functions, and, because selection is on different factors, each is likely to result in different choices.[6] Where techniques are different, it pays to disaggregate.

4. All case-selection strategies rest upon a case's relationship to a larger population of cases. For example, a deviant case is that case, or cases, in the studied population (or the observed sample) exhibiting the most deviant features. In addition, two general case-selection strategies (most-different and most-similar) require the researcher to consider the status of the chosen cases relative *to each other*.

5. Wherever case studies are oriented to causal inference, it is important to consider not only how a case compares to other potential cases at a particular point in time, but also how they compare *through time*. For example, it is much more informative to pinpoint the moment in time when values for a key variable changed than to know what its value was at time T. Thus, wherever possible, one

other cases in a study, e.g., the treatment and control cases in a most-similar analysis. The main point of interest in a placebo case is the values the case exhibits on X, Z, and Y – not the process connecting X with Y. Likewise, disparate results – where a placebo effect is found – do not necessarily falsify the hypothesis, as such a result might be credited to stochastic factors. This is a good illustration of how the incorporation of shadow cases approaches the conventional cross-case mode of investigation – where a large number of cases are analyzed in a schematic fashion.

[6] I preserve the common term (most-similar) in order to emphasize the common theme – similarity on Z – and also to avoid further confusion that might ensue if I invented neologisms for each of these strategies.

should consider ΔX rather than X, ΔZ rather than Z, and ΔY rather than Y.

6. Virtually all case-selection strategies may be executed in an informal ("qualitative") fashion or by employing a formal ("quantitative") algorithm. For example, a deviant case could be chosen based on a researcher's sense about which case, or cases, is poorly explained by extant theories, or it might be chosen by looking at residuals from a regression model. A full discussion of the pros and cons of algorithmic case selection is postponed until Chapter 6.

7. The factors that guide the case-selection process – D, X, Z, and/or Y – must be distinguished from features that the researcher wishes to discover, which by definition are unknown at the start of the research. If, for example, selection is conditional on Y, this means that the researcher knows the value of the outcome for cases that are under consideration for intensive study, but not the values of X or Z. If selection is conditional on Z and Y, the researcher is assumed to know the values for these dimensions of the case, but not the value for X. And so forth.

8. It is vital to clarify what the researcher knows, ex ante, prior to conducting the case study. Some aspects of a case are relevant for case selection while other aspects are irrelevant, and perhaps even counterproductive insofar as they may undermine the researcher's goals in conducting the case study. For example, if the goal of a case study is to estimate causal effects (for a population), it would be pointless to choose cases based on their values for the outcome, Y. Such a procedure, known as "cherry-picking," would obviously lead to a biased estimate.

9. While strategies of case selection refer to the *initial* decision to select cases, one must recognize that once a case is chosen it is likely to be exploited for all the information it can render. This includes possible hypotheses about Y (which may be regarded as part of a total explanation or as rival explanations *vis-à-vis* a favored hypothesis), and for each hypothesis, the causal effect,

the mechanism, the scope conditions, possible causal heterogeneity, and potential confounders. Intensively studied cases are mined for whatever information seems relevant to a research question.

10. Researchers occasionally wish their chosen cases to perform multiple functions, building this into their case-selection criteria from the very beginning. For example, in work focused on the causes of civil war, Paul Collier and Nicholas Sambanis (2005a, 2005b) choose cases that maximize variation along several independent variables of interest – regime type, violence, ethnic fragmentation, and resource dependence (*diverse* cases). Next, they select countries that fit their large-*C* model (*pathway* cases) and countries that do not (*deviant* cases) (Sambanis 2004: 6). Other examples of "composite" case-selection strategies are not hard to find (Fairfield 2013, 2015; Ostrom 1990; Pinfari 2012). However, the combination of multiple conflicting criteria in a selection of cases is relatively rare, and likely to remain so. In selecting a small basket of cases, one is forced to prioritize among various goals. Indeed, the examples of composite case selection that I have been able to find generally employ a fairly large basket of cases (typically, upwards of a dozen) – qualifying these studies as medium-*C* (for further discussion see Chapter 6).

11. Case selection sometimes occurs across *several levels*. For example, Fairfield (2013, 2015) first selects countries and then tax reform proposals within a specified period for each country. The latter are referred to as cases because they constitute the sort of event her theory tries to explain. However, the selection of countries – Argentina, Bolivia, and Chile – gets little attention. If cases are chosen at several levels, each level constitutes a distinct case-selection event, and deserves to be treated as such. For heuristic purposes, this book assumes that there are only two levels of analysis – the case level and the within-case level. But researchers can appreciate that things are often much more complicated.

12. The status of a case may *change* during the course of a researcher's investigation, which may last for years. For example, one might

choose a single extreme case and later add a second case to form a most-similar analysis. If cases are not chosen all at once, there is an issue of sequencing to resolve. Likewise, one might choose an extreme case and later decide that it conforms to a longitudinal design. Here, the case remains the same, but the description of the case changes. For example, Collier and Sambanis (2005a: 27) note that their case-selection guidelines "changed somewhat over time, as we moved away from the idea of using cases to test the theory and toward the idea of using the cases to develop theory and explore other issues such as mechanisms, sequences, measurement, and unit homogeneity."[7] The changing status of a case is virtually inevitable when the researcher starts out in an exploratory mode. Exploratory methods of case selection are quite vague, and are likely to morph into diagnostic designs once a specific hypothesis has been identified.

13. This derives from an important feature of case study research: case selection and case analysis are *enmeshed*. Indeed, the terms "case selection" and "research design" are virtually interchangeable. Choosing a case implies a method of analysis (though it does not entirely determine the method of analysis). Because case-selection methods also describe methods of analysis, it is useful to state the role of a case, ex post. If a case chosen for one purpose ends up serving another purpose, this is important information. And it need not cause confusion so long as the researcher is careful to distinguish between the ex ante method of case selection and the ex post method of case analysis (e.g., Fairfield 2015: 300).

14. This raises a final issue, that of *transparency*. Researchers should be clear about how they chose their cases and about any changes in their treatment of those cases as the research progresses. As Alan Stuart (1984; quoted in Henry 1990: 29) remarks, "The sample

---

[7] For another example of cases whose research design uses morph during the course of a case study, see Flyvbjerg (2006).

itself can never tell us whether the process that engendered it was free from bias. We must know what the process of selection was if we are not forever to be dogged by the shadow of selection bias." Unfortunately, many researchers are not as forthright as Collier & Sambanis or Fairfield. This is especially true for older studies, where methodological issues are generally not front-and-center.

Several features enhance ambiguity. First, researchers sometimes mean different things when they invoke case study terms, and rarely do authors differentiate between versions of the same generic design (e.g., most-similar exploratory, estimating, and diagnostic designs). Second, it is sometimes difficult to differentiate studies whose main purpose is descriptive from those whose main purpose is causal. This is because arguments are often rather loosely framed and may include a mixture of both elements. It is also because many case study researchers adopt a rather diffuse vision of causality (see Chapter 9). Third, it is often difficult to tell which features of the cases were known to the author prior to case selection. For example, it is often unclear when a researcher selected on X and when s/he selected on X and Y.[8]

Thus, in ascertaining case-selection techniques used in published studies, as I do in upcoming chapters, I am often forced to apply my own intuition. Others may disagree with my judgments. This is a solvable problem insofar as writers can do a better job of clarifying the technique they employed to select the chosen case, or cases (see Chapter 9).

3.3   Validation

Is there any way to determine empirically which of several strategies designed to achieve the same goal – as adumbrated in Table 3.1 – is most useful? Evidently, there are serious problems of *validation* to wrestle with.

---

[8] Glynn and Ichino (2015) discuss this problem.

Several attempts have been made to assess case-selection strategies using simulation techniques. Herron and Quinn (2016) assess estimating strategies, i.e., where the case is intended to measure causal effects. Seawright (2016b) assesses diagnostic strategies, where the case is designed to help confirm or disconfirm a causal hypothesis. Lucas and Szatrowski (2014) assess QCA-based strategies of case selection.

It would take some time to discuss these complex studies, so I shall content myself with several summary judgments. First, case-selection techniques have different goals, as shown in Table 3.1 – any attempt to compare them must focus on the goals that are appropriate to that technique. A technique whose purpose is exploratory (to identify a new hypothesis about Y) cannot be judged by its efficacy in identifying causal mechanisms, for example. Second, among these goals, estimating causal effects is the least common – and, by all accounts, the least successful – of these goals, so any attempt to gauge the effectiveness of case-selection methods should probably focus primarily on exploratory and diagnostic functions. Third, case-selection techniques are best practiced when taking into account change over time in the key variables, rather than static cross-sectional analyses, as emphasized above. Finally, and most importantly, it is difficult and perhaps impossible to simulate the complex features involved in an in-depth case analysis. The question of interest – which case, or cases, would best serve my purpose if I conducted an intensive analysis of it? – is hard to model without introducing assumptions that prejudge the results of the case study, and are in this respect endogenous to the case-selection strategy.[9]

In my opinion, testing the viability of case-selection strategies in a rigorous fashion would involve a methodological experiment of the

---

[9] For example, Herron and Quinn (2016: 9) make the assumption that the potential outcomes inherent in a case (i.e., the unit-level causal relationship) will be discovered by the case study researcher in the course of an intensive analysis of the case. Yet, "discoverability" is the very thing that case-selection techniques are designed to achieve. That is, a case-selection technique is regarded as superior insofar as it offers a higher probability of discovering an unknown feature of a case.

following sort. First, assemble a panel of researchers with similar background knowledge of a subject. Second, identify a subject deemed ripe for case study research, i.e., it is not well studied or has received no authoritative treatment and is not amenable to experimental manipulation. Third, select cases algorithmically, following the protocol laid out in Chapter 6. Fourth, randomly assign these cases to researchers with instructions to pursue all case study goals – exploratory, estimating, and diagnostic. Fifth, assemble a panel of judges, who are well versed in the subject of theoretical focus, to evaluate how well each case study achieved each of these goals. Judges would be instructed to decide independently (without conferring), though there might be a second round of judgments following a deliberative process in which they shared their thoughts and their preliminary decisions.

Such an experiment would be time-consuming and costly (assuming participants receive some remuneration), and it would need to be iterated across several research topics and with several panels of researchers and judges in order to make strong claims of generalizability. It presumes, furthermore, that expert judges are able to ascertain which approaches worked best, i.e., which yielded correct answers and/or and fruitful lines of inquiry. This is problematic, given that the ontological truth of the matter is probably contested. Nonetheless, it might be worth pursuing given the possible downstream benefits.[10]

---

[10] Note, however, that this experiment disregards qualitative judgments by researchers that might be undertaken after an algorithmic selection of cases. These qualitative judgments might serve as mediators. It could be, for example, that some case-selection strategies work better when the researcher is allowed to make final judgments – from among a set of potential cases that meet the stipulated case-selection criteria – based on knowledge of the potential cases. One must also consider a problem of generalizability that stems from the use of algorithmic procedures for selecting cases. It could be that subjects for which algorithmic case selection is feasible (i.e., where values for X, Z, and Y can be measured across a large sample) are different from subjects for which algorithmic case selection is infeasible. If so, we could not generalize the results of this experiment to the latter genre of case study research.

3.4   Summary

In this chapter, I present a typology of case-selection methods, intended to encompass the full (more or less) range of strategies employed in the social sciences. These are categorized according to their primary goal – descriptive or causal. If causal, the researcher's secondary goal may be categorized as exploratory (to identify a new hypothesis), estimating (to estimate the impact of X on Y), or diagnostic (to assess whether X is a cause of Y and, if so, what mechanisms might be at work and what scope conditions might apply). These goals determine what case-selection strategies are likely to be most availing, though the final choice must be made based on context-specific features (e.g., the hypothesis itself and the data available to explore it).

The final part of the chapter discusses efforts that have been undertaken, or might be undertaken, to validate different case-selection methods. My conclusion is that this is difficult to accomplish with simulation exercises, though it might be satisfactorily addressed with a set of experiments.

This chapter is rather diffuse as it deals with case selection in the abstract. Subsequent chapters explore these case-selection methods in greater depth with the assistance of numerous examples. They put the typology to work. It is hoped that the interplay between the general schema summarized in Table 3.1 and the specific applications of that schema is productive.

4 Descriptive case studies

Many case studies are primarily descriptive, which is to say they are not organized around a central, overarching causal hypothesis or theory. They may of course propose causal statements about the world, but these statements are peripheral to the main argument. Some of the best-known case studies are descriptive in this sense, as shown in the following tables.

Although writers are not always explicit about their selection of cases, most of these decisions might be described as following a *typical* or *diverse* case strategy. That is, they aim to identify a case, or cases, that exemplify a common pattern (typical) or patterns (diverse). In this respect, descriptive cases aim directly and explicitly at representativeness while other case-selection strategies do so only secondarily or more obliquely. This follows from the minimal goals of descriptive inference. Where the goal is to describe, there is no need to worry about more complex desiderata that might allow one to gain causal leverage on a question of interest.

Selection criteria for typical and diverse case studies are summarized in Table 4.1 and discussed in greater detail in the remaining sections of this chapter.

4.1 Typical

A case chosen by virtue of representing features that are common within a larger population may be described as *typical*. The typical case is intended to represent the central tendency of a distribution,

Table 4.1 Case-selection strategies for descriptive case studies

Goals/strategies	C	K	Criteria
Typical	1+	D	Mean, mode, or median of D
Diverse	2+	D	Typical sub-types

Notes: C = number of cases. K = factors relevant for case selection. D = descriptive features (other than those to be described in a case study).

which is of course not the same as the entire distribution. To say that a case is typical, therefore, does not mean that it is "representative" in the way that a larger sample might be representative of a population.

For example, Le Roy Ladurie (1978) focuses on a village in France ("Montaillou") that is thought to be representative of many other villages in the late Middle Ages. William Foote Whyte (1943/1955) chooses a street gang that is intended to be representative of many other street gangs in urban America. And Robert and Helen Lynd's (1929) study of "Middletown" focuses on a city (Muncie, Indiana) that was thought to be representative of many mid-sized cities across the United States.

The Lynds are more explicit about their case-selection criteria than most researchers. They state that they were looking for a city with

(1) a temperate climate; (2) a sufficiently rapid rate of growth to ensure the presence of a plentiful assortment of the growing pains accompanying contemporary social change; (3) an industrial culture with modern, high-speed machine production; (4) the absence of dominance of the city's industry by a single plant (i.e., not a one-industry town); (5) a substantial local artistic life to balance its industrial activity ... and (6) the absence of any outstanding peculiarities or acute local problems which would mark the city off from the midchannel sort of American community.[1]

After examining a number of options, the Lynds decide that Muncie, Indiana, is more representative than, or at least as representative as, other mid-sized cities in America.

---

[1] Lynd and Lynd (1929/1956), quoted in Yin (2004: 29–30).

Typical cases can be about anything at all, as our set of exemplars in Table 4.2 shows. Chosen studies focus on agencies, bureaucracies, cities, communities, corporations, cultures, delinquents, factories, families, gangs, legislative decisions, medical schools, peasant cultures, plants, poor communities, second-language learners, sidewalks, social groups, societies, tariff bills, towns, villages, and workers. The exemplars also span the universe of social science – from ethnographies, to social history, to economic history, and rational choice. Most samples are quite small – between one and three – and only one is fairly numerous ($C = 18$).

All of the chosen exemplars employ an informal ("qualitative") approach to case selection. Typicality may also be given a more precise rendering as the arithmetic mean, median, or mode. If all of the dimensions of concern to the Lynds were measurable, one can easily imagine that they might have used one of these algorithms to solve their case-selection dilemma. Note, however, that their last consideration is a catch-all residual category – *the absence of any outstanding peculiarities* – which, one imagines, would be impossible to measure systematically, and hence not amenable to an algorithmic approach to case selection.

4.2   Diverse

A descriptive case study might also focus on several cases that, together, are intended to capture the diversity of a subject. In effect, the researcher looks for typical cases of each envisioned type. From this perspective, a diverse case approach to case selection is an iterated typical-case approach to case selection. For example, Gabriel Almond and Sidney Verba (1963) choose to study political cultures in the United States, Germany, Mexico, Italy, and the United Kingdom with the idea that these countries, together, represent the diversity of political cultures in the world, which they conclude may be summarized in three ideal-types: participant, subject, and parochial.

Table 4.2 Typical case studies

Study	Field	Cites	SELECTION Algo.	SELECTION Non-algo.	CASES Phenomena	C
Allen (1965) *Nazi Seizure of Power*	HI	397		•	Towns	1
Banfield (1958) *Moral Basis of Backward Society*	PS	3,882		•	Villages	1
Becker (1961) *Boys in White*	SO	3,142		•	Medical schools	1
Benedict (1934) *Patterns of Culture*	AN	5,571		•	Cultures	3
Coase (1959) *Federal Communications Commission*	EC	1,410		•	Agencies	1
Dahl (1961) *Who Governs?*	PS	5,810		•	Cities	1
Duneier (1999) *Sidewalk*	AN	997		•	Sidewalks	1
Geertz (1978) *Bazaar Economy*	AN	892		•	Communities	1
Gouldner (1954) *Patterns of Industrial Bureaucracy*	SO	3,075		•	Factories	1
Handlin (1941) *Boston's Immigrants*	HI	488		•	Cities	1
Homans (1951) *Human Group*	SO	4,633		•	Groups	5
Hunter (1953) *Community Power Structure*	SO	2,393		•	Cities	1
Kanter (1977) *Men and Women of the Corporation*	SO	11,950		•	Corporations	1
Kaufman (1960) *Forest Ranger*	PS	1,073		•	Agencies	1
Lane (1962) *Political Ideology*	PS	695		•	Workers	18
Lerner (1958) *Passing of Traditional Society*	PS	4,912		•	Societies	1
Le Roy Ladurie (1978) *Montaillou*	HI	384		•	Peasant cultures	1
Lewis (1959) *Five Families*	AN	1,026		•	Families	5
Lynd and Lynd (1929) *Middletown*	SO	2,199		•	Cities	1
McAdam (1982) *Political Process and Black Insurgency*	SO	4,534		•	Social movements	1
Schattschneider (1935) *Politics, Pressures and the Tariff*	PS	740		•	Tariff bills	1
Scheper-Hughes (1992) *Death w/out Weeping*	AN	2,494		•	Poor communities	1
Schmidt (1983) *Interaction, Acculturation, Acquisition*	LI	515		•	2nd-lang. learners	1
Selznick (1949) *TVA and the Grass Roots*	SO	3,260		•	Agencies	1

Table 4.2 (*cont.*)

			SELECTION		CASES	
Study	Field	Cites	Algo.	Non-algo.	Phenomena	C
Shaw (1930) *The Jack Roller*	SO	654		•	Delinquents	1
Taylor (1911) *Principles of Scientific Management*	EC	13,344		•	Industrial plants	3
Warner and Lunt (1941) *Yankee City*	AN	239		•	Cities	1
Weber (1979) *Peasants into Frenchmen*	HI	3,367		•	Nation-building	1
Whyte (1943) *Street Corner Society*	SO	5,501		•	Gangs	3

Notes: C = number of cases. *Algo.* = case selection by algorithm.

Eight exemplars of this sort are listed in Table 4.3. They deal with constitutions, economic crises, firms, members of parliament (MPs) and their districts, nation-building, national civic cultures, and policy failures. The number of cases (*C*) ranges from four to 17. Diverse cases mandate a basket of cases, and the typical basket seems to be somewhat shy of a dozen.

As an in-depth example, we shall follow Richard Fenno's (1978) influential study, *Home Style*, which explores the relationship between members of the US House of Representatives and their districts. His lens on this question is the Member of Parliament (MP), rather than the constituent. While it might be interesting to know how different sorts of constituents view their MP, it is also important to know how the MP–constituent relationship appears to the elected official. This, at any rate, is Fenno's perspective on a time-honored subject. And it is one well suited to Fenno's chosen method of analysis – participant-observation, or ethnography. How better to obtain MPs' views than to observe them, up close, as they interact with constituents.

Cases – i.e., members of Congress – are chosen in a non-random fashion, presumably because subjects are hard to enlist. Not all will agree to submit to Fenno's intrusive "soaking and poking."

Table 4.3 Diverse case studies (descriptive)

Study	Field	Cites	SELECTION		CASES	
			Algo.	Non-algo.	Phenomena	C
Almond and Verba (1963) *Civic Culture*	PS	12,679		●	Political cultures	5
Anderson (1974) *Lineages of Absolutist State*	HI	2,508		●	Nation-building	10
Bendix (1978) *Kings or People*	SO	664		●	Nation-building	5
Chandler (1962) *Strategy and Structure*	EC	1,427		●	Firms	4
Fenno (1977, 1978) *Home Style*	PS	2,141		●	MPs and districts	17
Gourevitch (1986) *Politics in Hard Times*	PS	1,112		●	Economic crises	5
Scott (1998) *Seeing Like a State*	PS	8,634		●	Policy failures	6
Wilson (1889) *The State*	PS	268		●	Constitutions	10

Notes: C = number of cases. *Algo.* = case selection by algorithm.

Nonetheless, Fenno (1977: 884) can reasonably claim that the chosen group embodies diversity across the population of interest, the US House of Representatives. He writes modestly,

The seventeen include nine Democrats and eight Republicans. Geographically, three come from two eastern states; six come from five midwestern states; three come from three southern states; five come from three far western states. Since I began, one has retired, one has been defeated and one has run for the Senate. There is some variation among them in terms of ideology, seniority, ethnicity, race, sex, and in terms of safeness and diversity of district. But no claim is made that the group is ideally balanced in any of these respects.

Although all the exemplars in Table 4.3 choose cases in an informal, qualitative fashion, it is also possible to employ an algorithm to identify a small basket of diverse cases from a large population of potential cases. Specifically, the researcher may choose cases with different scores (e.g., high, medium, low) on parameters of interest, examine the intersection of different parameters (broken into discrete categories, if the variables are interval-level), or utilize more complex techniques such as factor analysis (Fabrigar and Wegener 2011) or cluster analysis (Everitt *et al.* 2011).

4.3   Summary

Arguably, case studies are better suited for descriptive analysis than for causal analysis. It is striking that the fields where case studies remain the dominant mode of analysis – e.g., anthropology, history, urban sociology, and political science "area studies" – are also fields where descriptive case studies remain the dominant mode of case study research. Where case studies are most often practiced, the case study format is most often descriptive. And many of our most renowned case studies arise from these fields.

These studies are also, one might argue, less problematic from a methodological point of view. They do not make clearly defined causal arguments, and as such are not subject to problems of causal inference. Of course, they are likely to make a multitude of small causal claims, but these are ancillary to an overall argument that is descriptive in nature. In this respect, one might say that they are less ambitious. Or, perhaps more appropriately, one might say that their ambition is focused on a different object.

Problems arise, however, if one considers the generalizability of many of these studies. As a rule, descriptive studies are less falsifiable than causal studies (Gerring 2012a). This pattern can be seen in descriptive case studies, where it is often difficult to specify a clearly defined population and a set of criteria that would allow one to verify, or falsify, the hypothesis within that larger population. These issues are taken up at greater length in Chapter 10.

5   Causal case studies

We turn now to case studies where the goal is to shed light on a causal argument.[1] Before we get into the weeds, several general points bear emphasis. (For further discussion, see Chapter 9.)

First, a case study is understood as causal if it is oriented around a central hypothesis about how X affects Y – the causal effect, symbolized as $X \rightarrow Y$. The study may embrace several interrelated hypotheses, where X is understood as a vector rather than a single factor (e.g., a *causes-of-effects* style of analysis). However, for heuristic purposes we usually restrict ourselves to a single causal factor.

Second, most case studies do not attempt to estimate a precise causal effect and an accompanying confidence interval, as would be expected from large-C research. Samples of one or several are not well suited to estimate population parameters.[2] Hence, in this book the notion of *causal inference* encompasses any statement about the impact of X on Y: precise (e.g., "An increase of one unit in X generates a two-unit increase in Y") or imprecise (e.g., "An increase in X causes an increase in Y").

---

[1] I shall not detain the reader with a long discussion of the meaning of causality and various frameworks for achieving causal inference. An introductory treatment may be found in Gerring (2012b) and more advanced treatments in Hernan and Robins (in process), Imbens and Rubin (2015), Morgan (2013), Morgan and Winship (2014).

[2] To be sure, one can sometimes estimate sample statistics. For example, if a single case allows one to observe the value of Y as X changes without an inordinate number of potential confounders, one may estimate the impact of X on Y with time-series models (Hamilton 1994). Alternatively, in a medium-n sample one may employ synthetic matching (Abadie, Diamond and Hainmueller 2015) or randomization inference (Glynn and Ichino 2015) to estimate causal effects. However, these procedures are not always applicable. Moreover, it seems highly unlikely that such precise estimates would be generalizable to a larger population.

Third, some case studies do not attempt to measure even a very imprecise causal effect. They adopt a theory about this causal effect, or rely on large-C analyses to estimate the effect. The case study is focused instead on other aspects of the relationship – measurement of key variables, mechanisms, potential confounders, scope conditions, and so forth. Thus, in saying that a case study is "causal" in orientation I do not mean to imply that the case provides the sole basis for the estimation of a causal effect.

Fourth, if a case (or set of cases) *is* relied upon to provide an estimate of causal effects, the case ought to exemplify *quasi-experimental* properties, i.e., replicate the virtues of a true experiment even while lacking a manipulated treatment (Gerring and McDermott 2007). Specifically, treatment assignment should be *as-if random* – as if it had been randomly assigned by a researcher (even though it is actually assigned by "nature"). This assures pre-treatment equivalence in a probabilistic fashion. Of course, one must also worry about post-treatment equivalence. A well-constructed experiment achieves causal comparability throughout the duration of the experiment. The expected value of Y, conditional on X and Z (a vector of observed background factors), should be equal for all units, and all time periods, under study. Otherwise stated, variation in X should not be correlated with other factors that are also causes of Y, which might serve as *confounders*, generating a spurious (non-causal) relationship between X and Y. This is the logic of experiments and it applies with equal force to most other research designs where the goal is causal inference.[3]

Fifth, case-selection criteria may be understood *cross-sectionally* or *longitudinally*. For example, the test of "deviance" might be a case's status at a particular point in time, or its change in status over an

---

[3] Two caveats should be added. First, exploratory case-selection strategies do not take account of a case's value on X because X is unknown. However, these strategies evolve into a different research design once the researcher identifies a hypothesis. At this point, the quasi-experimental ideal comes into play. Second, the analysis of *within-case* evidence builds on this experimental template but introduces additional elements, not all of which fall neatly into that template, as discussed in Chapter 8.

observed period of time. Sometimes, temporal changes are implicit in the case-selection format. For example, a case exhibiting an unusual outcome is presumed to show evidence of how that outcome came about. France is a "revolutionary" case because it experienced a dramatic and sudden reordering of social and political power at the end of the eighteenth century. Austria is a non-revolutionary case because it did not. Nonetheless, it is helpful to know when that change occurred – the eighteenth century is a more logical focus of study than the nineteenth century if one is interested in France's revolution.

Cases exhibiting change in key parameters of interest are usually more informative than cases that remain static through time. Moreover, ascertaining the precise point in time that a case underwent a change in X or Y can be extremely useful for analytic purposes. Thus, wherever possible, researchers should administer case-selection strategies using information about how cases perform through time in addition to how they compare to other cases at a particular point in time. Cross-sectional comparisons should be supplemented by longitudinal comparison.[4]

With this as background, we turn to case-selection strategies. Case studies enlisted for purposes of causal inference may serve *exploratory*, *estimating*, or *diagnostic* functions. Each of these functions calls forth a variety of case-selection strategies, as summarized in Table 5.1. We can now explore these functions and strategies in detail.

5.1   Exploratory

Many case studies aim to identify a new hypothesis and are therefore *exploratory*. Sometimes, the researcher begins with a factor that is

---

[4] This folk wisdom applies to all case-selection methods employed for causal inference, including those that incorporate an explicit cross-sectional (cross-case) comparison such as the *most-similar* and *most-different* case-selection strategies.

Table 5.1 Case-selection strategies for causal case studies

Goals/strategies	C	K	Criteria
1. Exploratory (to identify H_X)			
Extreme	1+	X or Y	Maximize variation in X or Y
Index	1+	Y	First instance of ΔY
Deviant	1+	$Z\,Y$	Poorly explained by Z
Most-similar	2+	$Z\,Y$	Similar on Z, different on Y
Most-different	2+	$Z\,Y$	Different on Z, similar on Y
Diverse	2+	$Z\,Y$	All possible configurations of Z (assumption: $X \in Z$)
2. Estimating (to estimate H_X)			
Longitudinal	1+	$X\,Z$	X changes, Z constant or biased against H_X
Most-similar	2+	$X\,Z$	Similar on Z, different on X
3. Diagnostic (to assess H_X)			
Influential	1+	$X\,Z\,Y$	Greatest impact on $P(H_X)$
Pathway	1+	$X\,Z\,Y$	$X \to Y$ strong, Z constant or biased against H_X
Most-similar	2+	$X\,Z\,Y$	Similar on Z, different on X and Y

Notes: C = number of cases. K = factors relevant for case selection. H_X = causal hypothesis of interest. $P(H_X)$ = the probability of H_X. X = causal factor(s) of theoretical interest. $X \to Y$ = apparent or estimated causal effect, which may be strong (high in magnitude) or weak. Y = outcome of interest. Z = vector of background factors that may affect X and/or Y.

presumed to have fundamental influence on a range of outcomes. The research question is: what outcomes $Y_{1...n}$ does X affect? More commonly, the researcher works backward from a known outcome to its possible causes. The research question is, therefore, what accounts for variation in Y? Or, if Y is a discrete event, why does Y occur? Specific exploratory techniques may be classified as *extreme, index, deviant, most-different, most-similar,* or *diverse,* and will be explored in detail below.

Exploratory case-selection strategies that select cases based on their outcome, Y, violate a well-worn piece of social science folk wisdom not to select based on the dependent variable.[5] This is indeed problematic if

---

[5] Geddes (1990). See also discussion in Brady and Collier (2004), Collier and Mahoney (1996), Rogowski (1995).

a number of cases are chosen, all of which lie on one end of a variable's spectrum (they are all positive *or* negative), and the researcher subjects this sample to cross-case analysis as if it were representative of a population.[6] Suppose that Theda Skocpol (1979) examined three revolutionary countries – France, Russia, and China – comparing them to each other in a quest to understand revolution. Or suppose that Peters and Waterman (1982) examined 42 highly successful firms, comparing them to each other to understand the causes of success. Results for these analyses would assuredly be biased (Collier and Mahoney 1996). Moreover, there will be little variation to explain since the outcome values of all cases are explicitly constrained.

However, this is not the proper or usual employment of cases chosen in an exploratory fashion. First of all, when cases are selected based on the outcome it is usually *change* in the outcome (ΔY) that is of primary interest. Skocpol looks at pre-revolutionary, revolutionary, and post-revolutionary periods for each chosen country. Peters and Waterman examine firm histories – how each firm achieved success. Second, some exploratory designs require variation in the outcome across cases ("negative" and "positive" cases), while other exploratory designs incorporate cross-case variation in Y in a less explicit fashion, as shadow cases. Thus, Skocpol compares revolutionary cases to cases of non-revolution or partial revolution and Peters and Waterman compare successful firms to unsuccessful firms. Background cases may also be formally integrated into a study through large-C analysis, generating a multimethod approach to research (Chapter 7).

Accordingly, the problem of "selecting on Y" may not be as severe as some writers have imagined. To be sure, selecting on Y is not the best way to select a representative sample. But this is only one of several goals informing case selection, as discussed in Chapter 3. When the

---

[6] The exception would be a circumstance in which the researcher intends to disprove a deterministic argument (Dion 1998).

goal is exploratory, it is difficult to envision a viable case-selection strategy that takes no notice of values for the outcome of interest.

Imagine a geologist who is trying to understand earthquakes but has no particular hypothesis in mind as she seeks to discover potential causes of these cataclysms. In her quest to avoid a biased sample, she refuses to consider the prevalence of earthquakes in her selection of a research site, ending up in Kansas – one of the world's more stable geological locations. Time spent in Kansas might be fruitful. However, it seems less likely to yield clues into the behavior of earthquakes than locations that lie along a major fault-line, where geologic activity is frequent and leaves many observable traces.

Extreme

An *extreme* case design maximizes variation in the variable of interest, either X or Y. This may be achieved by a single case or by a set of cases that, together, exhibit contrasting outcomes. William James writes that "moments of extremity often reveal the essence of a situation" (quoted in Singh 2015). It is not entirely clear how to understand "essence" in a social science context. Nonetheless, one may take the point that substantial variation in X or Y makes a relationship more transparent, and thus helps to identify hypotheses for further research.

Extreme cases are often regarded as prototypical or paradigmatic of a phenomenon. This is because concepts are often defined by their extremes, which may also be understood as a partial embodiment of an ideal-type. German fascism defines the concept of fascism because it offers the most extreme example of that phenomenon. Likewise, extreme cases may be intrinsically interesting – perhaps even strange, exotic – by virtue of their extremity or rarity. However, the prime methodological value of the extreme case derives from its promised variation in X or Y.

Table 5.2 lists fifteen extreme case studies. These exemplars stretch across the social science disciplines and cover a range of topics,

Table 5.2 Extreme case exemplars

Study	Field	Cites	SELECTION		CASES	
			Algo.	Non-algo.	Phenomena	C
Caldwell (1986) *Routes to Low Mortality*	DE	1,022		●	Mortality	3
Curtiss (1977) *Psycholinguistic Study of "Wild Child"*	PY	933		●	Human development	1
Fearon and Laitin (2008, 2014, 2015) *Random Narratives*	PS	85	●		Civil wars	25
Goldstone (1991) *Revolution and Rebellion*	SO	994		●	Revolutions	4
Harding *et al.* (2002) *Study of Rampage School Shootings*	SO	77		●	School shootings	2
Johnson (1983) *MITI and the Japanese Miracle*	PS	3,185		●	Industrial policies	1
Kindleberger (1996) *World Economic Primacy*	EC	213		●	Economic development	8
Linz and Stepan (1978a, 1978b) *Breakdown Demo. Regimes*	PS	1,765		●	Dem. breakdowns	11
Peters and Waterman (1982) *In Search of Excellence*	EC	17,443		●	Firms	43
Porter (1990) *Competitive Advantage of Nations*	EC	31,857		●	Economic development	10
Sagan (1993) *Limits of Safety*	PS	876		●	Nuclear accidents	4
Skocpol (1979) *States and Social Revolutions*	SO	5,227		●	Revolutions	3/6
Tilly (1964) *The Vendée*	SO	274		●	Counter-revs	1
Vaughan (1996) *Challenger Launch Decision*	SO	15		●	Space launches	1
Veenendaal (2015) *Microstates*	PS	11		●	Democracy	4

Notes: C = number of cases. *Algo.* = case selection by algorithm.

including democracy, economic development, human development, industrial policies, mortality, nuclear accidents, space launches, revolutions, school shootings, and the success/failure of firms. The number of cases varies from one to 43, with an average of about eight.

Most are focused on variation in Y, rather than X. The exception is Wouter Veenendaal's study of microstates, chosen on the basis of their diminutive size. Veenendaal is interested in how size affects the nature of politics, with particular attention to outcomes related to democracy. To do so, he chooses four tiny countries – Palau, St Kitts and Nevis, San Marino, and the Seychelles – which are then examined intensively through interviews, ethnography, and secondary sources.

Looking more closely, one may discern three versions of the extreme case. The first exhibits extreme values on X or Y (or ΔX or ΔY). Note that studies of welfare state development often focus on the world's largest welfare states, located in Northern Europe. Studies of war often focus on one of the two world wars. Studies of genocide often focus on the Holocaust.[7] By the same logic, those who risk their lives to save others provide more valuable information about altruism than those who make small donations to a cause (Monroe 1996). Companies that are supremely successful (Peters and Waterman 1982), or supremely unsuccessful, are more informative than companies that follow a middling trajectory. Countries with extremely high growth rates (Johnson 1983), or negative growth rates, may offer more insights than countries with modest growth rates. Countries with an extremely high (e.g., Guatemala), or extremely low (e.g., Japan), rate of violent crime may be more informative than those lying near the middle. And so forth.

A second version applies when an input or output is conceptualized in a binary fashion and one value (generally understood as the "positive" value) is especially rare. Case studies of war generally focus on wars – peace being the more common condition. Case studies of democratization generally focus on regime transitions – continuity being the more common condition. Case studies of revolution generally focus on revolution – non-revolution being the more common condition. Case studies of space launches focus on failures (Vaughan 1996).

---

[7] The "extreme" case approach to case selection (Seawright and Gerring 2008) is understood here as a sub-type of "outcome" case strategy.

The rarer the value the more important that positive case becomes. Harding *et al.* (2002) study "rampage" school shootings, noting that these events are extremely rare, numbering only 30 to 50 (depending upon how the event is defined) over three decades across the United States. This reinforces the authors' determination to focus on instances where the awful event occurred. (It would make little sense to study a school without violence.) They settle on two such events, one at Heath High School in West Paducah, Kentucky, on December 1, 1997, and the other at Westside Middle School, near Jonesboro, Arkansas, on March 24, 1998. (These cases were assigned to the researchers from a pool of positive cases by an agency implementing a mandate from the National Academy of Sciences.)

A third approach to achieving variation in the outcome is to choose cases lying at *both* tails of the distribution, i.e., *polar* cases. Here, comparisons can be made directly across the chosen cases. For example, a study of war may focus on cases exhibiting peace *and* war (e.g., Fearon and Laitin 2008, 2014, 2015).[8] Superficially, the polar case is quite different from the extreme or rare case since variation is built into the research design. However, one must bear in mind that studies focused on cases that lie on one side of the distribution are never focused exclusively on the chosen case(s); they always make implicit or explicit contrasts to other cases that have less extreme/rare values, which may be regarded as "shadow" cases.

All versions of the extreme case design maximize variation in X or Y, preferably variation through time (ΔX or ΔY). To identify such a case, or cases, from a large population of potential cases, an informal approach may be sufficient. Skocpol knew where revolutions had occurred, and where they had not. But not all settings are self-evident.

---

[8] In practice, we find that researchers generally focus on only one tail of the distribution. This, in turn, could reflect a persistent feature of the world. Long-tailed distributions – with especially large variance scores – may be accompanied by skew (to the right or the left). This is true by construction for phenomena such as income or mortality, both of which are bounded at 0.

Here one may employ an algorithm, selecting a case, or cases, that lies farthest from the mean, median, or mode of the distribution, or cases that lie on both tails of the distribution.

Admittedly, any case with an unusual value is also less likely to be representative of a larger population, posing a potential problem of generalizability. This is not true by definition. A case with an especially high value for *Y may* be perfectly predicted by *X*, once *X* has been discovered. It may lie right on the regression line, for example, if regression is used to model the interrelationship between *X* and *Y*. Extreme cases should not be confused with *deviant* cases, discussed below. To be sure, if all one knows about a case is its value for *Y*, and that value is far from the middle of the distribution, the possibility of sample bias is high. This is a cost that must be reckoned with. Nonetheless, if the goal of an extreme case study is exploratory – to identify a hypothesis – and if this is more likely to be perceived from examining an unusual example of a phenomenon, the risk may be worth the cost.

Index

An *index* case is the first instance of a phenomenon. In epidemiology, it refers to the first patient to contract a disease. Identifying the index case is useful for understanding the origin and spread of disease and for that reason a good deal of effort goes into the search for *patient zero*. In other social science disciplines, the focus on index cases is also motivated by the desire to understand the origins of a phenomenon. The presumption may be that the index case plays a causal role – as a prime mover or as an illustrative or standard-setting case, establishing a practice to emulate or avoid. The primacy of "firsts" is imprinted in natural language and in the social science lexicon, where new phenomena are often named after the person, place, or event of their first occurrence. In this fashion, the first instance of a case comes to *define* the case.

There is one additional reason for focusing on index cases. The first instance of a phenomenon cannot be influenced by other instances of that phenomenon. It occurs endogenously. By contrast, subsequent occurrences are likely to be influenced by the experience of the index case, assuming information has diffused through a population.

In some settings there may be multiple index cases. Subjects may contract a disease, discover a technology, or implement a policy independently of each other. Archaeologists speculate that writing was invented independently on two or more occasions.[9] A variety of features may impede diffusion. In the modern world, however, we can expect that diffusion processes are relatively efficient, which limits the number of cases that might qualify as indexical.

Wherever diffusion is at work, we may suspect that the occurrence of an event owes something to what has been learned from previous instances. This introduces a problem of non-independence across units (also known as Galton's problem). The advantage of an index case is that it – perhaps alone among all other instances of a phenomenon – is free from this confounder. (I am assuming that diffusion is of no theoretical importance to the researcher.)

Six index case studies are listed in Table 5.3. These involve the discovery of democracy (Athens, sixth century BC), the deployment of nuclear weapons (the United States, 1945), the imposition of limited government (England, sixteenth century), revolution (Britain, seventeenth century), class formation (Britain, nineteenth century), and tax revolts (California, 1973). The prominent position of historians, and British historians in particular, in the genre of index cases will not be missed.

Naturally, claims to representativeness are often suspect. The first example of something may be different from those that follow. Historians might dispute Steve Pincus's (2011) assertion that the English revolution is the first modern revolution. They might dispute the

---

[9] Daniels and Bright (1996).

Table 5.3 Index case exemplars

Study	Field	Cites	SELECTION		CASES	
			Algo.	Non-algo.	Phenomena	C
Alperovitz (1996) *Decision to Use Atomic Bomb*	PS	409		•	Nuclear deploy.	1
Martin (2008) *Permanent Tax Revolt*	SO	121		•	Tax revolts	1
North and Weingast (1989) *Constitutions and Commitment*	EC	3,462		•	Limited govt	1
Pincus (2011) *1688: First Modern Revolution*	HI	247		•	Revolutions	1
Raaflaub *et al.* (2007) *Origins of Democracy*	HI	98		•	Democratization	1
Thompson (1963) *Making of English Working Class*	HI	9,584		•	Class formation	1

Notes: C = number of cases. *Algo.* = case selection by algorithm.

contention that democracy in ancient Greece can teach us anything about the development of representative democracy in the eighteenth and nineteenth centuries. They might not agree that the fight for "Prop 13" in California is indicative of tax revolts elsewhere in the United States. Nonetheless, the claim of an index case rests on its status as first in a class of phenomena. If there is an earlier (known) precedent, or if later examples are not really examples of the same thing, then the status of a case changes. It no longer carries a methodological punch.

Deviant

A *deviant* case deviates from an expected causal pattern, as suggested by scientific theories or common sense, thereby registering a surprising result. The study of deviance may also be framed as the study of *anomalies*, which are widely acknowledged to play a central role in scientific progress (Elman and Elman 2002; Lakatos 1978).

The goal of a deviant, or anomalous, case study is to explain the oddball case and, in addition, to explain other similarly deviant cases, providing a generalizable hypothesis about the phenomenon of interest. The resulting explanation may involve a new causal factor, an inter-action (also known as contextual) effect between two or more causal factors, or a revision to the scope conditions of a theory. Note that interaction effects and scope conditions are two different responses to the issue of causal heterogeneity. In one setting, the source of causal heterogeneity is incorporated into a causal model; in the other setting, discordant cases are removed from the sample.

Barbara Geddes notes the importance of deviant cases in medical science, where researchers are habitually focused on that which is "pathological" (according to standard theory and practice). The *New England Journal of Medicine*, one of the premier journals of the field, carries a regular feature entitled Case Records of the Massachusetts General Hospital. These articles bear titles like the following: "An 80-Year-Old Woman with Sudden Unilateral Blindness" or "A 76-Year-Old Man with Fever, Dyspnea, Pulmonary Infiltrates, Pleural Effusions, and Confusion."[10]

Another example drawn from the field of medicine concerns the extensive study devoted to a small number of persons resistant to the HIV/AIDS virus (Buchbinder and Vittinghoff 1999; Haynes *et al.* 1996). Medical researchers are intrigued. Why are they resistant? What is different about these people? What can we learn about AIDS in other patients by observing people who have powerful defenses against this disease?

In psychology and sociology, case studies may be comprised of deviant persons or groups. Although this is a somewhat different use of the term, the goal of such studies is usually to bring "deviants" into the realm of theoretical understanding – that is, to explain why some

---

[10] Geddes (2003: 131). For other examples of case work from the annals of medicine, see "Clinical Reports" in *The Lancet*, "Case Studies" in *The Canadian Medical Association Journal*, and various issues of the *Journal of Obstetrics and Gynecology*, often devoted to clinical cases (discussed in Jenicek 2001: 7). For examples from the sub-field of comparative politics, see Kazancigil (1994).

people do not behave as others do. In economics, case studies may consist of countries or businesses that over-perform (e.g., Botswana; Apple) or under-perform (e.g., Britain through most of the twentieth century; Sears in recent decades) relative to some set of expectations. In political science, case studies may focus on countries where the welfare state is more developed (e.g., Sweden) or less developed (e.g., the United States) than one would expect, given a set of general expectations about welfare state development.[11]

Note that while extreme cases are judged relative to the mean of a single distribution (the outcome of interest, Y), deviant cases are judged relative to a general model of causal relations including both Z (a background factor or set of background factors) and Y (the outcome). The deviant case method selects cases which, by reference to a general large-C relationship, demonstrate a surprising value. They are "deviant" in that they are poorly explained.

In a regression model, deviance can be measured by the residual for a given case. If there is considerable distance between its predicted value and its actual value, we may feel justified in calling it deviant. Since deviance is usually a matter of degrees, the residual provides a convenient method of evaluating relative deviance among a large number of cases.

Because deviance can only be assessed according to a general (quantitative or qualitative) model, the relative deviance of a case is likely to change whenever that model is altered. For example, the US is a deviant case with respect to its "laggard" welfare state when a causal model includes only per capita GDP. But it is no longer deviant when certain additional factors measuring social and political institutions are included in the model. Deviance is always model-dependent, even if the model is of an informal (qualitative) sort. Thus, when discussing the

---

[11] For more examples and further discussion of deviant-case research designs in the social sciences, see Amenta (1991), Burawoy (1998), Burawoy et al. (1991), Eckstein (1975), Emigh (1997), Kendall and Wolf (1949/1955), Pearce (2002).

concept of the deviant case it is helpful to ask the following question: *relative to what general model* (set of background factors) is Case *A* deviant?

To reiterate, the purpose of deviant case analysis is to probe for novel explanations, i.e., new causes of *Y*. (If the purpose of a non-conforming case is to prove or disprove a pre-existing theory, it is an *influential case*, as discussed below.) Thus, the deviant case method is only slightly more determinate than the extreme case method. It, too, is an exploratory form of research. The researcher hopes that evidence found within the deviant case will illustrate some causal factor that is applicable to other (deviant) cases. This means that a successful deviant case study culminates in a general proposition – one that may be applied to other cases in the population.

As soon as that proposition is discovered, the case is no longer deviant; it has been explained. If the new explanation can be accurately measured as a single variable (or set of variables) across a larger sample of cases, then a new large-*C* model is in order. In that large-*C* model, the previously deviant case should receive a smaller residual. It is pulled toward the regression line.

Testing the new explanation in a larger sample is also important for alleviating concerns about representativeness. Naturally, when one chooses a highly deviant case for special attention one must be concerned about generalizing from that case. However, if the resulting proposition seems to fit other cases – beyond the studied case – worries about unrepresentativeness are mitigated.

Of course, deviant case analysis does not always culminate in a new, generalizable explanation for *Y*. It might culminate in the researcher's conclusion that the chosen case is deviant for idiosyncratic reasons – reasons that are accidental or do not apply to other cases. This would be a less satisfactory conclusion from the perspective of building theory. But it may be true to the facts, and in this sense plays an important role in the development of social science knowledge. Some deviant cases are just "different."

Table 5.4 Deviant case exemplars

			SELECTION		CASES	
Study	Field	Cites	Algo.	Non-algo.	Phenomena	C
Acemoglu *et al.* (2003) *African Success Story*	EC	638		●	Economic development	1
Alesina *et al.* (2001) *Why Doesn't US Have Welfare State?*	EC	824		●	Welfare state	1
Amenta (1991) *Theories of Welfare State: American Experience*	SO	40		●	Welfare states	1
Aymard (1982) *From Feudalism to Capitalism in Italy*	HI	22		●	Capitalism	1
Lieberman (2003) *Politics of Taxation Brazil, South Africa*	PS	172		●	Fiscal policy	2
Lijphart (1968) *Politics of Accommodation*	PS	2,026		●	Ethnic conflict	1
Lipset *et al.* (1956) *Union Democracy*	SO	1,211		●	Union democracy	1
Pearce (2002) *Integrating Survey and Ethnographic Methods*	SO	47	●		Fertility	28
Sombart (1906) *Why No Socialism in United States?*	SO	356		●	Socialism	1

Notes: C = number of cases. *Algo.* = case selection by algorithm.

Nine deviant case studies are listed in Table 5.4. These encompass various fields and topics, including economic development, welfare state development, capitalism, socialism, ethnic conflict, union democracy, and fertility. Most of these studies choose cases in an informal fashion and incorporate only one or two deviant cases in the analysis. Qualitative analysis dominates the deviant case study as it does other case study genres.

One study, by Lisa Pearce (2002), approaches the subject in an algorithmic fashion. Pearce begins her study of childrearing choices in Nepal with a standardized survey of ideal family size. The survey was conducted in the Chitwan Valley of south-central Nepal in 1996 and contains 5,271 respondents. Based on extant research and theoretical priors she constructs an initial model to predict preferences in family size. The model includes measures of religious and ethnic identity, gender, age, number of siblings, education, parents' education, media exposure, travel, distance to nearest city, and expectations of an inheritance. With this regression model, she identifies respondents whose preferences are not well predicted by the model. From these outliers, she chooses 28 subjects for in-depth analysis. These are her deviant cases. Following her theoretical interests, she chooses outliers that fall above the predicted line (they desire more children than the model predicts), possessing standardized residuals of 6+.

For each subject, she conducts in-depth interviews with open-ended questions designed to gauge un-measured factors that may influence family planning (Pearce 2002: 114). Insights gained from these interviews are then used to re-code features of the survey and re-specify the regression model. For example, Pearce is impressed with the degree to which religious practice centers on the family. Accordingly, she constructs indices from the survey to measure religious practices and beliefs at the household level. This becomes an important predictor in the revised model, which improves the overall fit and reduces the "deviant" status of her research subjects.

Most-similar (exploratory)

A *most-similar* research design (also known as Method of Difference) employs a minimum of two cases.[12] These cases exhibit similar

---

[12] The most-similar method (Przeworski and Teune 1970) may also be referred to as the *method of difference* (Mill 1843/1872), the *comparable cases* method, or the *comparative* method (Collier 1993; Glynn and Ichino 2015; Lijphart 1971, 1975). Frequently, this topic is addressed in tandem with other techniques for small-N cross-case selection and analysis under the rubric of *controlled comparison, paired comparison,* or *Millean* methods (Adcock 2008; Cohen and Nagel 1934; Gisselquist 2014; Meckstroth 1975; Sekhon 2004; Slater and Ziblatt 2013; Tarrow 2010).

Table 5.5 Exemplary most-similar (exploratory) case design

		Variables		
		X	Z	Y
Cases	A	?	0	1
	B	?	0	0

Notes: Exploratory most-similar design with binary factors, an exemplary setting. X = causal factor of theoretical interest (to be determined). Z = vector of background factors. Y = outcome. The assignment of 0s and 1s is an arbitrary coding choice. The key point is that cases A and B share the same values on all Z and differ on Y.

background conditions (Z) and different outcomes (Y). If these factors are binary, they may be represented in a simple diagram, as shown in Table 5.5. If these factors are ordinal or interval, the researcher would seek to maximize variance in Y and minimize variance in Z across the chosen cases. As always, the research design is more informative if it analyzes change through time rather than values at a particular point in time. Thus, one would prefer to compare values for ΔZ and ΔY.

Importantly, if background factors differ across the cases, they may still satisfy the desiderata of a most-similar design if (and only if) these differences bias the outcome *against* the actual finding. Let us imagine, for example, that Z_1 is a factor that we can assume (based on theoretical priors or extant studies) might have a positive effect on an outcome, Y, but could not possibly have a negative impact on Y. And let us say that the arrangement of the data is as follows:

Case A: $Z_1 = 0$, $Y = 1$
Case B: $Z_1 = 1$, $Y = 0$

Under these circumstances, we may safely discard Z_1 as a cause of Y (for these cases). Consequently, cases A and B qualify as most-similar – at least in these respects.

So much for the setup. Knowing values for Z and Y, the researcher hopes to uncover the identity of X – a previously unknown cause of Y.

Specifically, by exploring all possible causes of Y it is hoped that the researcher will stumble upon a factor that differs across the cases and seems – on theoretical grounds – as though it might serve as a cause of Y. This is the putative cause.

Naturally, one may uncover *multiple* factors that differ across the cases (and which seem like theoretically plausible causes of Y). In this circumstance, the most-similar design is not very helpful. Even so, one may be able to pare down the number of plausible suspects.

Often, fruitful analysis begins with an apparent anomaly: two cases are apparently quite similar and yet demonstrate surprisingly different outcomes. The hope is that intensive study of these cases will reveal one – or at most several – factors that differ across these cases and are plausible causes of Y.

Seventeen most-similar case studies are listed in Table 5.6, signaling the relative popularity of this form of analysis. Exemplars include all major disciplines, a wide range of topics, and a mix of algorithmic and qualitative case-selection strategies.

Consider John Snow's initial report on cholera in London, published in 1849.[13] At the time, physicians knew little about the source of this ghastly epidemic. Several theories were in circulation, including one based on the quality of the air (miasma). Snow conjectured that the source of contamination might be the water supply, so he had a working hypothesis. However, his initial selection of cases was not based on varying water sources (X). Instead, Snow compared city blocks where the disease was rampant with neighboring blocks where it was not – selection on Y, holding Z constant. Note that geography serves as a proxy for background factors that might affect the outcome of interest. People living cheek-by-jowl are assumed to share many

---

[13] This report precedes the more famous second edition, issued in 1855. The latter features Snow's description of the "Broad Street Pump," which, in recent years, has attracted great attention among epidemiologists and methodologists. My account follows Vinten-Johansen *et al.* (2003: 206–10). For other accounts, see Freedman (1991), Hempel (2007).

Table 5.6 Most-similar (exploratory) case exemplars

Study	Field	Cites	SELECTION Algo.	SELECTION Non-algo.	CASES Phenomena	C
Alston *et al.* (1996) *Property Rights*	EC	390		●	Brazilian states	2
Cornell (2002) *Autonomy as a Source of Conflict*	PS	256		●	Ethnic groups	9
Dreze and Sen (1989) *China and India*	EC	2,936		●	Economic development	2
Epstein (1964) *A Comparative Study of Canadian Parties*	PS	113		●	Party systems	2
Fiorina (1977) *Congress*	PS	1,866		●	US leg. districts	2
Geertz (1963) *Peddlers and Princes*	AN	977		●	Towns	2
Heclo (1974) *Modern Social Policies in Britain and Sweden*	PS	1,920		●	Social policies	2
Key (1949) *Southern Politics in State and Nation*	PS	3,238		●	US states	11
Lange (2009) *Lineages of Despotism and Development*	SO	69	●	●	Economic development	4/11
Luebbert (1991) *Liberalism, Fascism, or Social Democracy*	PS	356		●	Regime-types	15
Mahoney (2002) *Legacies of Liberalism*	PS	337		●	Regime-types	5
Miguel (2004) *Tribe or Nation: Kenya v. Tanzania*	EC	326		●	Nation-building	2
Putnam *et al.* (1993) *Making Democracy Work*	PS	29,712		●	Italian regions	20
Rosenbaum and Silber (2001) *Matching*	PH	50	●		Patients	76
Sahlins (1958) *Social Stratification in Polynesia*	AN	726		●	Societies	17
Snow (1849) *Communication of Cholera*	PH	1,369		●	City blocks	N/A
Ziblatt (2004, 2008) *Rethinking Origins of Federalism*	PS	36		●	Centralization	2

Notes: C = number of cases. *Algo.* = case selection by algorithm.

characteristics – a common assumption in most-similar research designs, whether the spatial units are blocks, neighborhoods, cities, or countries. In any case, the work of the case study consisted of delving into these incidents of the disease – interviewing medical practitioners, residents, water companies, and through direct observation of the sites themselves, which sometimes consisted of neighboring courts – in an attempt to rule out features that were common (Z), and therefore unlikely to cause the disease, and to isolate the discriminating feature (X), which Snow concluded was the water supply.

A second example of a very different sort is provided by Leon Epstein's (1964) study of party cohesion, which focuses on two neighboring countries. The two cases, United States and Canada, are assumed to share a large number of background characteristics – e.g., vast expanses of land rich in mineral and agricultural resources and lightly populated by indigenous peoples, a British colonial heritage, weak socialist traditions, heterogeneous populations, federal constitutions, and first-past-the-post electoral districts. Yet, Canada has highly disciplined parties whose members vote together on the floor of the House of Commons while the US has comparatively weak, undisciplined parties, whose members often defect on floor votes in Congress. In explaining these divergent outcomes, persistent over many years, Epstein points out that the two countries differ in one potentially important constitutional feature: Canada is parliamentary while the US is presidential. It is this institutional difference that Epstein identifies as the probable cause.

Most-different

The most-different design (also known as the Method of Agreement) is the mirror image of the most-similar design. Here, cases vary widely in background factors regarded as potential causes (Z), while sharing a common outcome (Y). The assumption is that background factors that differ across the cases are unlikely to be causes of Y since that outcome

Table 5.7 Exemplary most-different case design

		Variables					
		X	Z_a	Z_b	Z_c	Z_d	Y
Cases	A	?	1	0	1	0	1
	B	?	0	1	0	1	1

Notes: Most-different design with binary factors, an exemplary setting. X = causal factor of theoretical interest (to be determined). Z_{a-d} = vector of background factors. Y = outcome. The assignment of 0s and 1s is an arbitrary coding choice. The key point is that cases A and B differ on all Z and are similar on Y.

is constant across the cases. The hope is that if a potential causal factor (X) is constant across the cases, it might be the cause of Y.[14]

The basic setup is illustrated in Table 5.7 with two cases, coded in a binary fashion. If Z and Y are ordinal or interval, the researcher seeks to minimize variance in Z and maximize variance in Y.

As with other exploratory designs, it is often difficult to ascertain whether a case's value on X was known to the researcher prior to case selection and, if so, whether it influenced case selection. We leave this matter open for discussion. However, the most different design is classified as an exploratory design because we regard its implicit causal identification strategy as speculative, at best, and therefore useful for identifying potential causes but not so useful for testing a causal hypothesis, once identified.

Four most-different case studies are listed in Table 5.8. These exemplars – drawn from history, demography, and political science – examine colonial histories, demographic transitions, civil society, and economic development. Cases (C) range from two to seven.

[14] The most-different method is also sometimes referred to as the "method of agreement," following its inventor, J.S. Mill (1843/1872). See also DeFelice (1986), Lijphart (1971, 1975), Meckstroth (1975), Przeworski and Teune (1970), Skocpol and Somers (1980). For examples of this method, see Collier and Collier (1991/2002), Converse and Dupeux (1962), Karl (1997), Moore (1966), Skocpol (1979), Yashar (2005: 23). However, most of these studies are described as *combining* most-similar and most-different methods.

Table 5.8 Most-different case exemplars

			SELECTION		CASES	
Study	Field	Cites	Algo.	Non-algo.	Phenomena	C
Belich (2010) *Exploding Wests*	HI	5		●	Colonialism	7
Childs *et al.* (2005) *Tibetan Fertility Transitions*	DE	19		●	Demog transitions	3
Howard (2003) *Weakness Civil Society in Post-Communist*	PS	1,284		●	Civil society	2
Karl (1997) *Paradox of Plenty*	PS	1,892		●	Economic development	5/1

Notes: C = number of cases. *Algo.* = case selection by algorithm.

As an in-depth example, I follow Marc Howard's (2003) study of the enduring impact of communism on civil society in the post-Soviet region. Cross-national surveys show a strong correlation between former communist regimes and low social capital, controlling for a variety of possible confounders. Howard wonders why this relationship is so strong and why it persists – and perhaps even strengthens – in countries that are no longer socialist or authoritarian. In order to answer this question, he focuses on two most-different cases, Russia and East Germany. These two countries were quite different prior to the Soviet era, during the Soviet era (since East Germany received substantial subsidies from West Germany), and in the post-Soviet era, as East Germany was absorbed into West Germany. Yet, they both score near the bottom of various cross-national indices intended to measure the prevalence of civic engagement in the current era. Thus, Howard's case-selection procedure meets the requirements of the most-different research design: variance is found on many dimensions aside from the outcome of interest, which is constant (Howard 2003: 6–9). The factor holding constant across the cases is the communist heritage that both Russia and East Germany share. This is the anticipated cause (X).

Naturally, one must consider the possibility that additional factors – unmeasured in the analysis but shared by Russia and East

Germany – account for their low levels of civic engagement. Although these societies are different, they also share some cultural and historical characteristics (unrelated to communism) such as a legacy of autocracy. Likewise, the cause could be a product of an interaction among various factors – those that are measured and/or those that are omitted.

Howard's findings are stronger with the comparison of Russia and East Germany than they would be without. Yet, his study would not stand securely on the empirical foundation provided by most-different analysis alone. If one strips away the other elements of Howard's analysis,[15] there is little left upon which to base an analysis of causal relations. Indeed, most scholars who employ the most-different method do so in conjunction with other methods.[16] It is rarely, if ever, a stand-alone method.[17]

Generalizing from this discussion, I offer the following summary remarks on the most-different method of case selection.

Let us begin with the necessity of dichotomizing every variable in the analysis. Recall that differences across cases must generally be sizeable enough to be interpretable in an essentially binary fashion

---

[15] It should be noted that most-different analysis is not the only research design employed by Howard in his admirable study. These analyses do most of the analytic work, in my opinion.

[16] Karl (1997), which affects to be a most-different system analysis (20), is a particularly clear example of this. Her study, focused ostensibly on petro-states (states with large oil reserves), makes two sorts of inferences. The first concerns the (usually) obstructive role of oil in political and economic development. The second sort of inference concerns variation *within* the population of petro-states, showing that some countries (e.g., Norway, Indonesia) manage to avoid the pathologies brought on elsewhere by oil resources. When attempting to explain the constraining role of oil on petro-states, Karl usually relies on contrasts between petro-states and non-petro states (e.g., Chapter 10). Only when attempting to explain differences among petro-states does she restrict her sample to petro-states. In my opinion, very little use is made of the most-different research design.

[17] This was recognized, at least implicitly, by Mill (1843/1872: 258–9). Skepticism has been echoed by methodologists in the intervening years (e.g., Cohen and Nagel 1934: 251–6; Skocpol and Somers 1980). Indeed, explicit defenses of the most-different method are rare (but, see DeFelice 1986).

(e.g., high/low, present/absent) and similarities must be close enough to be understood as essentially identical (e.g., high/high, present/present). Otherwise, the results are not interpretable. The problem of "degrees" is especially worrisome if the variables under consideration are intrinsically continuous (e.g., GDP). This is a particular concern in Howard's analysis, where East Germany scores somewhat higher than Russia in civic engagement; they are both low, but Russia is quite a bit lower. Howard assumes that this divergence is minimal enough to be understood as a difference of degrees rather than of kinds, a judgment that might be questioned.

Granted, if the coding assumptions are sound, the most-different research design may be useful for *eliminating necessary causes*. Causal factors that do not appear across the chosen cases – e.g., Z_{a-d} in Table 5.7 – are evidently unnecessary for the production of Y. However, it does not follow that the most-different method is the *best* method for eliminating necessary causes.

Usually, case study analysis is focused on the identification (or clarification) of causal relations, not the elimination of possible causes. In this setting, the most-different technique is useful, but only if assumptions of causal uniqueness hold. By "causal uniqueness," I mean a situation in which a given outcome is the product of only one cause: Y cannot occur except in the presence of X. X is necessary, and in some situations (given certain background conditions) sufficient, to cause Y.[18]

Consider the following hypothetical example. Suppose that a new disease, about which little is known, has appeared in Country A. There are hundreds of infected persons across dozens of affected communities in that country. In Country B, located at the other end of the world, several new cases of the disease surface in a single community. In this setting, we can imagine two sorts of Millean analyses. The first

---

[18] Another way of stating this is to say that X is a "non-trivial necessary condition" of Y.

examines two similar communities within Country *A*, one of which has developed the disease and the other of which has not. This is the most-similar comparison, and focuses accordingly on the identification of a difference between the two cases that might account for variation across the sample. A second approach focuses on communities where the disease has appeared across the two countries and searches for any similarities that might account for these shared outcomes. This is the most-different research design.

Both are plausible approaches to this particular problem, and we can imagine epidemiologists employing them simultaneously. However, the most-different design demands stronger assumptions about the underlying factors at work. It supposes that the disease arises from the *same cause* in any setting. This is a reasonable operating assumption when one is dealing with natural phenomena (though there are certainly many exceptions), but it rarely holds in social-scientific settings. Most outcomes of interest to anthropologists, economists, political scientists, and sociologists have *multiple* causes. There are many ways to win an election, to build a welfare state, to enter a war, to overthrow a government, or – returning to Marc Howard's work – to build a strong civil society. And it is for this reason that most-different analysis is rarely applied in social science work – and, where applied, is rarely convincing.

If this seems a tad severe, there is a more charitable way of approaching the most-different method. Arguably, this is not a pure "method" at all, but merely a supplement, a way of incorporating diversity into the sub-sample of cases that provide the unusual outcome of interest. If the unusual outcome is revolutions, one might wish to encompass a wide variety of revolutions in one's analysis. If the unusual outcome is post-communist civil society, it seems appropriate to include a diverse set of post-communist polities in one's sample of case studies, as Howard does. From this perspective, the most-different method (so-called) might be better labeled a *diverse-case* method, as explored below.

Diverse (causal)

A final exploratory case-selection strategy has as its objective the identification of many – or perhaps all – of the causes of an outcome (assuming that outcome has multiple causes, i.e., equifinality). This is sometimes referred to as causes-of-effects study, in contrast to an effects-of-causes study, which focuses on a single $X \rightarrow Y$ relationship. The chosen cases are *diverse* if they represent all potential factors (Z), including causal conjunctures, that might explain variation in Y. The assumption is that the true causal factors (X) are to be found among the putative causal factors (Z).[19] George and Smoke, for example, wish to explore different types of deterrence failure – by "fait accompli," by "limited probe," and by "controlled pressure." Consequently, they wish to find cases that exemplify each causal factor.[20]

Where the potential causal factor is categorical (on/off, red/black/blue, Jewish/Protestant/Catholic), the researcher would normally choose one case from each category. For a continuous variable, one must construct cutoff points (based on theoretical understandings of the phenomenon or natural breakpoints in the data), e.g., dichotomizing or trichotomizing the variable, and then choosing cases with each discrete value. If one suspects that causal factors interact, then one will look for cases that represent all possible (or actual) intersections of these variables (understood as categorical variables). Two dichotomous variables produce a matrix with four possible cells, for example. If all

[19] This method has not received much attention on the part of qualitative methodologists; hence, the absence of a generally recognized name. It bears some resemblance to J.S. Mill's Joint Method of Agreement and Difference (Mill 1843/1872), which is to say a mixture of most-similar and most-different analysis, as discussed below. Patton (2002: 234) employs the concept of "maximum variation (heterogeneity) sampling."

[20] More precisely, George and Smoke (1974: 522–36, Chapter 18; see also discussion in Collier and Mahoney 1996: 78) set out to investigate causal pathways and discovered, through the course of their investigation of many cases, these three causal types. Yet, for our purposes what is important is that the final sample includes at least one representative of each "type."

variables are deemed relevant to the analysis, the selection of diverse cases mandates the selection of one case drawn from within each cell – assuming there are members in each cell. Let us say that an outcome is thought to be affected by sex, race (black/white), and marital status. Here, a diverse-case strategy of case selection would identify one case within each of these intersecting cells – a total of eight cases. It will be seen that where multiple categorical variables interact, the logic of diverse-case analysis rests upon a *typological* logic (Elman 2005; George and Bennett 2005; Lazarsfeld and Barton 1951).

In choosing a small basket of diverse cases from a large population of potential cases, the researcher may draw on qualitative comparative analysis (QCA) algorithms to identify the various possible conjunctures, selecting a case, or cases, from each configuration. Alternatively, within a regression framework, the researcher may explore various interaction effects, choosing cases that exemplify disparate interactions.

Eleven diverse case studies are included in Table 5.9. All stem from the fields of political science or sociology, and many would be described as comparative-historical analysis. Cases range from two to 22, with a mean of about seven, demonstrating that this particular case-selection strategy typically selects a basket of cases.

Of these studies, one stands out as especially influential, and thus serves as our in-depth exemplar. Barrington Moore's (1966) *Social Origins of Dictatorship and Democracy* is sometimes regarded as the fountainhead of modern comparative-historical inquiry, influencing a generation of scholars in the adjoining fields of sociology and political science. The study is extraordinarily ambitious – the subtitle reads "Lord and Peasant in the Making of the Modern World" – and written with a vivid narrative that manages to weave events and analysis together in a lucid fashion. Although lengthy, this book is readable to an extent that few works of social science in the contemporary era can match. No doubt, this helps to account for its enduring influence on scholarship. With respect to case selection, I follow Theda Skocpol's (1973) synopsis of the book, summarized in Table 5.10 below. This

Table 5.9 Diverse (causal) case exemplars

Study	Field	Cites	SELECTION		CASES	
			Algo.	Non-algo.	Phenomena	C
Bunce (1981) *Do New Leaders Make a Difference?*	PS	114		•	Succession	2
Collier and Collier (1991) *Shaping the Political Arena*	PS	2,171		•	State-labor relations	8
Downing (1992) *Military Revolution and Political Change*	PS	398		•	Statebuilding	7
Evans (1995) *Embedded Autonomy*	SO	5,281		•	Economic development	3
George and Smoke (1974) *Deterrence in US Foreign Policy*	PS	894		•	Crises	11
Kohli (2004) *State-Directed Development*	PS	723		•	Industrial policies	4
Levi (1988) *Of Rule and Revenue*	PS	1,821		•	Fiscal policy	4
Moore (1966) *Social Origins of Dictatorship and Democracy*	SO	6,573		•	Regime-types	8
Rueschemeyer *et al.* (1992) *Capitalist Development*	SO	2,727		•	Regime-types	22
Tsai (2007) *Accountability without Democracy*	PS	227		•	Village governance	4
Wood (2000) *Forging Democracy from Below*	PS	353		•	Regime-types	2

Notes: C = number of cases. *Algo.* = case selection by algorithm.

shows that there are essentially three routes to modernity, with two or three cases serving to represent each route in Moore's study.

In classifying Moore (1966) and other case studies listed in Table 5.9 as exploratory, I am making an important assumption: that the authors used the chosen cases to develop their theories – selecting on Y and Z and working their way to X. An alternative reading of these works is that the authors developed their theories ex ante, using the cases in a confirmatory fashion (to provide further confirmation or disconfirmation of the theory) – thus selecting on X and Y (and perhaps also Z). If so, these case studies should be classified as diagnostic rather

Table 5.10 Diverse cases in Moore (1966)

	Routes to modernity			
	1		2	3
Cases	UK, USA France		Germany, Japan	Russia, China
Common starting point	Agrarian bureaucracy		Agrarian bureaucracy	Agrarian bureaucracy
Key variable clusters				
Bourgeois impulse	Strong	Strong	Medium	Weak
Mode of commercial agriculture	Market	Labor-repressive	Labor-repressive	Labor-repressive
Peasant revolutionary potential	Low	High	Low	High
Critical political event	Bourgeois revolution		Revolution from above	Peasant revolution
Major systemic political outcome	Democratic capitalism		Fascism	Communism

Source: Reproduced from Skocpol (1973: 10).

than exploratory. As is often the case with case study research, it is difficult to say for sure what the authors knew and when they knew it. Suffice it to say that, regardless of how these particular studies are classified, there remains an important role for case studies that employ a diverse case-selection strategy – namely, wherever a researcher suspects there may be multiple routes to *Y* but is not sure what they are.

5.2   Estimating

Thus far, I have dealt with case study research designs that are exploratory, i.e., designed to identify a causal hypothesis. I turn now to case studies whose goal is to test a hypothesis by estimating a causal effect. Estimating may mean a precise point estimate along with a confidence interval (as might be obtained from a time-series or synthetic matching analysis), or a less precise estimate of the "sign" of a relationship, i.e., whether X has a positive, negative, or no relationship to Y. The latter is more common, as we have observed, not only because of the small size of the sample (at the case level), but also because it is more likely to be generalizable (see discussion in Chapter 10). In either situation, case selection must rest on information about X and Z – not Y. Two general approaches are viable for estimating causal effects in a small-C setting – *longitudinal* and *most-similar* – as outlined below.

Before entering into this discussion, it may be appropriate to observe that this is not the most common use of case study research. I have been able to identify only a few exemplars, as demonstrated in the following tables. I am not even sure that those case studies classified as estimating actually qualify as such (insofar as it is sometimes difficult to discern whether researchers considered outcome values (Y) in their selection of cases).

The reason for the rarity of causal estimation from case studies arises from a logistical feature of the world. In situations where a researcher has identified a specific hypothesis (H_x) that pertains to a broad population, it is usually possible to estimate that relationship across a large number of cases, generating a large-C research design. This mode of analysis is generally able to provide a stronger test of the hypothesis and is therefore the preferred research design.

Nonetheless, there are some circumstances in which it is possible, and advisable, to estimate the impact of X on Y using a very small sample of cases. The justification for this small-sample approach lies in the inability, or inadvisability, of extending the sample to include additional cases. That is, the longitudinal evidence provided by a single case, perhaps accompanied by one or several "control" cases, provides stronger grounds for inference than the corresponding large-C design – presumably because additional cases are heterogeneous and would therefore introduce potential confounders to the analysis.

Longitudinal

A longitudinal case study mimics a one-group experiment, where X changes in an as-if random fashion while Z remains constant and Y is observed before and after the intervention. It might also be referred to as an *interrupted time-series* (Campbell 1968/1988) or a *repeated measures* (or *repeated observations*) design, and is consistent with a time-series analysis of a continuously observed case (Hamilton 1994).

The caveat of course is that in order to qualify as a case study, the number of cases must be limited and the intensiveness of study devoted to them must be correspondingly great. More specifically, the researcher must examine the chosen case(s) closely to see if any potential confounders can be identified, and if so, see whether they might bias the data-generating process towards the hypothesis of interest. If not, that is if potential confounders exert a "conservative" bias, the case may be acceptable.

Five longitudinal exemplars are listed in Table 5.11. All focus on policy changes – monetary policy, fiscal policy, traffic control policy, and irrigation management policy. For example, in order to understand

Table 5.11 Longitudinal case exemplars

			SELECTION		CASES	
Study	Field	Cites	Algo.	Non-algo.	Phenomena	C
Campbell (1968/1988) *Connecticut Crackdown*	PY	384		●	Speeding laws	1
Friedman and Schwartz (1963) *Monetary History of US*	EC	6,208		●	Monetary policy	1
Hsieh and Romer (2001) *Was Federal Reserve Fettered?*	EC	19		●	Monetary expansions	1
Romer and Romer (2010) *Effects of Tax Changes*	EC	800		●	Fiscal policy	1
Uphoff (1992) *Learning from Gal Oya*	PS	467		●	Irrigation projects	1

Notes: C = number of cases. *Algo.* = case selection by algorithm.

the interrelationship between monetary policy and economic fluctuations, Milton Friedman and Anna Schwartz (1963) look closely at US history, identifying four occasions when the stock of money changed due to policy choices largely unrelated to the behavior of the economy (and hence exogenous to the research question). These four interventions consisted of "the increase in the discount rate in the first half of 1920, the increase in the discount rate in October 1931, the increase in reserve requirements in 1936–1937, and the failure of the Federal Reserve to stem the tide of falling money in 1929–1931" (Miron 1994: 19). It turns out that each was followed by a substantial change in the behavior of the stock of money, validating a central pillar of monetarist theory.

To identify a longitudinal case, or cases, from a large population of potential cases, one may look for instances where change in X is not accompanied by a change in Z. This information is not easy to tease out of a large-C sample, as it demands that X and Z be measured in a panel format for all potential cases, and Z is of course very difficult to identify in an a priori fashion (without knowing the details of each case). It is perhaps not coincidental that none of the exemplars chooses cases in an algorithmic fashion.

Most-similar (estimating)

Estimating a causal effect with a most-similar design is similar to a longitudinal design with the notable addition of a control case – which (ideally) experiences no change on either X or Z.[21] That is, chosen cases exhibit different values on X and similar values on Z. Under these circumstances, and with a variety of assumptions, realized outcomes across the cases (Y) allow one to estimate a causal effect.

---

[21] This is the version of most-similar analysis discussed in Glynn and Ichino (2015) and Lijphart (1975).

Table 5.12 Exemplary most-similar (estimating) case design

		Variables		
		X	Z	Y
Cases	A	1	0	?
	B	0	0	?

Notes: Estimating most-similar design with binary factors, an exemplary setting. X = causal factor of theoretical interest. Z = vector of background factors. Y = outcome (values to be determined). The assignment of 0s and 1s is an arbitrary coding choice. The key point is that cases A and B share the same values on all Z and differ on X.

As with the exploratory most-similar design, differences and similarities may manifest themselves in a binary fashion, as illustrated in Table 5.12. Or, they may be matters of degree, in which circumstance one seeks cases that maximize variance in X and minimize variance in Z. If one is seeking to identify a small number of most-similar cases from a large population of potential cases, the researcher may employ matching algorithms that achieve these desiderata.[22] As always, the research design is more informative if it analyzes change through time rather than values at a particular point in time. Thus, one would prefer to measure X and Z as ΔX and ΔZ.

Five most-similar (estimating) case studies are listed as exemplars in Table 5.13. These focus on diverse subjects and are conducted by researchers in several fields. They seem to share little in common except their most-similar design.

As an initial example, let us consider Jeffrey Mondak's (1995) study of two cities – Cleveland and Pittsburgh – that are regarded as similar in background conditions. One of the cities experiences a newspaper strike, exhibiting a change in the causal factor of theoretical interest. The goal of the study is to determine to what extent the absence of a newspaper affects citizen knowledge of politics, as measured through a

---

[22] See Nielsen (2016) and accompanying web application: https://rnielsen.shinyapps.io/caseMatch/

Table 5.13 Most-similar (estimating) case exemplars

Study	Field	Cites	SELECTION		CASES	
			Algo.	Non-algo.	Phenomena	C
Abadie and Gardeazabal (2003) *Costs of Conflict*	EC	867		●	Spanish regions	1/17
Mondak (1995) *Newspapers and Political Awareness*	PS	95		●	Cities	2
Posner (2004) *Political Salience of Cultural Difference*	PS	376		●	Ethnic groups	4
Skendaj (2014) *International Insulation from Politics*	PS	2		●	Agencies	4
Useem and Goldstone (2002) *Riot and Reform US Prisons*	SO	32		●	Prisons	2

Notes: C = number of cases. *Algo.* = case selection by algorithm.

post-test survey of political awareness. A weakness of this study is that it measures the outcome only *after* the newspaper strike (post-treatment). Ideally, one would prefer to measure change through time across the two cases, eliminating a large number of potential confounders that are static in nature (specific to each city).

An extension of the most-similar method called *synthetic control* has been developed by Alberto Abadie and colleagues (Abadie *et al.* 2015). Here, there is typically a single "treatment" case (where *X* varies) and a larger number of control cases (where *X* is constant) that are well matched on background characteristics. For example, to test the impact of violent conflict on growth performance, Abadie and Gardeazabal (2003) look closely at one region of Spain that has been riven by conflict – the Basque country – which they contrast with other regions of the country observed over the same time period. Spain is a fairly decentralized polity, so each region enjoys a fair bit of autonomy and the problem of non-independence across units is therefore minimized. The researchers note that a simple time-series analysis focused on the Basque region could shed light on the economic impact of ETA-sponsored terrorism. However, this "intervention" began slowly in the 1960s and 1970s (there was no well-defined point of onset) and was coincident with a general economic downturn in Spain. Thus, temporal patterns are difficult to interpret.

Abadie and Gardeazabal identify a series of covariates that might help to identify a territory – or territories – in Spain that is most-similar to the Basque region with respect to various factors that might affect growth performance but has not experienced violent conflict. These covariates include real per capita GDP, investment, population density, the shape of the economy (e.g., agriculture, industry, and other sectors), as well as various measures of human capital. However, there is no perfect match for the Basque country among the 16 other Spanish regions. Rather than consigning themselves to a less-than-perfect comparison, the authors instead construct a hypothetical case from the two cases that match relatively well with the Basque region, Madrid and Catalonia. Each is weighted according to the strength of the match (with the Basque region) along the various dimensions noted earlier; the two are then combined into a single case. This composite case is looked upon as providing a best "control" case for the treatment case, the Basque region. "Our goal," the authors explain, "is to approximate the per capita GDP path that the Basque Country would have experienced in the absence of terrorism. This counterfactual per capita GDP path is calculated as the per capita GDP of the synthetic Basque Country" (Abadie and Gardeazabal 2003: 117). Based on this synthetic counterfactual, the authors conclude that the Basque region experienced a 10% loss in per capita GDP due to terrorist violence over the course of two decades (the 1980s and 1990s).

5.3   Diagnostic

Case studies, finally, may perform a *diagnostic* function – helping to confirm, disconfirm, or refine a hypothesis (garnered from the literature on a subject or from the researcher's own ruminations) and identifying the generative agent at work in that relationship. Specific strategies may be classified as *influential*, *pathway*, or *most-similar*, as discussed below.

Since all elements of a causal model – X, Z, and Y – are generally involved in the selection of a diagnostic case, the reader may wonder what is left for case study research to accomplish. Actually, a good deal remains on the table. Diagnostic case studies may assess:

- *Measurement error*: Are X, Z, and Y properly measured? (Seawright 2016b)
- *Scope conditions*: Is the chosen case rightly classified as part of the population? What are the appropriate scope conditions for the hypothesis? (Ragin 2000; Skocpol and Somers 1980)
- *Causal heterogeneity*: Are there background factors that mediate the $X \rightarrow Y$ relationship? (Harding and Seefeldt 2013: 98)
- *Confounders*: Is the actual data-generating process consistent with the chosen causal model? What is the assignment mechanism? Are there pre- or post-treatment confounders? (Dunning 2012; Harding and Seefeldt 2013; Seawright 2016b)
- *Causal mechanisms*: What is the pathway through which X affects Y? (see below)

Of particular interest is the latter feature – the mechanisms (M) connecting X to Y (if indeed the relationship is causal).[23] Mechanisms not only help to confirm or disconfirm a hypothesis, they also explain it – in specifying a mechanism, we also specify the generative process by which X causes Y. Note that when there is no strong theoretical prior about the nature of the mechanism, the case analysis assumes an

---

[23] Mechanism-focused case studies do not usually attempt to estimate the precise causal effect of X on M and M on Y, as one might in an experimental context or – with many caveats – in a large-N observational context (Imai *et al.* 2010). The effort is more modestly pitched: to shed light on whether a mechanism is at work, and hence responsible for some of the causal effect of X on Y (Goertz 2017).

open-ended, inductive quest – to identify M. When there is a theoretical expectation, the analysis assumes a deductive format – to test the existence of a pre-specified pattern thought to be indicative of M (e.g., Dafoe and Kelsey 2014). This is sometimes referred to as *congruence testing, pattern-matching,* or *implication analysis.*

In sum, there is a quite lot to occupy a case study researcher engaged in a diagnostic case study, even though preliminary values for X, Z, and Y are known. Information gleaned from a case study may be used to confirm, reject, or refine a theory or to revise a large-C model, e.g., by helping to re-specify that model (Gordon and Smith 2004; Seawright 2016b).

Diagnostic cases are probably the most complex sort of case study from a research design perspective so this section is somewhat longer than the previous sections and will include in-depth discussion of several examples.

Influential

An *influential* case is one whose status has a profound effect on the (subjective) probability of a hypothesis being true, $P(H_x)$. We may understand influence in a counterfactual fashion. That is, if values for key variables – X, Z, M, or Y – for that case were to be reassigned, our assessment of $P(H_x)$ would change. Because the values for this case matter more than the values for other cases, intensive analysis is warranted. Case study analysis is likely to affect our assessment of the hypothesis – either strengthening or weakening $P(H_x)$.

The most influential case is one that, by itself, falsifies a hypothesis. This is possible if the proposition is strictly deterministic (Dion 1998). Suppose that $X = 1$ is regarded as a necessary condition of an outcome, $Y = 1$. A falsifying case would have the attributes $X = 0$, $Y = 1$. If, on the other hand, $X = 1$ is regarded as a sufficient condition of an outcome, $Y = 1$, a falsifying case would exhibit the attributes $X = 1$, $Y = 0$.

(Necessary and sufficient conditions are mirror images of each other – which terminology one uses is a matter of clarity and convenience.)

The most prominent deterministic hypothesis in political science today is probably the democratic peace – the idea that democratic dyads do not wage war on each other.[24] There are a number of possible exceptions to this "universal" law including the Spanish–American war, the Kargil War, the Paquisha War, Lebanese participation in the Six Day War, the French–Thai war, and the Turkish invasion of Cyprus. Each has drawn considerable attention from supporters and skeptics of the democratic peace hypothesis (Bremer 1992, 1993; Elman 1997; Gleditsch 1992; Owen 1994; Ray 1993). Thus far, this research has not yielded a knockout blow to democratic peace theory. There is a problem of measurement insofar as apparent exceptions are often hard to classify cleanly as democratic/autocratic or peaceful/bellicose. More fundamentally, many researchers take a probabilistic view of the theory – in which case, a few exceptions are not so worrisome for the theory. For present purposes, what is important is that these cases are influential. Whether the theory is interpreted as deterministic or probabilistic, these cases have greater bearing on the validity of the theory than other cases that might be chosen for intensive analysis, which explains their centrality in the ongoing debate over the democratic peace.

Influential cases are often outliers, or apparent outliers – cases that do not seem to fit the theory, as seen in the case of the democratic peace. This is true for other subjects as well, including subjects that are understood by pretty much everyone as probabilistic. In Jeremy Weinstein's (2007) study of civil conflict, four outliers are identified – Algeria (1962–4), Algeria (1992–2000), Colombia (1949–63), and Lebanon (1975–91). Here, conflict deaths during civil wars were higher than

---

[24] Not everyone views the democratic peace as deterministic; but some do (Brown *et al.* 1996). For a list of additional hypotheses that take a deterministic form, see Goertz and Starr (2003).

predicted by Weinstein's theory, which hinges on access to material resources. Weinstein finds that two of these outliers – Algeria (1962–4) and Lebanon – are the product of measurement errors, which are then corrected in subsequent analyses (Weinstein 2007: 324). In Colombia and Algeria (1992–2000), in-depth case exploration reveals additional factors that seem to contribute to insurgent violence, allowing Weinstein an opportunity to re-specify the background features of his causal model (to account for causal heterogeneity) or to establish narrower scope conditions for the theory. In this fashion, case exploration leads to theory development.[25]

Sometimes, influential cases take the form of the "dog that didn't bark," i.e., a case that should have exhibited a positive outcome but in the event did not. For example, in Stathis Kalyvas's (1996) study of Christian democracy in Europe, the case of France – a Catholic country that never develops a well-institutionalized Christian democratic party – looms large. Consequently, Kalyvas devotes greater attention to this case than to the more well-deserved cases. "Difficult" cases often deserve more detailed attention, whether their difficulty arises from problems of measurement, classification, ambiguity in the theory, confounders, or stochastic features of the world. The researcher must come to terms with them.

Note that while influential cases are usually outliers – and in this sense appear to mirror deviant cases (discussed above) – they may also be conforming. Indeed, they may *define* the relationship of interest (e.g., least-likely cases, discussed below). What makes a case influential is not its fit with the model but its influence on the model. Likewise, even when an influential case is deviant, the purpose of these two genres is quite different. A deviant case is designed for discovery (to identify a new hypothesis) while an influential case is designed for diagnostic purposes (to assess an existing hypothesis).

---

[25] My exposition of Weinstein (2007) follows Soifer (2015). For another example of this sort, one may consider the case of Denmark in Ertman (1997), discussed by Munck (2004: 118).

Influential cases may take the form of *crucial* cases if certain background conditions hold (Eckstein 1975; Rapport 2015). If the goal is to prove a hypothesis, the crucial case is known as a *least-likely* case. Here, the hypothesized relationship between X and Y holds even though background factors (Z) predict otherwise. With respect to democratic peace hypothesis, a least-likely case would be a dyad composed of two democratic countries with background characteristics that seem to predispose them to war but nonetheless are at peace. If the goal is to disprove a hypothesis, the crucial case is known as a *most-likely* case. Here, the hypothesized relationship between X and Y does not hold even though background factors (Z) predict that it should. With respect to the democratic peace hypothesis, a most-likely case would be a dyad composed of two democratic countries with background characteristics that seem to predispose them to peace (e.g., they are rich, culturally similar, and economically co-dependent), but who nonetheless engage in violent conflict. Distinguishing most- from least-likely cases depends upon the hypothesis, which may be formulated in different ways. For example, if one chooses to frame the outcome as "war" rather than "peace" (an arbitrary decision, in most respects), then the terminology is flipped. The logic that informs the crucial case remains the same, however.

As another example, one might consider the well-worn claim that diverse countries are less likely to establish and maintain a democratic form of government (Diamond and Plattner 1994). A most-likely case is provided by Papua New Guinea (PNG), which exhibits what is probably the highest level of ethnolinguistic heterogeneity of any country in the world (X) along with a very low level of modernization (Z), a background factor that should also discourage democratization. Despite these features, PNG has sustained a vibrant multiparty democracy since independence in 1975. In a detailed case study, Ben Reilly (2000/2001) points out that this constitutes strong evidence against the prevailing view of social diversity.

A variety of influential case studies are listed in Table 5.14. All derive from political science or sociology (though I see no particular reason

Table 5.14 Influential case exemplars

| Study | Field | Cites | SELECTION | | CASES | |
			Algo.	Non-algo.	Phenomena	C
Allison and Zelikow (1999) *Essence of Decision*	PS	9,113		●	Foreign crises	1
Bennett *et al.* (1994) *Burden-Sharing in the Persian Gulf War*	PS	90		●	Alliances	1
Kalyvas (1996) *Christian Democracy in Europe*	PS	556		●	Christian demo. parties	6
Kemp (1986) *Urban Spatial Conflict*	SO	5		●	Local ethnic conflict	1
Michels (1911) *Political Parties*	SO	4,231		●	Parties	2
Ray (1993) *Wars between Democracies*	PS	157		●	Wars	5
Reilly (2000/2001) *Democracy, Ethnic Fragmentation*	PS	80		●	Regime-types	1
Rosenberg (1991) *Hollow Hope*	PS	2,761		●	Legal cases	2
Snyder and Borghard (2011) *Cost of Empty Threats*	PS	78		●	Crises	4

Notes: C = number of cases. *Algo.* = case selection by algorithm.

why this sort of work should be focused on these particular disciplines). Samples are small, ranging from 1 to 6.

Although all studies listed in Table 5.14 were chosen in an informal fashion, most could also have been chosen in an algorithmic fashion. To identify an influential case, or cases, for deterministic hypotheses from a large population of potential cases, the researcher need only compare values for X and Y, looking for those that seem to disconfirm the theory. To identify an influential case, or cases, for probabilistic hypotheses from a large population of potential cases in a regression context, the researcher may draw on a well-developed body of influence statistics designed to identify those cases that play an influential role – understood as cases, which, if removed from the sample, would have the largest impact on the total model or – more usefully – on estimated coefficients for a particular independent variable, as revealed by the

DFBETA statistic (Andersen 2008; Belsey, Kuh and Welsch 2004; Bollen and Jackman 1985).

Pathway

A *pathway* case is one where the apparent impact of X on Y conforms to theoretical expectations and is strong (in magnitude), while background conditions (Z) are held constant or exert a "conservative" bias (Gerring 2007a, 2007b; Weller and Barnes 2014). This might also be called a *conforming, typical, on-line,* or *illustrative* case since it conforms to, typifies, or illustrates a causal relationship of interest (Lieberman 2005; Schneider and Rohlfing 2013). Generally, the chosen case is *positive*, i.e., where $X = 1$ and $Y = 1$, with the assumption that these sorts of cases embody change through time that might be fruitfully studied (Goertz 2017). The label "pathway" is used here in order to emphasize additional criteria not captured by these other terms (even though these additional features are not always possible to ascertain).

Let us now consider some settings in which pathway cases might be usefully employed.

In a setting where the relationship between X and Y is highly uncertain – perhaps because it has not yet been (or cannot be) tested in a large-C format – the pathway case serves an illustrative function. By showing that the theory fits the chosen case, the case study illustrates the contents of the theory and demonstrates its plausibility. If it works here, the logic goes, it may apply elsewhere.[26] Economic models often lead to case studies that perform an illustrative function (Bates *et al.* 1998; Goemans and Spaniel 2014; Kuehn 2013; Lorentzen *et al.* 2015; Pahre 2005). This is presumably because the abstract quality of the theory, perhaps laid out with a mathematical model, must be related to the real world. Without a concrete illustration – a case – the theory is

---

[26] Goertz (2017: Chapter 6) refers to this genre of case study as an "empirical existence proof."

disembodied. Note also that formal theories are generally focused on *mechanisms*, which are often difficult to test in a large-*C* setting (Goertz 2017: Chapter 6).

Other theories, not rooted in formal models, also seek illustrative cases. For example, in presenting the theory of path dependence, Paul David (1985) draws on the curious case of the "QWERTY" keyboard. This peculiar arrangement of keys was adopted by the developers of the typewriter as a way to slow down the action of the keys so they would not jam up – a constant problem on early typewriters, even with the QWERTY arrangement. Later on, as technology advanced, typewriters could accommodate faster keyboard action and developers suggested new arrangements of the keyboard that promised to speed up the typing process. However, David shows that these innovations never caught on. The QWERTY system had "locked in" with both consumers and producers, illustrating the theory of path dependence.

In a setting where the relationship between *X* and *Y* is well established – perhaps as a result of large-*C* analysis (the researcher's or someone else's) – the pathway case is usually focused specifically on causal mechanisms (*M*). An example is provided by Edward Mansfield and Jack Snyder's (2005) research on regime transitions and war. The authors find a strong relationship between (incomplete) democratization and bellicose behavior in their large-*C cross*-national analysis. To ascertain whether their hypothesized causal mechanisms are actually at work in generating this relationship, they look closely at ten countries where the posited covariational pattern between *X* and *Y* clearly holds, i.e., where democratization is followed by war.[27]

Fourteen pathway case exemplars are listed in Table 5.15. Several are selected by algorithm (Dafoe and Kelsey 2014; Teorell 2010), though

[27] Mansfield and Snyder's large-*C* results have been critiqued, as has their approach to case selection. In particular, Narang and Nelson (2009) allege that the authors' case-selection model is not true to their theory, an issue I am not competent to judge. (I disregard the criticism of "selecting on the dependent variable," for reasons discussed above.)

Table 5.15 Pathway case exemplars

Study	Field	Cites	SELECTION		CASES	
			Algo.	Non-algo.	Phenomena	C
Adamson (2001) *Democratization*	PS	53		●	Foreign policies	1
Dafoe and Kelsey (2014) *Observing the Capitalist Peace*	PS	2	●		Nation dyads	6
David (1985) *Clio and the Economics of QWERTY*	EC	6,473		●	Path dependence	1
Dunning (2008) *Crude Democracy*	PS	**395**		●	Democratization	5
Khong (1992) *Analogies at War*	PS	564		●	Crises	4
Kuehn (2013) *Game Theory Models and Process Tracing*	PS	3		●	Civil-military rel.	2
Mansfield and Snyder (2005) *Electing to Fight*	PS	627		●	Conflicts	10
Martin (1992) *Coercive Cooperation*	PS	700		●	Sanctions	4
Richards (2011) *Cultural Explanations of War*	AN	8		●	Wars	2
Ross (2004) *How Do Natural Resources Influence Civil War?*	PS	566		●	Civil wars	13
Schultz (2001) *Democracy and Coercive Diplomacy*	PS	590		●	Crises	4
Simmons (1994) *Who Adjusts?*	PS	348		●	Econ. policy crises	3
Tannenwald (1999, 2007) *Nuclear Taboo*	PS	480		●	Nuclear-use occasions	4
Teorell (2010) *Determinants of Democratization*	PS	153	●		Regime-types	14

Notes: C = number of cases. *Algo.* = case selection by algorithm.

most are selected in an informal fashion. Samples range from one to 14 and cover a wide range of topics.

In previous sections, we have not spent much time on algorithmic case selection, except to note the methods that might be employed. Since these methods – usually variants of regression – are well known (or at any rate well plowed by statistics texts), there was little point in producing a detailed discussion. Using an algorithm to choose a

Table 5.16 Pathway case design with binary factors

		Variables		
		X	Z	Y
Cases	A	1	1	1
	B	0	0	0
	C	0	1	1
	D	0	0	1
	E	1	0	0
	F	1	1	0
	G	0	1	0
	H	1	0	1

Notes: X = causal factor of theoretical interest. Z = vector of background factors.
Y = outcome. The N for each case type is indeterminate. H = pathway case.

pathway case is not, however, well-tilled ground, so we shall spend considerable time on this aspect of case selection. Doing so should also help to illustrate the procedure, and the underlying purpose, of pathway case analysis.

The logic of the pathway case is clearest in situations where all factors of interest (both causes and outcomes) may be understood in a binary fashion (0 or 1). For heuristic purposes, I shall stipulate that if X is a cause of Y, there is a positive relationship between the two, i.e., a change from $X = 0$ to $X = 1$ enhances the probability of $Y = 1$. Likewise, I shall stipulate that all background factors (represented by the vector Z) have a positive relationship to Y. I shall also assume that the impact of X on Y is independent of Z (the vector Z does not serve as a mediator). And I shall assume that positive values for X and Y correspond to a change in those variables at some point in the past (and which therefore may be observable), whereas negative values correspond to stasis (no change).

In this scenario, we can classify case types into eight categories, illustrated in Table 5.16. Note that the total number of combinations of values depends on the number of control variables, which we have represented with a single vector, Z. If this vector consists of a single variable, then there are only eight case types. If this vector consists of two variables (Z_1, Z_2). then the total number of possible combinations increases from eight (2^3) to 16 (2^4). Identifying these case types is a relatively simple matter, and can be accomplished in a small-C sample by the construction of a truth-table or in a large-C sample by the use of cross-tabs.

The pathway case, following the logic of the crucial case, is one where the causal factor of interest is positive $(X = 1)$ and correctly predicts Y while all other possible causes of Y (represented by the vector, Z) make "wrong" predictions. This is depicted as Case H in Table 5.16. If X is a cause of Y, this relationship should be most visible where other potential confounders are not at work – or, more accurately, *probably* not at work. This does not presume that the relationship (as manifested in a larger population) is mono-causal; it merely supposes that in a given case the relationship may be mono-causal, i.e., where $X = 1$ is causally sufficient to produce $Y = 1$. It does not presume causal determinism; there may be many instances where $X = 1$ and $Y = 0$ (case types E and F). (Naturally, if X is a cause of Y, we would expect to find fewer instances of E and F than of other types.)

Now, let us approach a more complicated scenario, when all (or most) variables of concern to the model are continuous rather than dichotomous. Here, the job of case selection is considerably more complex, for causal "sufficiency" (in the usual sense) cannot be invoked. It is no longer plausible to assume that a given cause can be entirely partitioned, i.e., rival factors eliminated. However, the search for a pathway case may still be viable in a large-C setting.

What we are looking for in this scenario is a case that satisfies two criteria: (1) it is not an outlier, or at least not an extreme outlier, in the full model (so it does not violate the criterion of representativeness in an obvious way) and (2) its score on the outcome (Y) is strongly influenced by the theoretical variable of interest (X), taking other factors into account (Z). This is the continuous-variable analog of Case

H in Table 5.16. In this sort of case, it should be easiest to "see" causal mechanisms that may lie between X and Y.

To identify this case, a three-step procedure is needed. First, the researcher constructs a *minimal* specification with all relevant background factors (those that might serve as confounders),

$$Y = Z + \varepsilon_1 \tag{5.1}$$

Second, the researcher constructs a *full* specification, including the causal factor of interest,

$$Y = Z + X + \varepsilon_2 \tag{5.2}$$

The potential pathway case is that case – or set of cases – which shows the greatest difference between the absolute value of the residual for the minimal specification and the absolute value of the full specification (ΔResidual),

$$\text{Pathway} = |\varepsilon_1 - \varepsilon_2|, \text{if } |\varepsilon_1| > |\varepsilon_2| \tag{5.3}$$

Note that the residual for a case must be smaller in the full specification than in the minimal specification; otherwise, the addition of the variable of interest (X) pulls the case *away* from the regression line. We want to find a case where the addition of X pushes the case towards the regression line, i.e., it helps to "explain" that case, according to the terms of the theory that is being assessed.

As an example, let us suppose that we are interested in exploring the effect of mineral wealth on the prospects for democracy in a society. According to a good deal of work on this subject, countries with a bounty of natural resources – particularly oil – are less likely to democratize. Yet, even for those who are convinced of the argument, the causal mechanisms remain rather obscure. Consider the following list of possible causal pathways, summarized by Michael Ross (2001: 327–8):

A "rentier effect" … suggests that resources rich governments use low tax rates and patronage to relieve pressures for greater accountability; a "repression effect" … argues that resources wealth retards democratization by enabling governments to boost their funding for internal security; and a "modernization effect" ... holds that growth based on the export of oil and minerals fails to bring about the social and cultural changes that tend to produce democratic government.

Are all three causal mechanisms at work? Are they present in all cases, and to equal degrees? Although Ross attempts to test these factors in a large-C cross-country setting, his answers remain rather speculative.[28] Let us see how this might be handled by a pathway-case approach.

The factor of theoretical interest, oil wealth, may be operationalized as per capita oil production (barrels of oil produced, divided by the total population of a country [derived from Humphreys 2005]). We measure democracy with a variable, Polity2, drawn from the Polity IV dataset. Additional factors in the model include GDP per capita (logged), Muslims (as percent of the population), European language (percentage speaking a European language), and ethnic fractionalization.[29] These are all regarded as background variables that may affect a country's propensity to democratize (Z). We shall analyze these in a simple cross-sectional ordinary least squares regression model focused on a recent year (1995). To simplify the equations, we present coefficients for all right-side variables, but not standard errors and p-values (readers may assume that all factors are statistically significant at standard threshold levels). The *minimal* specification includes all factors except the factor of theoretical interest.

---

[28] Ross tests these various causal mechanisms with cross-country data, employing various proxies for these concepts in the benchmark model and observing the effect of these – presumably intermediary – effects on the main variable of interest (oil resources). This is a good example of how cross-case evidence can be mustered to shed light on causal mechanisms; one is not limited to case study formats, as discussed in Chapter 1. Still, as Ross (2001: 356) notes, these tests are by no means definitive. Indeed, the coefficient on the key oil variable remains fairly constant, except in circumstances where the sample is severely constrained.

[29] GDPpc data are from World Bank (2003). Muslims and European language are coded by the author. Ethnic fractionalization is drawn from Alesina *et al.* (2003).

Table 5.17 Example of pathway cases with continuous variables

	ε_1 (Eq. (5.4))	ε_2 (Eq. (5.5))	$\varepsilon_1 - \varepsilon_2$
Iran	−0.282	−0.456	0.175
Turkmenistan	−1.220	−1.398	0.178
Mauritania	−0.076	−0.255	0.179
Turkey	2.261	2.069	0.192
Switzerland	0.177	−0.028	0.205
Venezuela	0.148	0.355	−0.207
Belgium	0.518	0.310	0.208
Morocco	−0.540	−0.776	0.236
Jordan	0.382	0.142	0.240
Djibouti	−0.451	−0.696	0.245
Bahrain	−1.411	−1.673	0.262
Luxembourg	0.559	0.291	0.269
Singapore	−1.593	−1.864	0.271
Oman	−1.270	−0.981	−0.289
Gabon	−1.743	−1.418	−0.325
Saudi Arabia	−1.681	−1.253	−0.428
Norway	0.315	1.285	−0.971
United Arab Emirates	−1.256	−0.081	−1.175
Kuwait	−1.007	0.925	−1.932

Notes: ε_1 = standardized residual from the minimal specification, without Oil (Eq. (5.4)). ε_2 = standardized residual from the full specification, with Oil (Eq. (5.5)).

$$\text{Polity2} = -.831 \text{ Constant} + .909 \text{ GDP} + -.086 \text{ Muslim} + 2.242 \text{ European} + -3.023 \text{ Ethnic fract} + \varepsilon_1$$
$$R^2\text{adj} = .428n = 149 \tag{5.4}$$

The full specification – adding Oil – is as follows:

$$\text{Polity2} = -3.71 \text{ Constant} + 1.258 \text{ GDP} + -.075 \text{ Muslim} + 1.843 \text{ European} + -2.093 \text{ Ethnic fract} + -7.662 \text{ Oil} + \varepsilon_2$$
$$R^2\text{adj} = .450 \ n = 149 \tag{5.5}$$

What does a comparison of the residuals across equations (5.4) and (5.5) reveal? Table 5.17 displays the highest ΔResidual cases. Several of these may be summarily removed from consideration by virtue of the fact that $|\varepsilon_1| < |\varepsilon_2|$. Thus, we see that the inclusion of oil increases the residual for Norway; this case is apparently better explained *without* the inclusion of the variable of theoretical interest. Needless to say, this is not a good case to explore if we wish to examine causal mechanisms. (It probably serves as an influential case, however, as discussed in the previous section.)

Among cases where the residual declines from the minimal to the full specification, several are obvious choices as pathway cases. The United Arab Emirates and Kuwait have the highest ΔResidual values signifying that the variable of theoretical interest (resource wealth) is an important influence on those cases (within the assumptions of the models), UAE, but not Kuwait, also has a modest residual in the full specification, signifying that it fits the model rather well and, on that account, is more likely to be representative of the larger population (if not its outliers). The analysis suggests, therefore, that researchers seeking to explore the effect of oil wealth on regime type might do well to focus on these two cases (or at least on UAE) since their patterns of democracy are not well explained by other factors – e.g., economic development, religion, European influence, or ethnic fractionalization. The presence of oil wealth in these countries would appear to have a strong *independent* effect on the prospects for democratization in these cases. This is not to say, of course, that other cases can be ignored, or should be ignored. It is to say, quite simply, that if one is constrained to focus on one or a few cases, the United Arab Emirates and Kuwait should be among them.

The foregoing examples of pathway case selection focus on cross-sectional variation (across cases). Longitudinal variation, which is generally more useful, is implied. However, it is also possible to incorporate temporal information into the case-selection algorithm (as suggested by Teorell 2010: Appendix D). Suppose one is able to measure relevant features of the sample through time and that there is considerable variation in X and Y in the resulting panel, Under these circumstances, one may regress Y on X (along with Z, if measurable) for each case, a simple time-series analysis for each unit in the panel dataset. The ideal case is one in which βX is strong (and statistically significant), while controlling for all relevant background factors (Z).

Continuing with our stylized example, one might regress democracy on oil, controlling for background factors that might influence a country's regime type. Because this is a single-unit analysis, factors that are constant through time – such as Muslim, European, or ethnic fractionalization – are omitted. The resulting time-series model has only two right-side factors,

$$\text{Polity2} = \text{GDP} + \text{Oil} + \varepsilon_1 \tag{5.6}$$

Accordingly, a country in which changes in per capita oil production have the strongest (negative) relationship to democracy over the observed period is a country that fits the pathway paradigm. Here, one is most likely to view the causal mechanism of interest at work.

To assure that the case is not idiosyncratic (according to the terms of the model), one may construct a fixed-effect panel analysis with dummies representing each case. The dummy for the chosen case(s) should not have a high estimated coefficient in the fixed-effect model.

Most-similar (diagnostic)

When employed for diagnostic purposes, the most-similar design consists of a pathway case (as above) plus a control case, which exhibits minimal variation in X and Z.[30] That is, chosen cases exhibit different values on X, similar values on Z, and different values on Y. As discussed (in connection with the exploratory most-similar design), values for Z may differ if (and only if) such differences cannot account for variation in Y across the cases given plausible theoretical assumptions.

When factors of theoretical interest are all binary, the research design may be illustrated in a schematic fashion, as shown in Table 5.18. When factors are ordinal or interval, the researcher seeks to minimize variance (across cases) in Z while maximizing variance in X and Y. In this context, one is more or less assuming that values for X, Z, and Y represent values for the cases that are realized over time rather than

---

[30] For work on the most-similar method, generally understood, see work cited for the most-similar (exploratory) method above.

Table 5.18 Exemplary most-similar (diagnostic) design

		Variables		
		X	Z	Y
Cases	A	1	0	1
	B	0	0	0

Notes: Diagnostic most-similar design with binary factors, an exemplary setting. X = causal factor of theoretical interest. Z = vector of background factors. Y = outcome. The assignment of 0s and 1s is an arbitrary coding choice. The key point is that cases A and B share the same values on all Z and differ on X and Y.

at just one point in time. Thus, one may read X, Z, and Y in Table 5.18 as ΔX, ΔZ, and ΔY.

These research design features may be identified in a large sample of potential cases by employing matching algorithms that maximize differences across cases in X and Y (or ΔX and ΔY) in ways that are consistent with the hypothesis while minimizing differences on the vector Z (or ΔZ).[31]

Ten exemplars of the most-similar (diagnostic) design are listed in Table 5.19. These are drawn from a range of disciplines and pertain to a variety of phenomena – industrial policies, banking systems, health policies, social movements, clinics, water and irrigation agencies, and party systems. Samples are limited to a narrow range of two to four.

As an in-depth example, let us consider a recent study by Karen Lutfey and Jeremy Freese (2005). The authors are interested in uncovering the mechanisms at work in a persistent, and oft-noted, relationship between socioeconomic status and health. Poor people experience poor health, which is presumably – at least in some respects – a product of their poverty. (Illness may also contribute to poverty, but we shall not consider this feedback loop here.) Lutfey and Freese compare high and low status individuals who suffer from diabetes, with the knowledge that the latter

---

[31] See Nielsen (2016) and accompanying web application: https://rnielsen.shinyapps.io/caseMatch/

Table 5.19 Most-similar (diagnostic) case exemplars

			SELECTION		CASES	
Study	Field	Cites	Algo.	Non-algo.	Phenomena	C
Dobbin (1994) *Forging Industrial Policy*	SO	745		●	Industrial policies	3
Dunlavy (1994) *Politics and Industrialization*	HI	125		●	Industrial policies	2
Haber (2010) *Politics, Banking, and Economic Development*	HI	3		●	Banking systems	3
Immergut (1992) *Health Politics*	PS	1,008		●	Health policy	3
Kitschelt (1986) *Political Opportunity Structures and Protest*	PS	1,760		●	Social movements	4
Lutfey and Freese (2005) *SES and Health in Routine Clinic*	SO	144		●	Clinics	2
Madrigal *et al.* (2011) *Community-Based Orgs*	EC	20	●		Water agencies	4
Shefter (1977) *Party and Patronage*	PS	237		●	Party systems	3/2
Wade (1997) *How Infrastructure Agencies Motivate Staff*	PS	71		●	Irrigation agencies	2
Walter (2002) *Committing to Peace*	PS	821		●	Civil wars	2

Notes: C = number of cases. *Algo.* = case selection by algorithm.

are more likely to succumb to the effects of the disease. This is accomplished by focusing on two endocrinology clinics, one located in an affluent neighborhood and the other in a poor neighborhood. Cases are thus selected on X (patient socioeconomic status) and Y (mortality rates from diabetes), with the assumption that other background factors that might contribute to mortality (Z) are equivalent across the clinics. The focus of the study is on factors inside the clinic (continuity of care, in-clinic educational resources, bureaucratic organization), outside the clinic (financial limitations, occupational constraints, social support networks), and among the patients (motivation, cognitive ability) that might affect compliance with an exacting medical regime. These are regarded as prima facie causal mechanisms in the relationship between socioeconomic status (SES) and health.

5.4   Summary

In this chapter, I have discussed case-selection strategies that are intended to identify, measure, or assess a causal hypothesis. For each of these goals, several strategies are possible. These are laid out in brief form, with several examples, and advice on how to select a case, or small set of cases, from a large set of potential cases.

An important "take-home" message of this chapter is that there are many aspects of causal inference, each of which calls for a somewhat different method of case selection. To be sure, these goals tend to mush together in the finished product, as researchers want to squeeze as much juice from the fruit as they can. It would be wasteful for a researcher to try to measure a causal effect without any attention to potential mechanisms, for example. Nonetheless, the researcher's *initial* goal rightly structures the selection of cases, with other goals trailing behind (to be handled, as best as they can, once the case is chosen).

6 Algorithms and samples

All case-selection strategies may be implemented in an informal ("qualitative") fashion by reviewing potential cases known to the researcher according to the criteria listed in Table 3.1. For example, let us say that the goal is to describe social life within mid-sized cities in the United States, an iteration of the Lynds' *Middletown*. For this purpose, one might prefer a typical case. Accordingly, one might think about those cities that one is familiar with in order to determine which is most representative of the population of interest. One might also conduct some preliminary research based on the secondary literature, a survey of urbanists, or initial field research.

Another approach would be to employ an *algorithm* to choose cases. This approach, also known as *quantitative, ex ante, automatic, formalized, systematic,* or *model-based* case selection, will occupy us in the present chapter.[1]

The simplest algorithm is random selection, i.e., sampling randomly from the population so that each unit has an equal chance of selection. The first section of the chapter deals with this much-discussed (but little-practiced) approach. The second section deals with other approaches, building on the menu of case-selection techniques laid out in Table 3.1. The third section revisits the "size" question by exploring the viability of medium-sized samples (comprising from one to several dozen cases). This chapter thus combines two topics

---

[1] See Dafoe and Kelsey (2014), Gerring (2007a), Goertz (2017), Herron and Quinn (2016), Lieberman (2005), Nielsen (2016), Schneider and Rohlfing (2013, 2016), Seawright (2016b), Seawright and Gerring (2008).

that are difficult to distinguish from one another – the size of the sample and the method of case selection.

6.1   Random sampling

Random sampling means that each case in a given population has an equal chance of being selected. This may be achieved by a random draw from an urn, a random number generator, or a systematic sampling technique. The key point is that if cases are selected randomly and the resulting sample is large, the sample is likely to be representative of the overall population with regard to any particular feature.[2]

Random sampling is the preferred approach to case selection in most large-*C* contexts. However, it is not widely practiced in case study research. To understand why this is so, we need to appreciate two problems – *stochastic error* and *leverage*.

The first problem with random sampling as an approach to case selection with very small samples – i.e., in case study research – is that the resulting sample is much less likely to be representative. Resulting errors (deviations from the population mean) may be understood as stochastic, e.g., measurement error, error in the data-generation process, and/or error as a fundamental feature of the universe. But they are still worrisome since one wishes to draw inferences about the population from that (quite possibly biased) sample.

To dramatize this point, let us consider two sampling exercises, one with large samples and the other with small samples. Figure 6.1 shows a histogram of the mean values from 500 random samples, each consisting of 1,000 cases. For each case, one variable has been measured: a

---

[2] The exception involves features of the population that are very rare, and which must therefore be over-sampled. To restore representativeness, the observations can be weighted by their prevalence in the population. For a general introduction to sampling, see Henry (1990).

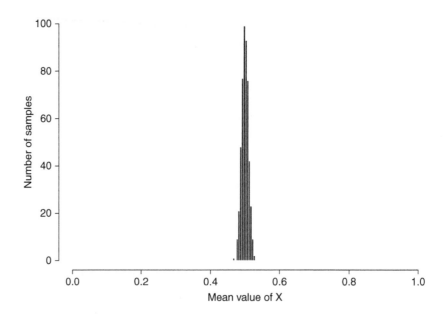

Figure 6.1   Sample means of large-sample draws

Notes: Samples = 500. Sample size (C) = 1,000. Graph shows the distribution of mean values across all samples. Population mean = 0.5.

continuous variable that falls somewhere between 0 and 1. In the population, the mean value of this variable is 0.5. As can be seen, all of the sample means are close to the true (population) mean. In this respect, random sampling is successful, and each of the 500 samples turns out to be fairly representative of the population.

Now consider what happens if we reduce sample size from 1,000 cases to five (C = 5). Results, shown in Figure 6.2, show that small random samples are again centered on the true mean, and thus unbiased. However, many of the sample means lie far from the population mean, and some are quite far indeed. Thus, even though this case-selection technique produces representative samples *on average*, any given sample may be wildly unrepresentative. In statistical terms, the problem is that small sample sizes tend to produce estimates with a great deal of variance – sometimes referred to as a problem of precision (or, somewhat misleadingly, of "efficiency"). For this reason, random

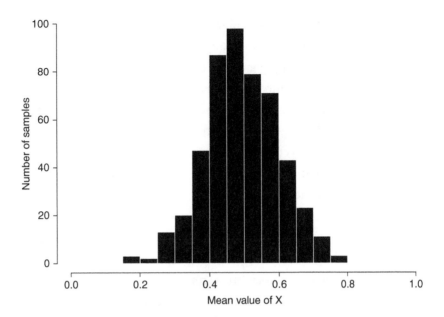

Figure 6.2   Sample means of small-sample draws
Notes: Samples = 500. Sample size (*C*) = 5. Graph shows the distribution of mean values across all samples. Population mean = 0.5.

sampling is inherently unreliable in case study research insofar as case study research involves a limited number of cases and a much larger population.

To be sure, random sampling with small samples is more defensible when the population of theoretical interest is very small. Several countries chosen randomly from Western Europe (*N*~10) offer a more precise representation of that population than several countries chosen randomly from the world can represent the population of all sovereign countries (*N*~200). This is reflected in the *finite population correction factor*, as employed in sampling statistics (Knaub 2008). However, this is a rather unusual circumstance. Typically, the population of interest, even if finite, is much larger than the sample. In this circumstance, the finite population correction factor has minimal impact on the precision of the resulting estimates.

The second problem with random sampling as an approach to case selection in case study work may be summarized as one of *leverage*. There is no guarantee that a few cases, chosen randomly, will provide leverage into the research question that animates an investigation. The sample might be representative but still uninformative, or less informative than other cases that could have been chosen using a purposive case-selection strategy. (*Stratified* random sampling is another matter entirely for it allows one to specify the type of case that is likely to provide the greatest leverage on the question of interest. Indeed, almost all of the methods of case selection outlined in Table 3.1 are amenable to stratified random sampling, as discussed below. However, it is important to bear in mind that stratified random sampling is still subject to stochastic error if the resulting sample is small.)

These two problems – stochastic error (sampling variance) and leverage – limit random sampling as a strategy for case selection in case study research. Indeed, I do not find even a single example of it in my canvas of case studies in the social sciences.[3]

6.2   Algorithmic ("quantitative") case selection

While large-C research aspires to collect observations randomly from a known universe, case study research does not, for reasons discussed above. Instead, researchers select based on particular dimensions of the potential cases – D, X, Z, and/or Y – as summarized in Table 3.1. This is sometimes referred to as *purposive* case selection. However, there is no reason why a specification of dimensions cannot be combined with a random element – a *stratified* random sample – as we shall see.

---

[3] Note that Fearon and Laitin (2008, 2014, 2015), who appear to advocate random sampling, in fact utilize a stratified random sampling technique for their "random narratives" project in which countries are stratified by outcome and region.

Purposive case selection does not mean that case selection must be entirely qualitative. It may enlist a pre-specified algorithm.

Algorithmic (also known as quantitative, statistical) case selection follows a set of rules executed in a sequence of steps, which I envision in the following fashion.

1. Define the research question and the population of theoretical interest.
2. Identify a sample of potential cases. Ideally, this sampling frame should be representative of the population of interest.
3. Measure relevant features of the cases – e.g., D, X, Y, and/or Z (as specified in Table 3.1) – across the sample.
4. Combine diverse indicators of D, X, Y, and/or Z into indices, if necessary.
5. Construct a causal model, if required.
6. Apply a case-selection algorithm to identify the case, or cases, eligible for investigation (as discussed in Chapters 4–5).
7. If more than one case satisfies the criteria, select cases randomly from within the subset of eligible cases (stratified random sampling).

Algorithms might be simple, as they are for the typical case, where the case – or cases – lying closest to the mean, median, or mode is usually regarded as typical, as discussed in Chapter 4. Or they might be more complex, involving causal models, as discussed in Chapter 5. Our discussion focused mostly on regression or matching estimators as these are the most common large-C estimation techniques. But one might also employ algorithms drawn from the qualitative comparative analysis (QCA) family (e.g., crisp-set, fuzzy-set, or temporal QCA).[4]

---

[4] I suspect that methods of case selection relying on QCA (Qualitative Comparative Analysis) also follow the strategies listed in Table 5.1, at least insofar as cases are chosen according to a pathway strategy (where each configuration constitutes a pathway and cases are chosen from each pathway) or an influential strategy (focused on cases that do not fit the general patterns discovered by the QCA). On this topic, see Schneider and Rohlfing (2013), as well as Rohlfing and Schneider (2013),

Table 6.1 Algorithmic case selection

			CASES	
Study	Field	Cites	Phenomena	C
Collier and Sambanis (2005a, b) *Understanding Civil War*	PS	430	Civil wars	21
Dafoe and Kelsey (2014) *Observing the Capitalist Peace*	PS	2	Nation dyads	6
Fearon and Laitin (2008, 2014, 2015) *Random Narratives*	PS	85	Civil wars	25
Lange (2009) *Lineages of Despotism and Development*	SO	69	Economic development	4/11
Madrigal *et al.* (2011) *Community-Based Orgs*	EC	20	Water agencies	4
Pearce (2002) *Integrating Survey and Ethnographic Methods*	SO	47	Fertility	28
Pinfari (2012) *Peace Negotiations and Time*	PS	0	Negotiations	4
Rosenbaum and Silber (2001) *Matching*	PH	50	Patients	76
Teorell (2010) *Determinants of Democratization*	PS	153	Regime-types	14

Note: C = number of cases.

Whatever the chosen technique, it deserves to be emphasized that all case-selection strategies may be implemented in an algorithmic fashion. At the same time, readers should be aware that this approach to case selection is still fairly unusual. Among the 151 exemplars listed in Table 1.2, only nine utilize algorithmic case-selection procedures, as listed in Table 6.1.[5] Nonetheless, it is now an established method of case selection and appears to be growing in importance, so it warrants close attention.

Schneider and Rohlfing (2016). For a note of caution, see Lucas and Szatrowski (2014).

[5] In one of these studies (Lange 2009), the initial analysis is supplemented by further deliberation, ex post, prior to final case selection.

Advantages

Four main advantages may be credited to the algorithmic approach. First, case selection is explicit and replicable. It would be difficult, by contrast, to describe and to replicate the complex judgments involved in qualitative case selection.

Second, the algorithm assists researchers in identifying the best case, or cases, wherever case-selection criteria are complicated and/or the number of potential cases is large – perhaps numbering in the hundreds, thousands, or even millions. So long as a criterion can be reduced to a formula, and so long as it can be measured across the potential cases, the algorithmic approach is seaworthy.

Third, claims to sample representativeness – relative to a larger population – are easier to define and to defend. That is, it is clearer what the chosen case(s) might be a case of (what population one is sampling from). Of course, that population might not be coterminous with the population of the hypothesis that results from the research. For example, if one chooses the case(s) to maximize variation in Y, one would not claim that the resulting sample of the extreme case(s) is representative of the population of cases for which $X \rightarrow Y$ (once X has been identified). But one might claim that the sample is representative of a population for which Y is "high" or "low."

Fourth, the algorithmic approach allows for (but does not by itself assure) a clear separation between theory generation and theory testing. Only in this fashion can the problem of "cherry-picking" (choosing cases that fit the researcher's theory or preconceptions) be avoided.

For all these reasons, an algorithmic approach to case selection is worth considering.

Limitations

There are also reasons to be dubious of "automatic" algorithmic procedures.

First, the protocol for algorithmic case selection outlined above is demanding. One must have a clearly defined research question and population of theoretical interest. One must possess data sufficient to measure the relevant parameters for a large sample of cases, and the data must be relatively reliable. If a causal model is required, one must be able to construct a model that is plausible. If any of these requirements is not satisfied, then one may be better off with an informal method of case selection.

Second, concerns about separating theory formation and theory testing are irrelevant if the goal of the case study is exploratory, i.e., to discover a new cause of Y. Exploratory work always entails an interplay between theory and evidence (Rueschemeyer 2009), a function that the case study format is well suited to facilitate.

Third, while algorithmic case selection might make sense when choosing a medium-sized sample of cases, most case studies focus on only one or several cases. In a sample this small, problems arise with a purely algorithmic selection procedure. Specifically, any given sample is quite likely to fall far from the population parameter of theoretical interest, as shown in the previous section of this chapter. Moreover, detailed knowledge of a case may be sufficient to call into question the representativeness of a case. If, after close examination, a case seems unrepresentative, it may make more sense to jettison that case – based on "qualitative" considerations – rather than to persist with a case that is obviously flawed.

Most important, some criteria, almost by definition, are hard to measure, ex ante, across a large sample of cases and therefore are not features that an algorithmic case-selection method can condition on. Foremost among these "un-measurables" are omnibus criteria (discussed in Chapter 3) such as the independence of a case, the availability and suitability of within-case evidence, and logistics.

For cases that serve a role in causal inference, one must also consider the degree to which the chosen case, or cases, exhibits experimental qualities, as discussed in Chapter 5. A case with many potential confounders is less useful – indeed, perhaps not useful at all – than a case that is relatively "clean," e.g., where X changes without corresponding changes in Z. While case-selection algorithms often attempt to control for background characteristics, confounders are notoriously devious and therefore not always easy to measure – especially in a large-C framework. If quasi-experimental cases could be identified by algorithms, we could find good natural experiments simply by running selection algorithms across thousands of potential sites of investigation. In practice, researchers must invest an enormous amount of time looking into the fine details of a site before it can be ascertained whether – or in what respects – it satisfies the methodological criteria of a natural experiment, i.e., as-if random assignment and the absence of post-treatment confounders. What is true of sites (suitable for large-C natural experiments) is also true for cases (suitable for small-C natural experiments): there are no mechanical tools for finding them (Dunning 2012).

Conclusions

Algorithmic case selection makes good sense if one is choosing a medium-C sample of cases, for all the same reasons that it makes sense for large samples. Here, traditional sampling theory applies. Indeed, it is not clear how one would select several dozen cases in an informal (qualitative) fashion. When a sample is expanded beyond a dozen, one is more or less presuming that an automated selection criterion can be applied. The most outspoken proponents of model-based case selection, James Fearon and David Laitin (2008, 2014, 2015), incorporate 25 country cases in their "random narratives" project, each of which is intensively studied. With a sample of this size, it makes good sense to apply an algorithmic selection procedure because threats from stochastic error are minimized and sufficient leverage on factors of theoretical interest are likely to be contained in the resulting sample.

Even where the sample is very small, i.e., in traditional case study work, case-selection algorithms are probably an under-utilized tool. However, the algorithmic choice should probably not be followed slavishly in the final selection of cases for all the reasons discussed above. A case that looks good from the perspective of an algorithm may not look so appealing when one becomes familiar with the intricacies of the setting.

Having considered the pros and cons of algorithmic case selection, I offer a final thought on why this approach to case selection is elusive, and likely to remain so. Recall that algorithmic selection requires a great deal of information gathered across a large sample as well as a reliable descriptive or causal model. These are demanding criteria. If the criteria are not satisfied, one is probably ill-advised to choose cases in an algorithmic fashion. If, on the other hand, the criteria are satisfied, the need for additional analysis focused on one or several cases is minimized. This is the paradox.

The less we know about a population of interest, the more we can learn from a case study. At the same time, our ignorance about the population makes it difficult to employ algorithmic case-selection procedures with confidence. That is perhaps why algorithmic case selection is not commonly employed for exploratory case studies.

The more we know about a population, the better we can devise algorithms to help us choose cases – but, at the same time, the less informative a case study is likely to be. If a case study is conducted in such a scenario, it is likely to play a supporting role. That is probably why algorithmic case selection is most commonly employed for diagnostic case studies.

6.3   The size question revisited

Thus far, I have assumed that case studies will incorporate a very small sample of cases, e.g., one or several. However, the advantages of a somewhat larger sample – *medium-C*, comprising ten or more cases – are probably apparent. In particular, a medium-C sample can be chosen algorithmically, achieving all of the advantages of algorithmic selection (including stronger claims to representativeness) without sacrificing leverage on the problem at hand (since the chosen cases are likely to provide sufficient variation in the dimensions of interest). In light of these advantages, it may behoove case study researchers to follow Fearon and Laitin's lead. Perhaps the problems of case study research can be mitigated by the simple expedient of increasing C, the size of the sample. If case studies are good, more cases may be even better.[6]

To help us wrap our heads around this question, all case study exemplars with more than ten cases (not counting shadow cases) are listed in Table 6.2. The reader will perceive that, although a distinct minority, this approach to case study research is by no means rare. Twenty-two examples are identified, embracing diverse topics and a variety of disciplines.

In evaluating the viability of medium-C case studies, let us begin with a fairly obvious point. If all things were equal, medium-C samples would indeed be preferred to small-C samples. However, tradeoffs are inevitable when a larger number of cases are incorporated into a study. Studying additional cases intensively requires additional time and resources – to access informants or research sites, to learn new languages, to process the information and write up the results, and so forth. Sometimes, these tasks can be divided up among a team of researchers – this, of course, requires a greater manpower than the traditional case study (usually undertaken by an individual researcher, perhaps with the help of a research assistant), and raises coordination problems. Yet, if the only obstacles to medium-C case study research were logistical, one would expect it to occur more frequently. After all,

---

[6] For further discussion and examples, see Goertz (2017: Chapter 8). For discussion from a non-positivist angle, see Stake (2006).

Table 6.2 Medium-C case studies

| Study | Field | Cites | SELECTION | | CASES | |
			Algo.	Non-algo.	Phenomena	C
Anderson (1974) *Lineages of Absolutist State*	HI	2,508		●	Nation-building	10
Collier, Sambanis (2005a, 2005b) *Understanding Civil War*	PS	430	●		Civil wars	21
Fairfield (2013, 2015) *Going Where Money Is*	PS	7		●	Tax reform proposals	32
Fearon and Laitin (2008, 2014, 2015) *Random Narratives*	PS	85	●		Civil wars	25
Fenno (1977, 1978) *Home Style*	PS	2,141		●	MPs and districts	17
George and Smoke (1974) *Deterrence in US Foreign Policy*	PS	894		●	Crises	11
Key (1949) *Southern Politics in State and Nation*	PS	3,238		●	US states	11
Lane (1962) *Political Ideology*	PS	695		●	Workers	18
Linz and Stepan (1978a, 1978b) *Breakdown Demo. Regimes*	PS	1,765		●	Dem. breakdowns	11
Luebbert (1991) *Liberalism, Fascism, or Social Democracy*	PS	356		●	Regime-types	15
Mansfield and Snyder (2005) *Electing to Fight*	PS	627		●	Conflicts	10
Ostrom (1990) *Governing the Commons*	PS	20,073		●	Common pool res.	~14
Pearce (2002) *Integrating Survey and Ethnographic Methods*	SO	47	●		Fertility	28
Peters and Waterman (1982) *In Search of Excellence*	EC	17,443		●	Firms	43
Porter (1990) *Competitive Advantage of Nations*	EC	31,857		●	Economic development	10
Putnam *et al.* (1993) *Making Democracy Work*	PS	29,712		●	Italian regions	20
Rosenbaum and Silber (2001) *Matching*	PH	50	●		Patients	76
Ross (2004) *How Do Natural Resources Influence Civil War?*	PS	566		●	Civil wars	13

Table 6.2 (*cont.*)

			SELECTION		CASES	
Study	Field	Cites	Algo.	Non-algo.	Phenomena	*C*
Rueschemeyer *et al.* (1992) *Capitalist Development*	SO	2,727		●	Regime-types	22
Sahlins (1958) *Social Stratification in Polynesia*	AN	726		●	Societies	17
Teorell (2010) *Determinants of Democratization*	PS	153	●		Regime-types	14
Wilson (1889) *The State*	PS	268		●	Constitutions	10

Notes: C = number of cases. *Algo.* = selection of cases by algorithm.

teamwork is increasingly common in the social sciences and some projects are able to draw on large budgets and a sizeable staff.

A more fundamental issue arises when one considers what to do with the results of 25 case studies. (I shall assume that the population of interest is much larger – numbering in the hundreds, thousands, or millions.) To integrate results from 25 cases, some sort of data reduction is required, i.e., the cases will need to be reduced to numbers. This might be a simple count of the number of cases that seem to show a particular causal mechanism at work, or the number of cases that validate or invalidate the hypothesis of interest, or some new causal factor that is suggested by the cases. It might be a causal model, to be run on the sample of 25. The point is that once a sample reaches into the dozens it is no longer possible to analyze patterns in a purely informal, qualitative manner.

If the end-product of a medium-*C* study is a quantitative analysis, the question arises: does medium-*C* offer any advantages over large-*C*? The large-*C* study might involve hand-coding cases or collecting data from extant sources – following, in either case, a standardized protocol that mitigates problems of cross-case equivalence and vastly enhances the efficiency of the case analysis relative to the laborious task of open-ended case-based research.

An example of standardized coding across cases is provided by a recent study by Stephan Haggard and Robert Kaufman (2012), who examine over 100 regime transitions in order to determine the role of distributional conflict in these events. The case profiles are housed in a lengthy on-line document. The published study presents the data derived from this extensive analysis, condensed into tabular formats. The role of the in-depth qualitative investigation is thus to arrive at a binary coding of each case, as "distributive" or "non-distributive." It is an ingenious study, and evidence of extraordinary labor on the part of a coordinated research team. However, it is hardly a case study in the sense in which I have defined the term. Indeed, the protocol is indistinguishable from any large-C data collection project in which the authors conduct careful, nose-to-the-grindstone coding and preserve their notes in a codebook.[7]

The point, then, is that a large sample of cases can be integrated through careful case-based knowledge if data collection is directed by a systematic survey protocol. The process may be centralized (a few researchers do all the coding, as in the Haggard and Kaufman projects) or decentralized (coding is conducted by experts on different subjects or different parts of the world, as in the Varieties of Democracy project [Coppedge *et al.* 2015]). In either case, the resulting study has stronger claims to representativeness and greater protection against stochastic error than the corresponding medium-C analysis. It would, in short, seem superior to medium-C analysis in all respects that medium-C analysis is superior to small-C analysis.

This foreshadows our conclusion. Medium-C case studies are much more expensive (in terms of time and resources) than small-C case studies, and the end-result is generally inferior to large-C analysis. As such, medium-C case-based analysis is a hybrid form of research that

---

[7] See, e.g., Kreuzer (2010), Mainwaring and Pérez-Liñán (2014), Narang and Nelson (2009), Snyder and Borghard (2011), and the Archigos codebook (Goemans *et al.* 2009). For further discussion, see Goertz (2017: Chapters 7–8).

seems to have no area in which it enjoys comparative advantage relative to the small-*C* and large-*C* alternatives. For these reasons, both logistical and methodological, I regard case study research in a traditional fashion, i.e., as a small-*C* endeavor. While it might make sense in some circumstances to accumulate a medium-sized sample of cases, each studied intensively, I suspect this will remain a relatively rare approach to social science research.[8]

6.4   Summary

Chapters 3–5 focused on specific case-selection strategies. This chapter explores several generic features of this process.

The first section discusses the application of *random sampling* to the selection of cases in case study research. It was shown that this approach suffers two flaws. The chosen sample of cases, if small, is subject to serious threats from stochastic error and is also unlikely to yield sufficient leverage on the question of theoretical interest.

The second section takes on the subject of *algorithmic* case selection, where a formula governs the selection of a case, or cases, from a large number of potential cases. I set out a protocol for algorithmic case selection and discuss its pros and cons. My view, in a nutshell, is that algorithms are useful wherever a large number of potential cases are available and wherever data for those cases allow for the application of a suitable algorithm. However, I do not believe that an algorithm should provide the final choice among cases if the sample of chosen cases is very small – as it typically is in case study research. This is because it is difficult, if not impossible, to incorporate all the desiderata of case selection into an algorithm. Some things, like the

---

[8] Ragin (2000: 25) provides a revealing histogram of social science studies understood in terms of their number of cases. The histogram displays a U-shaped curve, with many small-*C* studies, many large-*C* studies, and very few medium-*C* studies.

quasi-experimental qualities of a case, can only be known from in-depth knowledge of the case. If, on the other hand, the researcher wishes to incorporate a larger number of cases – a medium-C sample – the use of algorithms becomes defensible, and probably indispensable.

In the final section, I comment on the viability of *medium-C* samples (comprising several dozen cases). While I am impressed by recent studies that utilize a large basket of cases, I am unsure that this method offers the most efficient method of investigation. Medium-C case studies are much more labor-intensive than small-C case studies, and also demand that researchers possess in-depth knowledge of a large number of cases. The resulting material – lengthy studies of each case – is hard to integrate except by quantitative methods, which of course require a more reductionist approach to the cases, a vast simplification of what has been learned. The process begins to look more like coding, where a systematic questionnaire is applied to each case, and less like case studies. In short, medium-C studies seem to occupy a nebulous methodological zone in between small- and large-C studies. I suspect that researchers' time and money would be better spent doing one or the other, or combining both in a multimethod study, as discussed in the next chapter.

Part III

Analyzing cases

7

A typology of research designs

Having explored methods of case selection in Part II, we turn now to methods of analysis – what to do with the cases once they are chosen. Of course, these two moments in a case study are never entirely divorced from each other. A key characteristic of case study research is the intermingling of case selection and case analysis. Any method of choosing cases implies a method of analyzing them, and some methods (specifically, those that are oriented toward estimating a causal effect or diagnosing a causal hypothesis) are fairly explicit about how to do so. Consequently, this chapter revisits some issues introduced in Chapters 3–6. Nonetheless, it is worth covering this ground carefully as it is by no means redundant.

In this chapter, I lay out a typology of research designs, beginning with the core contrast between large- and small-C studies, with *multimethod* research describing the union of those two formats.

These archetypal methods may be distinguished according to whether they exploit *cross-case*, *longitudinal*, or *within-case* variation, and according to whether this variation is analyzed *qualitatively* (with causal-process observations) or *quantitatively* (with matrix observations). The intersection of these concepts provides a three-part typology of research designs, shown in Table 7.1, that will guide our discussion.

Briefly, a *case study* enlists cross-case variation in a qualitative fashion, as the number of cases is very limited. (These may be cases that are formally defined or they may be shadow cases.) It also enlists longitudinal evidence, which may be analyzed qualitatively or quantitatively (a time-series). And it enlists within-case evidence, which may also be analyzed qualitatively or quantitatively. In short, the case study enlists evidence at three levels and generally combines qualitative and

Table 7.1 Typology of research designs

	ANALYSIS		
	Cross-case	Longitudinal	Within-case
Small-C	Yes (Qual)	Yes (Qual and/or Quant)	Yes (Qual and/or Quant)
Large-C	Yes (Quant)	Maybe (TSCS)	No
Multimethod	Yes (Quant)	Yes (Qual and/or Quant)	Yes (Qual and/or Quant)

quantitative observations – except for cross-case analysis, which must be qualitative by virtue of the tiny sample of cases. C is small but N may be large, facilitating quantitative analysis at other levels.

A *large-C* study embraces a large number of cases and – following from the size of the sample – a quantitative form of analysis. The analysis may rest on cross-sectional comparisons and/or longitudinal comparisons (a panel or repeated cross-section). There is little opportunity for exploiting within-case variation.[1]

A *multimethod* study, occupying the final row in Table 7.1, combines both formats and thus appears as a hybrid form of research – the union of small- and large-C methods.

We now proceed to provide more flesh to this bare-bones account. I begin with a discussion of case study evidence, understood as cross-case, longitudinal, or within-case. Next, I explore the composite genre of multimethod studies.

Here, as elsewhere in this book, my primary focus is on causal analysis. However, much of what I have to say is also applicable to descriptive analysis. Indeed, the two forms of inference are not always easy to distinguish.

---

[1] One might make a partial exception for hierarchical models. However, such models are generally theoretically focused on the lowest level of analysis, data from higher levels serving a model-specification role (Arceneaux and Nickerson 2009). For example, a model that combines national- and individual-level data will probably be focused on explaining individual-level behavior. As such, the individual level must be regarded as the cases of theoretical interest and there is no within-case evidence.

7.1   Case study evidence

I have stipulated that case study evidence may be categorized as cross-case, longitudinal, or within-case. Now, we can examine these categories in greater detail.

Cross-case

Cross-case analysis is mandated by some case-selection methods, i.e. those that assume a *most-similar* or *most-different* format. Here, variation across studied cases provides essential and explicit evidence for reaching causal inferences, as described in Chapter 5.

Virtually all case studies make reference to additional cases in an informal fashion, i.e., as *shadow cases*. For example, Louis Hartz (1955), in his influential study of the US political culture, refers repeatedly to European countries that seem to offer starkly contrasting developmental trajectories. "Any attempt to uncover the nature of an American society without feudalism can only be accomplished by studying it in conjunction with a European society where the feudal structure and the feudal ethos did in fact survive," Hartz (1955: 4) writes. The importance of shadow cases is apparent in most other case studies, even if they are not always acknowledged in such a forthright fashion (Soifer 2015).

It follows that *C* (number of cases) in a case study is generally greater than the author's stated case load. This is especially true for studies focused on a single case. We have noted that the meaning and interpretation of that case is always contingent upon comparisons with other cases. An extreme case or deviant case cannot be understood without a frame of reference, and this frame of reference stands in the background of any proposed explanation. Thus, although case studies may appear to be ridiculously myopic, cross-case analysis is never entirely absent. Other cases are smuggled in, one might say, through the back door – i.e., through implicit comparisons with a larger population of cases.

Longitudinal

Case studies always employ some form of *longitudinal* analysis, focused on the chosen case(s) over time. The timeline might extend for centuries, e.g., the history of Italy from the Middle Ages to the twentieth century (Putnam *et al.* 1993) or for days, e.g., the 13 days of the Cuban Missile Crisis (Allison 1971). Whatever the chosen period, there is generally variation over time along key dimensions – X (the causal factor or factors), Y (the outcome), or D (the descriptive factor or factors).

Very occasionally, a case does not show change in variables of theoretical interest – the proverbial dog that does not bark. For example, Nina Tannenwald's (1999, 2007) influential work focuses on the non-use of nuclear weapons by the United States after World War II. However, this period of restraint is implicitly contrasted with the deployment of nuclear weapons at the end of the war. In this respect, Tannenwald incorporates temporal variation in the variable of interest.

Within-case

The most important element of any case study is the opportunity to exploit variation "inside" or "within" the case of theoretical interest. If cases are nation-states, these humungous entities may be decomposed into regions, cities, or individuals. If cases are political parties, these may be decomposed into elected officials, activists, voters, and ideological factions. Any unit may be decomposed, and evidence drawn from each of these sub-units is likely to provide vital information for the main argument, pitched at the level of the primary case.

Given the ubiquity of within-case evidence, it seems fair to assert that all case study research is also cross-level research. The case study operates at the level of the principal units of analysis (the cases) as well as within selected cases. This is where the advantages of scoping down kick in. These are the sorts of micro-level foundations that are generally impossible to replicate in a large-*C* format (Campbell 1975/1988; George and McKeown 1985; King *et al.* 1994; Smelser 1976).

At the same time, these observations involve an additional complexity not encountered with latitudinal and longitudinal variation. Specifically, the researcher must infer features of the case (at the macro level) from features derived from a lower level of analysis (at the micro level). This leap "up" is perhaps less complicated than the leap "down" from a larger unit to its components, for which we have a recognized term (*ecological inference*). But it is rarely self-evident. The *aggregation fallacy* assumes that behavior at the aggregate level can be inferred from behavior at lower levels. This is sometimes true, and sometimes not. In any case, it cannot be taken for granted (Achen and Shively 1995; Alexander *et al.* 1987).

Tentative conclusions

It seems fair to conclude that all case studies combine all three kinds of evidence – cross-case, longitudinal, and within-case. They are sometimes clearly separable, e.g., in different chapters or under different headings within a chapter or article. More typically, they are *gemischt*.

Whatever the mode of presentation, combining these styles of evidence provides a valuable form of triangulation. A proposition is more secure if it has been corroborated with cross-case, longitudinal, *and* within-case evidence.

But all evidence is not equal, and it may be helpful to discern the "weak legs" and the "strong legs" of case study research before quitting this subject. Over time, a consensus seems to have arisen about the utility of within-case evidence. Few methodologists question the value-added of peeking inside the box, looking at a lower level of analysis for evidence that might further corroborate, or weaken, a causal inference.

Likewise, no one would argue with the adage to exploit over-time variation. Cases that change on key parameters are more useful than cases that do not.

By contrast, there is considerable skepticism about the utility of cross-case comparisons in case study research (George and Bennett 2005: 152; Glynn and Ichino 2015; Goertz 2017; Seawright 2016b; Sekhon 2004; but see Slater and Ziblatt 2013). Since shadow cases do not bear a heavy burden in any study's causal inference (by definition) and most-different case designs are rare (as discussed in Chapter 5), our discussion will focus on the dominant cross-case design, the *most-similar* case study. Here, we consider all three versions (*exploratory*, *estimating*, and *diagnostic*) together, since they all draw upon the same logic of inference once cases are selected.

Recall that most-similar analysis depends upon finding cases that are similar in background characteristics (Z) and different in the causal factor of interest (X). To be sure, cases chosen for exploratory purposes select conditional on Y and Z, rather than X. However, in order for these cases to serve their function – identifying a new cause of Y – they must provide the requisite cross-case variation conditional on X.

It turns out that this configuration is not very common in the terrain of social science. One rarely finds cases that are similar in all but one potential cause of Y. Cases that are similar to each other conditional on Z also tend to be similar to each other conditional on X, and vice-versa.

And when a situation presents itself that seems to embody a most-similar comparison, it often turns out that there are *many* potential cases with this characteristic, a setting that lends itself to large-C analysis. Large-C natural experiments are rare (Dunning 2012); case study natural experiments (where only one or several cases embody the treatment and control conditions) are even rarer. Skepticism about cross-case comparisons in case study research is thus a product of the social world as it presents itself.

This skepticism is not limited to case study settings. Even in a large-C setting, methodologists are suspicious of inferences based solely, or primarily, on cross-case (cross-sectional) comparisons of observational data. Recall that any causal inference rests on the core assumption of causal comparability: the expected value of Y, conditional on X, must be equal for all units, and all time periods, under study. (Whether this criterion is understood in a deterministic or probabilistic manner need not concern us here.) Wherever the treatment is not randomly assigned (i.e., in non-experimental settings), this assumption is unlikely to be met by observing cross-sectional variation. Cases exposed to the treatment ($X = 1$) are likely to differ from cases that exhibit the control condition ($X = 0$) in ways that affect the outcome, introducing confounding. In a large-C setting, one may attempt to control for these confounders by conditioning on covariates (in a regression framework) or by restricting the analysis to cases that are well matched on key covariates (in a matching framework). However, there are bound to be doubts about whether all the relevant background conditions are correctly identified, measured, and controlled, and whether irrelevant factors (perhaps affected by X) are avoided. Challenges to causal inference are formidable.

By way of contrast, it is somewhat more likely that the assumption of causal comparability will be met when comparing a case to itself, pre- and post-treatment. Frequently, X changes while other background conditions (represented by the vector Z) remain constant. Longitudinal natural experiments (where X changes in an as-if random fashion) are more common than latitudinal natural experiments. For this reason, longitudinal comparisons are often judged to be more plausible than cross-sectional comparisons, at least with respect to causal effects understood as average treatment effects on the treated (ATT). This rule of thumb is reflected in the general preference for causal models that privilege change over time (e.g., difference-in-difference or fixed-effect models) over causal models that privilege comparisons across units (e.g., pooled cross-sections).

These methodological norms are based on our general sense of the way the world works. Naturally, there are plenty of exceptions, accounting for the persistence of cross-case analysis in both large- and small-C

settings. Every research setting must be evaluated on its own terms. Still, it is important to note the general preference for longitudinal over latitudinal evidence, which seems to be shared by nearly everyone dealing with observational data, whether in qualitative or quantitative formats.

Having said all this, we do not want to lose sight of a more important point. All styles of evidence are useful, and all are generally combined in a case study. When it comes to analyzing cases, there is no "pure" most-similar analysis, where causal inference rests only on cross-case comparisons. Most-similar case studies, like other kinds of case studies, rest as much on longitudinal analysis for the "treatment" case (where there is an observable change in X) as they do on cross-case analysis. And all case studies employ some form of within-case analysis. In this light, it is pedantic to dwell excessively on the comparative advantages and disadvantages of different styles of evidence. They are all good.

7.2   Multimethod studies

Some studies combine the intensive study of one or several cases with a large-C analysis, generating a *multimethod* (or mixed-method) style of research. This form of study seems increasingly common, and is often praised by methodologists.[2]

Seventeen exemplars are listed in Table 7.2.[3] Some select cases (for intensive study) by algorithm and others do not. All employ a

---

[2] "Multimethod," broadly construed, refers simply to the combination of diverse methods, e.g., experimental and observational, qualitative and quantitative, game theory and empirics, cross-level inference, and so forth (Seawright 2016b). Here, the term is used in a narrower fashion, i.e., as a study – or, occasionally, a research stream – that combines large- and small-C analysis (Goertz 2017; Kauffman 2012; Lieberman 2005, 2015). For critiques of this approach, see Ahmed and Sil (2012), Rohlfing (2008).

[3] For additional examples, see Goertz (2017: Appendix A).

quantitative analysis of cross-case variation – this, of course, is what qualifies them as "multimethod" in our lexicon. Some also analyze within-case observations in a quantitative fashion. (All utilize qualitative methods to analyze within-case variation; this is more or less assumed in a case study.)

Consider Alesina *et al.*'s (2001) study of the welfare state. The authors employ regression analysis to look at welfare state outcomes (measured by expenditures). Their favored explanation is ethnic fractionalization, which is negatively correlated with welfare state development across the OECD, suggesting that in diverse countries citizens feel less of an obligation to provide social protections for other citizens. This is corroborated by case-level evidence drawn from the United States.

An important question arises with respect to the sequencing of large- and small-*C* analysis in multimethod studies. Logically, there are three possibilities: one may precede the other or they may occur in tandem (or in a back-and-forth fashion, which I shall consider equivalent to being in tandem).

Case study first

If case study research precedes large-*C* analysis, then the case study plays a seminal role – as in the approach to research known as "grounded theory" (Glaser and Strauss 1967). The case study identifies the topic, i.e., the relevant variables and hypotheses, which large-*C* research can test in a broader – and perhaps more systematic – fashion. Readers will be familiar with case study research that starts out with a case and then generalizes – perhaps in the final section of a book or article – to a larger population. If the latter analysis is formal, i.e., carried out with an algorithm drawn from logic or statistics, then it fits our definition of multimethod.

Alternatively, the move to large-*C* analysis may be carried out by later studies. In this vein, there have been attempts to generalize the

Table 7.2 Multimethod exemplars

Study	Field	Cites	SELECTION Algo.	SELECTION Non-algo	CASES Phenomena	C	QUANT Cross-case	QUANT Within-case
Alesina *et al.* (2001) *Why Doesn't US Have Welfare State?*	EC	824		●	Welfare state	1	●	
Collier and Sambanis (2005a, 2005b) *Understanding Civil War*	PS	430	●		Civil wars	21	●	●
Dafoe and Kelsey (2014) *Observing the Capitalist Peace*	PS	2	●		Nation dyads	6	●	
Fearon and Laitin (2008, 2014, 2015) *Random Narratives*	PS	85	●		Civil wars	25	●	
Lange (2009) *Lineages of Despotism and Development*	SO	69	●	●	Economic development	4/11	●	
Lieberman (2003) *Politics of Taxation Brazil, South Africa*	PS	172		●	Fiscal policy	2	●	
Madrigal *et al.* (2011) *Community-Based Orgs*	EC	20	●		Water agencies	4	●	●
Mansfield and Snyder (2005) *Electing to Fight*	PS	627		●	Conflicts	10	●	
Martin (1992) *Coercive Cooperation*	PS	700		●	Sanctions	4	●	
Pearce (2002) *Integrating Survey and Ethnographic Methods*	SO	47	●		Fertility	28	●	
Pinfari (2012) *Peace Negotiations and Time*	PS	5	●		Negotiations	4	●	●
Romer and Romer (2010) *Effects of Tax Changes*	EC	800		●	Fiscal policy	1	●	
Ross (2004) *How Do Natural Resources Influence Civil War?*	PS	566		●	Civil wars	13	●	

Table 7.2 (*cont.*)

| Study | Field | Cites | SELECTION | | CASES | | QUANT | |
			Algo.	Non-algo	Phenomena	C	Cross-case	Within-case
Schultz (2001) *Democracy and Coercive Diplomacy*	PS	590		●	Crises	4	●	
Simmons (1994) *Who Adjusts?*	PS	348		●	Econ. policy crises	3	●	
Teorell (2010) *Determinants of Democratization*	PS	153	●		Regime-types	14	●	
Walter (2002) *Committing to Peace*	PS	821		●	Civil wars	2	●	

Notes: C = number of cases. *Algo.* = selection of cases by algorithm.

theory of social capital associated with Robert Putnam *et al.*'s (1993) case study of Italian regions (e.g., Knack and Keefer 1997), and the theory of party cohesion developed in Leon Epstein's (1964) most-similar comparison of the United States and Canada has been carried out for a much larger sample in later studies (Carey 2007). However, for present purposes I shall reserve the term "multimethod" for work that incorporates both elements in the same study.

Large-*C* first

If a researcher already knows a good deal about a topic from large-*C* analysis (her own or someone else's), the case study plays a supplemental role, as outlined in the "nested analysis" approach to multimethod research (Lieberman 2005). Here, algorithmic selection of cases is also common.

In descriptive work, it may be possible to measure certain features across a large number of cases, leaving other – perhaps more difficult to measure – features for in-depth case analysis. In causal work, it may be possible to establish a robust association between X and Y in a large sample, leaving questions about influential cases or mechanisms to in-depth case analysis. The latter may be essential to establishing causal inference, especially if the large-C correlation between X and Y is subject to numerous confounders. But even if large-C evidence is able to establish causal inference, as might be the case in an experimental or quasi-experimental setting, the job is by no means finished. Researchers want to establish not only what the causal effect of X on Y is, but also how – by what mechanism(s) – it is generated. The latter is essential to building theory, which is to say, generalizing beyond the sample, extending the results to new topics, and connecting it with extant research.

To explore the viability of two theories of civil war – one generated by Paul Collier and Anke Hoeffler (2001) (CH) and the other by James Fearon and David Laitin (2003) (FL) – a series of case studies were undertaken by a team headed by Paul Collier and Nicholas Sambanis. Sambanis (2004: 259–60) summarizes the payoff from these cases as follows:

- They help us identify a number of causal mechanisms through which independent variables in the CH and FL models influence the dependent variable – i.e., the risk of civil war onset. It quickly becomes clear that the CH model's distinction between "greed" and "grievance" as competing motives for civil war is illusory, because greed and grievance are usually shades of the same problem.
- They question assumptions and premises of the quantitative studies and make clear that CH and FL are often right for the wrong reasons yet also wrong for the wrong reasons. (In other words, the cases identify mechanisms that are different from those underlying their theories, both where the statistical models make good predictions and where they make bad predictions.)
- They sometimes point to a poor fit between the empirical proxies and the theoretically significant variables – i.e., they identify measurement problems in the statistical studies.

- They help us identify new variables that might explain civil war but are omitted from CH and FL (e.g., external intervention, or diffusion and contagion from violence in the "neighborhood"). Adding these variables to quantitative models might reduce the risk of omitted-variable bias and facilitate inductive theory building.
- They highlight interactive effects between variables in the statistical models and help us identify exogenous and endogenous variables by presenting the narratives of the series of events and the processes that led to civil war.
- They suggest substantial unit heterogeneity in the data, as the mechanisms that lead to civil war seem to differ substantially across different sets of countries and types of civil war.

To say that case studies are supplementary to a large-*C* analysis does not mean they are unimportant.

Part of their importance, it might be noted, is in refining large-*C* models. Collier and Sambanis (2005a: 25) acknowledge that "case studies can ... feed back into the statistical analysis, as new candidate variables are identified to expand the theory of civil war onset, and these variables are coded so that they can be integrated in the dataset. With the new, refined proxies added to the dataset, the new and expanded CH model can be reestimated in another iteration of this research." This offers a convenient segue into our next section.

In tandem

A final possibility is that large- and small-*C* research occur together, or in a continual back-and-forth fashion. For example, Lisa Pearce's (2002) study of childrearing choices in Nepal, discussed in Chapter 6, begins with a regression model of ideal family size, drawn from the literature and from her theoretical priors. She then conducts in-depth research on deviant cases, which she uses to re-specify her model. Likewise, Evan Lieberman's study of tax policy utilizes in-depth knowledge of country cases – South Africa and Brazil – along with cross-national statistical analysis. According to the author, both elements of the research proceeded in tandem.[4]

This may be the most common approach for scholars who do multimethod research, since researchers generally begin with some background knowledge about the population and about a few specific cases that they happen to have visited or studied, and proceed iteratively.

Conclusions

The role of a case study within a multimethod work varies according to its sequence in the process. When a small-C analysis follows large-C analysis, it plays a supplemental role. When a case study precedes the large-C analysis, it plays a seminal role. And when the two elements are conducted in tandem, their roles are difficult to distinguish. This much seems clear.

However, one should be aware that the actual work performed by a case study is not always easy to discern from the final product, i.e., a published article, book, dissertation, or report. It is especially difficult to reconstruct the sequences followed by multimethod studies such as those listed in Table 7.2. Authors are rarely transparent about the protocols employed, leaving questions about which procedure was conducted at which point in the research.[5]

I suspect that case study research often plays a guiding role at an early stage, as the researcher fishes around for a topic and a thesis. This might be followed by a large-C analysis, which then becomes the evidentiary backbone of the project. The original case study may be elided entirely, or mentioned only briefly, in the final report.

---

[4] Personal communication (2015).

[5] This serves as a reminder that quantitative methods do not translate automatically into replicable work. In addition, there must be clarity about the protocols followed.

Alternatively, a study may begin with large-C analysis, which is then supplemented by a carefully chosen case whose role is to assess influential cases or elucidate causal mechanisms. In this scenario, it is possible to imagine that the case study plays a fairly prominent role in the final report, even though it has played a minor role in developing and testing the argument.

Thus, it is quite possible that the influence of a case study in a project is inversely proportional to its prominence in the final product – with case studies highlighted where they play an auxiliary function and downplayed where they play a generative function. We cannot know for sure. What can be safely concluded is that the order in which case studies are enlisted in a multimethod study structures their role in the research process.

7.3   Summary

This chapter has set forth a simple typology of case study research designs, which allows us to distinguish (a) small-C (case) studies, (b) large-C studies, and (c) multimethod studies by examining the type of evidence they enlist and the type of analysis they perform. The schema, summarized in Table 7.1, provides further clarity to the problem of definition, which we encountered initially in Chapter 2.

It also demonstrates that case study analysis is complex, involving variation across cases, through time, and within cases (at a lower level of analysis). By contrast, large-C studies generally exploit only one level of analysis, remaining at the level of the case.

Note, finally, that while cross-case analysis in case study research must be undertaken in a qualitative fashion (because of the limited number of cases), longitudinal and within-case analysis may be conducted qualitatively and/or quantitatively. This means that case analysis is open-ended and essentially coterminous with social science methodology. The only thing that is categorically rejected is the quantitative analysis of cross-case variation – the distinctive characteristic of large-*C* research. However, multimethod research does precisely this, combining large- and small-*C* methods. This leads to the topic of the next chapter, where we investigate the qualitative/quantitative distinction.

8

Quantitative and qualitative modes of analysis

Traditionally, the case study has been identified with qualitative methods and large-C analysis with quantitative methods. This is how Franklin Giddings (1924: 94) conceptualized the matter in his influential textbook, published nearly a century ago. There, he contrasted two fundamentally different procedures:

> In the one we follow, the distribution of a particular trait, quality, habit or other phenomenon as far as we can. In the other we ascertain as completely as we can the number and variety of traits, qualities, habits, or what not, combined in a particular instance. The first of these procedures has long been known as the statistical method ... The second procedure has almost as long been known as the case method.

In the intervening years, this dichotomy has become ever-more entrenched: a contrast between statistics and narrative, variables and cases, quant and qual.[1]

As we shall see, the traditional view is partly true, and partly not. Specifically, large-C samples must be analyzed quantitatively. However, case studies may contain both quantitative and qualitative evidence. To clarify this point, we first need to clarify the key terms.[2]

---

[1] Abbott (1990), Abell (1987), Bendix (1963), Bernard (1928), Burgess (1927), Giddings (1924: 94), Jocher (1928: 203), Meehl (1954), Przeworski and Teune (1970: 8–9), Ragin (1987; 2004: 124), Rice (1928: Chapter 1), Stouffer (1941: 349), Znaniecki (1934: 250–1). An overview of these two ways of viewing the social world is provided by Goertz and Mahoney (2012).

[2] Alternate definitions (mostly, but not entirely, consistent with my own) can be found in Berg and Lune (2011), Brady and Collier (2004), Denzin and Lincoln (2000), Goertz and Mahoney (2012).

I define *quantitative* analysis as any formal analysis based on matrix observations. A matrix observation is the conventional sort, represented as a row in a rectangular dataset (illustrated in Figures 2.1 and 2.2). Each observation is coded along a number of dimensions, understood as columns in the matrix and as variables in an analysis. All observations are regarded as examples of the same general phenomenon and are presumed to have been drawn from the same population. Each is regarded as comparable to all the others (with some degree of error) with respect to whatever analysis is undertaken. The analysis is "formal" insofar as it rests on an explicit framework of inference such as logic/set theory, Bayesian statistics, frequentist statistics, or randomization inference.[3]

By contrast, *qualitative* analysis refers to an informal analysis of non-comparable observations. Non-comparable observations cannot be arrayed in a matrix format because they are examples of different things, drawn from different populations. The analysis is "informal" insofar as it is articulated with natural language and is unconnected to an explicit and general framework of inference. When applied in the context of causal inference, this sort of evidence may be referred to as *causal-process observations* (Brady 2004), *clues* (Collier 2011; Ginzburg 1983; Humphreys and Jacobs 2015), *colligation* (Roberts 1996), *congruence* (Blatter and Blume 2008), *genetic explanation* (Nagel 1961), *narrative analysis* (Abell 2004; Abbott 1990; Griffin 1993; Roth 1994), or *process tracing* (Bennett and Checkel 2015; Trampusch and Palier 2016; Waldner 2012).[4]

---

[3] Few writers have attempted to define quantitative analysis, though one may infer that it is a residual category defined by qualitative analysis, as below.

[4] I do not mean to imply that these terms are identical, merely that they are overlapping. Process tracing (the main alternative to "qualitative analysis") is usually defined as an investigation of causal mechanisms (Bennett and Checkel 2015: 5–9). It is generally implied that the investigation takes the form of qualitative observations: a time-series analysis, by itself, does not qualify. My reading of the term is that it refers to qualitative data enlisted to shed light on causal mechanisms. So defined, the term seems too narrow for present purposes, since we need to talk about the interrelationship of causal factors (X) and outcomes (Y), as well as their interconnections (M). We also want to talk about other clues to causal inference such

My use of the terms qualitative and quantitative thus embraces two elements: the type of *data* (matrix/non-matrix) and the type of *analysis* (formal/informal). These are conjoined – perhaps not of necessity but certainly by habit and convenience. Note also that there is an elective affinity between quantitative analysis and large samples, as well as between qualitative analysis and small samples. One would be hard-pressed to apply informal styles of analysis to a sample of 1,000. Likewise, one would be hard-pressed to apply a formal analysis to a sample of two. The size of a sample thus influences the style of analysis. However, it does not determine it. This is apparent in the middle range. A sample of 20 may be analyzed formally or informally. Thus, when we use the terms quantitative and qualitative, the reader should understand that the former usually (but not always) corresponds to large samples and the latter usually (but not always) corresponds to small samples. The qual/quant distinction is not solely a matter of N.

Building on these definitions, I proceed to discuss the application of quantitative analysis to case study methods, an area that is not well understood. The rest of the chapter is devoted to qualitative analysis, including a consideration of general standards that might guide this mode of inquiry, along with a set of informal "rules of thumb."

8.1 Quantitative analysis

A quantitative mode of analysis comes into play in three areas of case study research. First, it may be employed to choose cases, referred to as

---

as prior causes, confounders, alternate outcomes, and pattern-matching/congruence. These additional factors seem to strain the boundaries of process tracing, as traditionally defined (even though they are often included in published works under the heading of "process tracing"). For all these reasons, we have chosen the more general term – "qualitative analysis." But readers should be aware that contemporary discussions of process tracing cover much the same ground. For further discussion of the qualitative/quantitative divide, see Gerring (2017).

"algorithmic" case selection, as discussed in Chapter 6. Roughly 6% of the studies reviewed in Table 1.2 utilize this method of case selection.

Second, it may be enlisted to analyze a large number of cases in a large-C format. When combined with a case study, this is referred to as multimethod research, discussed in the previous chapter. Roughly 13% of the studies reviewed in Table 1.2 are multimethod in this special sense.

Third, quantitative analysis may be enlisted to conduct within-case analysis. For example, if the primary unit of theoretical interest (the "case") is the nation-state, within-case observations might be constructed from provinces, localities, groups, or individuals. The possibilities for within-case analysis are, in principle, infinite. In their pathbreaking study of the International Typographical Union, Lipset *et al.* (1956: 422) note the variety of within-case evidence, which included union locals, union shops (within each local), and individual members of the union.

Importantly, (within-case) observations (N) often swamp cases (C), as noted by Donald Campbell (1975) many years ago. This is bound to be true wherever individuals comprise within-case observations. A single national survey will produce a much larger sample than any conceivable cross-country analysis. There are only so many countries.

Indeed, a recent review of natural resource management studies found that sample size varies inversely with geographic scope. Specifically, case studies focused on single communities tend to have large samples since they often employ individual-level (within-case) observations. Large-C studies are more likely to treat communities as comprising observations, and hence have smaller samples (Poteete and Ostrom 2005: 11).

This common pattern stretches back to the beginnings of modern social science. Robert and Helen Lynd's (1929/1956) study of Muncie, Indiana, featured surveys of hundreds of respondents in "Middletown." *Yankee City* (Warner and Lunt 1941), another pioneering community study, included interviews with 17,000 people. Not surprisingly, within-case analysis is the most common setting for quantitative analysis within a case study format, characterizing roughly 18% of the studies surveyed in Table 1.2.

We may conclude that quantitative analysis is a regular feature – and, by all appearances, an increasingly common feature – in studies classified as case studies. Still, we must take note of the fact that in our (admittedly non-random) sample only a minority of case studies employ original quantitative analyses. Most depend solely, or primarily, upon a qualitative analysis of the data at hand. Because of this, and because standards of qualitative analysis are less well established – and much more contentious – the rest of this chapter is devoted to non-quantitative modes of analysis.

8.2   Qualitative analysis

While a large body of research explores the inferential foundations of quantitative modes of analysis, comparatively little has been written about qualitative modes of analysis. (This is starting to change, as witnessed by the compendium of references in this book.) Because of its centrality to case study research, it is important to get a sense for what the latter offers and the sorts of settings in which it might be useful. Our focus will be on causal inference, where the role of qualitative data is most controversial (Beck 2010). My approach to the subject builds on examples of qualitative observations at work. This follows from the fact that informal methods do not have a clearly prescribed format and thus are best understood in a context of use.

To begin, let us consider Theda Skocpol's (1979) theory of social revolution, which hinges critically upon the breakdown of the French state in the decades leading up to 1789. James Mahoney (1999) explicates this element of the argument in meticulous detail, identifying three general causal factors – agrarian backwardness, international pressure, and state autonomy – which are, in turn, broken down into 37 discrete steps. The entire argument is reproduced in Figure 8.1.

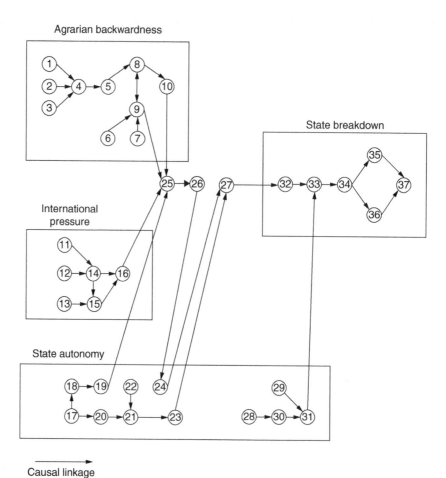

Causal linkage

Figure 8.1   Skocpol's explanation of breakdown of the French state (1789)

1. Property relations prevent introduction of new agricultural techniques. 2. Tax system discourages agricultural innovation. 3. Sustained growth discourages agricultural innovation. 4. Backwardness of French agriculture. 5. Weak domestic market for industrial goods. 6. Internal transportation problems. 7. Population growth. 8. Failure to achieve industrial breakthrough. 9. Failure to sustain economic growth. 10. Inability to successfully compete with England. 11. Initial military successes under Louis XIV. 12. Expansionist ambitions of state. 13. French geographical location *vis-à-vis* England. 14. Sustained warfare. 15. State needs to devote resources to both army and navy. 16. Repeated defeats in war. 17. Creation of absolutist monarchy; decentralized medieval institutions still persist. 18. Dominant class often exempted from taxes. 19. State faces obstacles generating loans. 20. Socially cohesive dominant class based in proprietary wealth. 21. Dominant class possesses legal right to delay royal legislation. 22. Dominant class exercises firm control over offices. 23. Dominant class is

Figure 8.1 (*cont.*) capable of blocking state reforms. 24. Dominant class resists financial reforms. 25. Major financial problems of state. 26. State attempts tax-financial reforms. 27. Financial reforms fail. 28. Recruitment of military officers from privileged classes. 29. Military officers hold grievances against the crown. 30. Military officers identify with the dominant class. 31. Military is unwilling to repress dominant class resistance. 32. Financial crisis deepens. 33. Pressures for creation of the Estates-General. 34. King summons the Estates-General. 35. Popular protests spread. 36. Conflict among dominant class members in the Estates-General; paralysis of old regime. 37. Municipal revolution; the old state collapses. *Source:* Adapted from Mahoney (1999: 1166) after Skocpol (1979).

For our purposes, what is noteworthy is that the evidence for each step in this causal chain is unique, which is to say that the evidence mustered to prove step (1) is different in character from the evidence adduced for step (2), and so forth, all the way down the line. Each is a separate argument, nested within a larger argument about the causes of state breakdown in France in 1789. And this, in turn, is nested within a larger argument about social revolution in the modern world. Mahoney (1999: 1168) points out that Skocpol's overall theory is rendered more plausible by her ability "to order numerous idiosyncratic features of French, Russian, and Chinese history into meaningful accounts of unfolding processes that are consistent with a broader, overarching macrocausal argument." Qualitative observations allow for an account of causal mechanisms that simply would not be possible were Skocpol restricted to a formal analysis with matrix observations.

Each piece of evidence brought to bear on Skocpol's case – the French Revolution – is relevant to the central argument. Yet, they do not comprise observations in a larger sample. They are more correctly understood as a series of one-shot observations ($N = 1$). Although the procedure seems messy, we may be convinced by her conclusions. Thus, we may conclude that, in some circumstances at least, inferences based on qualitative observations offer a reasonable approach to a problem, even though the "method" borders on the ineffable.

Our confidence rests on specific propositions and specific observations; it is, in this sense, ad hoc. While matrix observations can be understood according to their covariational properties, qualitative observations invoke a more complex logic – one invoked by detective work, legal briefs, journalism, and traditional historical accounts. The analyst seeks to make sense of a congeries of disparate evidence, some of which may shed light on a single event or decision. The research question is always singular. What caused the French Revolution? Who shot JFK? Why did the US invade Iraq? What caused the outbreak of World War I? However, the explanation drawn from a focused account based on qualitative observations may be quite general. Skocpol's explanatory sketch enlists the minutiae of French history to demonstrate a much larger, macro-theoretical account pertaining to all countries (without a colonial past) in the modern era.

Note also that qualitative observations may be either numerical or non-numerical. However, because each numerical observation is quite different from the rest they do not collectively constitute a sample. Each observation is sampled from a different population. This means that each observation is qualitatively different – reinforcing my argument that it is the non-comparability of adjacent observations, not the nature of individual observations, that differentiates qualitative and quantitative modes of analysis.

Note, finally, that because each observation is qualitatively different from the next, the total number of observations in a study is indeterminate. To be sure, the cumulative number of qualitative observations may be quite large. However, because these observations are not well defined, it is difficult to say exactly how many there are. Non-comparable observations are, by definition, difficult to count. In an effort to count, one may resort to lists of what appear to be discrete pieces of evidence. This approximates the numbering systems employed in legal briefs ("There are 15 reasons why X is unlikely to have killed Y.") But lists can always be composed in multiple ways, and each individual argument carries a different weight in the researcher's overall assessment. So the total number of observations remains an open question. We do not know, and by the nature of the analysis cannot know, precisely how many observations are present in Skocpol's study of revolution or in other qualitative accounts such as Richard Fenno's (1978) *Homestyle* or Herbert Kaufman's (1960) *The Forest Ranger*.

Qualitative observations are not different examples of the same thing; they are *different things*. Consequently, it is not clear where one observation ends and another begins. They flow seamlessly together. We cannot re-read the foregoing studies with the aid of a calculator and hope to discover their true *N*; nor would we gain any analytic leverage by doing so. Quantitative researchers are inclined to assume that if observations cannot be counted, they must not be there, or – more charitably – that there must be very few of them. Qualitative researchers may insist that they have many "rich" observations at their disposal, which provide them with the opportunity for thick description. But they are unable to say, precisely, how many observations they have or how many observations are needed for thick analysis. The observations remain undefined.

This ambiguity is not necessarily troublesome, for the number of observations in a study based on qualitative observations does not bear directly on the usefulness or truthfulness of that study. While the number of observations in a sample drawn from a well-defined population contains information directly relevant to any inferences that might be drawn from that sample, the number of observations in non-sample-based study has no obvious relevance to inferences that might be drawn from that study. Consider that if it was merely quantity that mattered, we might conclude that longer studies, which presumably contain more qualitative observations, are more reliable or valid than shorter studies. Yet, it is risible to assert that long books are more convincing than short books. It is the quality of the observations and how they are analyzed, not the quantity of observations, that are relevant in evaluating the truth-claims of a study based (at least in part) on qualitative observations. In some circumstances, one lonely observation is sufficient to prove an inference. If we are inquiring into the cause of Joe's demise, and we know that he was shot at close range, we can eliminate suspects who were not in the general vicinity. One observation – say, a videotape from a surveillance camera – is sufficient to provide conclusive proof that a suspect was not, in fact, the killer.

We should not jump to the conclusion that qualitative observations are superior to matrix observations. It all depends. And what it depends on are all the circumstances of the case. There is nothing inherently good or bad about qualitative observations. But there are circumstances when we might judge them useful.

Briefly, qualitative observations are useful wherever matrix observations cannot be collected, for one reason or another, or where a large-sample analysis does not pass the laugh test (face validity). They are also often utilized in conjunction with quantitative analysis. In this context, qualitative data serve as a cross-check, a triangulation, within the context of mixed-method research. Studies based on a formal research design and a set of matrix observations will sometimes note parenthetically that their account is consistent with "anecdotal" or "narrative" evidence, i.e., with evidence that falls outside the formal research design. It makes sense of the statements made by the actors, of their plausible motives, and so forth. This is often extremely important evidence and deserves a more respectful label than "anecdotal" and a more revealing label than "narrative" (what is the evidentiary status of a narrative?). To say that a method is informal is not to say that the evidence drawn from that method is weak or peripheral to the point at issue. It is to say only that the information cannot be (or need not be) understood as a series of comparable observations.

A good example of qualitative observations as an adjunct mode of analysis is provided by a recent study examining the behavior of the US Federal Reserve during the Great Depression. The central question is whether the Fed was constrained to adopt tight monetary policies because any deviation from this standard would have led to a loss of confidence in the nation's commitment to the gold standard (i.e., an expectation of a general devaluation), and hence to a general panic.[5] To test this proposition, Chang-Tai Hsieh and Christina Romer (2001) examine an incident in monetary policy during the spring of 1932, when the Federal Reserve embarked on a brief program of rapid monetary expansion. "In just fourteen weeks," the authors note, "the Federal Reserve purchased $936 million worth of US government securities, more than doubling its holdings of government debt." To determine whether the Fed's actions fostered investor insecurity, Hsieh and Romer track the forward dollar exchange rate during the spring of 1932, which is then compared to the spot rate, using "a measure of expected dollar devaluation relative to the currencies of four countries widely thought to have been firmly attached to gold during this period" (Hsieh and Romer 2001: 2). A time-series regression analysis reveals no such devaluation, suggesting that the reigning theory is false – investor confidence could not have constrained the Fed's actions during the Great Depression. This is the standard quantitative evidence that we are accustomed to – especially among studies by economists.

However, this conclusion would be questionable were it not bolstered by additional evidence bearing on the likely motivations of officials at the Federal Reserve. In order to shed light on this matter, the authors survey the *Commercial and Financial Chronicle* (a widely read professional journal, presumably representative of the banking community) and other documentary evidence. Hsieh and Romer (2001: 2) find that "the leaders of the Federal Reserve . . . expressed little concern about a loss of credibility. Indeed, they took gold outflows to be a sign that expansionary open market operations were needed, not as a sign of trouble." This informal evidence is instrumental in helping the authors' argument. It also sheds light on a new theory about Fed behavior during this critical era.[6] Granted, the qualitative observations enlisted

---

[5] This line of argumentation is pursued by Eichengreen (1992).

[6] "Our reading of the Federal Reserve records suggests that a misguided model of the economy, together with infighting among the twelve Federal Reserve banks, accounts for the end of concerted action. The Federal Reserve stopped largely because it

by Hsieh and Romer might have been converted into standardized (quantitative) observations. For example, the authors might have conducted a content analysis of the *Commercial and Financial Chronicle* and/or of Federal Reserve records. This would have required coding sentences (or some other linguistic unit) according to whether they registered anxiety about a loss of credibility. Here, the sentence becomes the unit of analysis and the number of sentences comprises the total N in a quantitative research design.

In principle, it is *always* possible to convert informal analyses into formal analyses. Non-comparable bits of evidence can be transformed into comparable bits of evidence – i.e., standardized observations – simply by getting more bits of evidence and coding them according to type. This is one of the functions of qualitative software programs such as NVivo.[7]

However, it may not be possible to do so *in practice*. Moreover, there may be little advantage in doing so. In the previous example, it is not clear that anything would be gained from this sort of formalization. If there is, as the authors claim, no evidence whatsoever of credibility anxieties in the documentary evidence, then the reader is not likely to be more convinced by an elaborate counting exercise (coded as 0, 0, 0, 0, 0, . . .). More useful, I would think, are specific examples of what leaders of the Fed actually said, as provided by the authors of this study. Sometimes quantification is useful, and sometimes not.

8.3   Standards for qualitative inquiry

Because it is informal, the nature of qualitative evidence is more than a little mysterious. Quantitatively inclined scholars often regard it with

thought it had accomplished its goal and because it was difficult to achieve consensus among the twelve Federal Reserve banks" (Hsieh and Romer 2001: 3).

[7] Franzosi *et al.* (2013). See also Lieberman (2010), who discusses the systematic collection of historical data.

suspicion, while qualitatively inclined scholars are apt to be more trusting (perhaps, too trusting). In any case, it is hard to articulate what a convincing inference might consist of, or how to recognize it when one comes across it. What standards apply to qualitative inquiry?

To remedy this situation, a number of recent works try to make sense of case-level qualitative data (sometimes referred to as process tracing), imposing order on the seeming chaos. The proposed framework might take the form of set theory (Mahoney 2012; Mahoney and Vanderpoel 2015), acyclic graphs (Waldner 2015b), or – most commonly – Bayesian inference.[8] This set of studies reinforces my sense that qualitative and quantitative data do not partake of different epistemological worlds. They can be understood as part of a unified framework of inference.

However, establishing a general framework does not necessarily produce a practical guide for the conduct of inquiry. To date, the proposed frameworks seem to be focused on making sense of qualitative analysis rather than providing advice to researchers. One may wonder whether it is possible to formalize a process of analysis that is – arguably, by its very nature – informal.

Consider the fourfold typology of tests, first proposed by Van Evera (1997), that has become a touchstone for methodologists across all of the foregoing frameworks (Bennett and Checkel 2015: 17; George and Bennett 2005; Mahoney and Vanderpoel 2015; Waldner 2015b). Briefly, a *hoop* test is necessary (but not sufficient) for demonstrating a hypothesis, H_x. A *smoking-gun* test is sufficient (but not necessary) for demonstrating H_x. A *doubly decisive* test is necessary and sufficient for demonstrating H_x. A *straw-in-the-wind* test is neither necessary nor sufficient, constituting weak or circumstantial evidence. These concepts, shown in Table 8.1, are useful for classifying the nature of evidence according to the researcher's judgment. However, the hard

---

[8] Beach and Pedersen (2013: 83–99), Bennett (2008, 2015), Crandell *et al.* (2011), George and McKeown (1985), Gill *et al.* (2005), Humphreys and Jacobs (2015), McKeown (1999), Rohlfing (2012: 180–99).

Table 8.1 Qualitative tests and their presumed inferential role

		Inferential role	
		Necessary	*Sufficient*
Tests	*Hoop*	✓	
	Smoking-gun		✓
	Doubly decisive	✓	✓
	Straw-in-wind		

question – the judgment itself – is elided. When does a particular piece of evidence qualify as a hoop, smoking-gun, doubly decisive, or straw-in-the-wind test (or something in between)?

Likewise, Bayesian frameworks can help combine evidence from diverse quarters in a logical fashion with the use of subjective assessments, e.g., the probability that a hypothesis is true, ex ante, and assessments of the probability that the hypothesis is true if a piece of evidence (stipulated in advance) is observed. The hard question, again, is the case-specific judgment.

Consider the lengthy debate that has ensued over the reasons for electoral system choice in Europe (Kreuzer 2010). Humphreys and Jacobs (2015) use this example to sketch out their application of Bayesian inference to qualitative research. In particular, they explore the "left threat" hypothesis, which suggests that the presence of a large left-wing party explains the adoption of proportional representation (PR) in the early twentieth century (Boix 1999). The authors point out that "for cases with high left threat and a shift to PR, the inferential task is to determine whether they would have . . . or would not have . . . shifted to PR without left threat" (Humphreys and Jacobs 2015: 664). Bayesian frameworks do nothing to ease this inferential task, which takes the form of a counterfactual thought experiment. Similar judgments are required by other frameworks – set theory, acyclic graphs, and so forth.

To get a feel for the level of detail required in qualitative research, we may benefit from a closer look at a particular inquiry. Helpfully, Tasha

Fairfield (2013: 55–6; see also 2015) provides a blow-by-blow account of the sleuthing required to reach each case-level inference in her study of how policymakers avoid political backlash when they attempt to tax economic elites. One of her three country cases is Chile, which is observed during and after a recent presidential election. Fairfield explains,

> During the 2005 presidential campaign, right candidate Lavín blamed Chile's persistent inequality on the left and accused President Lagos of failing to deliver his promise of growth with equity. Lagos responded by publicly challenging the right to eliminate *57 bis*, a highly regressive tax benefit for wealthy stockholders that he called "a tremendous support for inequality." The right accepted the challenge and voted in favor of eliminating the tax benefit in congress, deviating from its prior position on this policy and the preferences of its core business constituency.
>
> The following three hypotheses encompass the main components of my argument regarding why the right voted in favor of the reform:
>
> Hypothesis 1. Lagos' equity appeal motivated the right to accept the reform, due to concern over public opinion.
>
> Hypothesis 2. The timing of the equity appeal – during a major electoral campaign – contributed to its success.
>
> Hypothesis 3. The high issue-salience of inequality contributed to the equity appeal's success.
>
> The following four observations, drawn from different sources, provide indirect, circumstantial support for Hypothesis 1:
>
> Observation 1a (p. 48): The Lagos administration considered eliminating *57 bis* in the 2001 Anti-Evasion reform but judged it politically infeasible given business-right opposition (interview: Finance Ministry-a, 2005).
>
> Observation 1b: The Lagos administration subsequently tried to reach an agreement with business to eliminate *57 bis* without success (interview, Finance Ministry-b, 2005).
>
> Observation 1c: Initiatives to eliminate the exemption were blocked in 1995 and 1998 due to right opposition. (Sources: congressional records, multiple interviews)
>
> Observation 1d: Previous efforts to eliminate *57 bis* did not involve concerted equity appeals. Although Concertacíon governments had mentioned

equity in prior efforts, technical language predominated, and government statements focused much more on *57 bis'* failure to stimulate investment rather than its regressive distributive impact (congressional records, La Segunda, March 27, 1998, El Mercurio, April 1, 1998, Interview, Ffrench-Davis, Santiago, Chile, Sept. 5, 2005).

Inference: These observations suggest that right votes to eliminate *57 bis* would have been highly unlikely without some new, distinct political dynamic. Lagos' strong, high-profile equity appeal, in the unusual context of electoral competition from the right on the issue of inequality, becomes a strong candidate for explaining the right's acceptance of the reform.

The appendix continues in this vein for several pages, focused relentlessly on explaining the behavior of one particular set of actors in one event, i.e., why members of the right-wing favored reform. This event is just one of a multitude of events discussed in connection with the Chilean case study, to which must be added the equally complex set of events occurring in Argentina and Bolivia (her other country cases). Clearly, reaching case-level inferences is a complicated and time-consuming business, requiring a great deal of local knowledge.

One may conclude that *if researchers agreed on case-level judgments*, then general frameworks might be successful in cumulating these judgments into a higher-level inference, accompanied by a (very useful!) confidence interval. But if one cannot assume case-level consensus, conclusions based on qualitative judgments combined through a Bayesian framework represent nothing more than one researcher's views, which might vary appreciably from another's. Readers who are not versed in the intricacies of Chilean politics will have a hard time ascertaining whether Fairfield's judgments are correct.

This problem could be partially overcome with a crowd-based approach to research. Specifically, one might survey a panel of experts – chosen randomly or with an aim to represent diverse perspectives – on each point of judgment. One could then cumulate these judgments into an overall inference with a confidence interval that reflects (among other things) the level of disagreement among experts. Unfortunately, not just any crowd will do. The extreme difficulty of case study research derives in no small part from the expertise that case study researchers bring to their task. I cannot envision a world in which lay coders, recruited through Amazon Turk or Facebook, would replace that expertise, honed through years of work on a particular problem and in a particular site (a historical period, country, city, village, organization . . .).

To be credible, a crowd-based approach to the problem of judgment would need to enlist the small community of experts who study a subject and can be expected to make knowledgeable judgments about highly specific questions such as the "left-wing threat" in France in the early twentieth century or political economy of contemporary Chile. This procedure is conceivable, but difficult to implement. How would one identify a random, or otherwise representative, sample? (What is the sampling frame?) How would one motivate scholars to undertake the task? How would one elicit honest judgments about the specific questions on a questionnaire, uncorrupted by broader judgments about the theoretical question at hand (which they would probably be able to infer)?

Likewise, if one goes to the trouble of constructing a common coding frame (a questionnaire), an on-line system for recording responses, a system of recruitment, and a Bayesian (or some other) framework for integrating judgments, the considerable investment in time and expense of such a venture would probably justify extending the analysis to many cases, chosen randomly, so that a representative sample can be attained and stochastic threats to inference minimized. In this fashion, procedures to integrate qualitative data into a quantitative framework seem likely to morph from small-C qualitative research into large-C coding exercises. This is not to argue against the idea. It is simply to point out that any standardization of procedures tends to work against the intensive focus on one or several cases, which defines case study research.

8.4   Rules of thumb for qualitative inquiry

My tentative conclusion, based on the discussion in the previous section and pending further developments in this fast-moving field, is that it is hard to improve upon the informal "rules of thumb" that have been honed and practiced by qualitative researchers over many centuries. They have their faults (see Part IV). But remedying those faults may not be possible within the constraints of a case study framework.

In this final section of the chapter, I try to identify procedures that guide (or at any rate ought to guide) the elucidation of causal relationships for a single case utilizing within-case evidence of an informal (qualitative) nature.[9] My suggestions build on the expanding literature cited above and cover several interrelated topics: (a) the use of sources, (b) the identification of a hypothesis or theory, (c) adjudicating among rival explanations, (d) constructing testable hypotheses, (e) counterfactual thought experiments, (f) analyzing temporal relations, and (g) examining assumptions.

Utilizing sources

The case study method is not defined by its sources of evidence. Nonetheless, it may be helpful to categorize these sources in a rough-and-ready fashion so we have a sense of the sorts of evidence that this genre typically elicits. Accordingly, I distinguish among five sources in Table 1.2: *ethnography* (participant-observation research), *interview*

---

[9] Naturally, the specific goals of the case study (as discussed in Chapter 2) affect this discussion. Nonetheless, there are certain generic features of within-case qualitative analysis that apply broadly, regardless of the author's specific goals. This section builds on the following works: Beach and Pedersen (2013), Bennett and Checkel (2015), Brady and Collier (2004), Collier (2011), George (1979), Hall (2006), Jacobs (2015), Mahoney (2012), Roberts (1996), Schimmelfennig (2015), Waldner (2012, 2015a, 2015b), Winks (1969).

(structured or unstructured personal interviews), *survey* (information collected – by the researcher or by someone else – from expert or non-expert informants with a standardized questionnaire and limited response options), *primary sources* (other than those listed above), and *secondary sources* (including extant datasets if they rest on non-survey sources).

In Table 1.2, each study was coded according to the sorts of evidence that it enlists, which may be one or several. A category is recognized only if it forms an important part of the entire body of evidence considered in the study (scattered references do not count). Naturally, these categories are not neat and tidy; distinguishing between primary and secondary sources, for example, is always a matter of judgment. Nonetheless, it gives us a sense of the lay of the land.

Judging by the tally in the bottom row of Table 1.2, the most common source of evidence in case studies is primary sources (67.5%), followed by secondary sources (43.2%), interviews (32.4%), ethnography (23.6%), and surveys (15.5%). But the more important point may be that case studies typically combine evidence from several sources. There are few "pure" ethnographies – untainted by research into primary and secondary sources – for example. A panoply of evidence drawn from different kinds of sources seems to be the norm.

I do not offer further discussion of the data-gathering aspect of case study research as this would take us far afield, and is in any case well covered by other texts.[10] However, it is important to say something about how diverse sources might be integrated into a within-case analysis. After all, interpretations of a case are based on interpretations of sources, and sources do not always agree. Indeed, they do not even address the same issues. Suppose that sources 1–3 suggest one interpretation while sources 4–6 suggest another. To make matters worse,

---

[10] For recent surveys, see Gerring and Christenson (2017), Kapiszewski *et al.* (2015). For ethnographic data collection, see Bernard (1988). See also sources listed under various headings in the Methods Coordination Project (https://qdr.syr.edu/mcp).

there is always the possibility that sources 7–9, unknown to the researcher, provide yet another angle, or offer "smoking-gun" evidence for one or the other perspective. Evidently, one's conclusions about a subject rest, in part, on the sources one happens to consult – and on one's understanding of those sources.[11]

The problem of evaluating divergent social science evidence is no different from the problem of evaluating journalistic, historical, or criminal evidence. Sources matter, and because they matter social scientists must judge the quality of their sources.

In making these judgments, the following considerations come into play:

- *Relevance:* The source speaks to the question of theoretical interest.
- *Proximity:* The source is in a position to know what you want to know. It is close to the action.
- *Authenticity:* The source is not fake or doctored, or under the influence of someone else.
- *Validity:* The source is not biased. Or it is biased in ways that (a) are readily apparent and can therefore be taken into account or (b) do not affect the theoretical question of interest.
- *Diversity:* Collectively, the chosen sources exemplify a diversity of viewpoints, interests, and/or data collection methods, allowing one to triangulate across sources that may conflict with one another.

Let us explore these issues in greater detail, with particular attention to potential problems of bias.

---

[11] For work relevant to various points raised in this section, see Chandler *et al.* (1994), Fischer (1970), Gilovich (1993), Ginzburg (1991), Gottschalk (1969), Harzing (2002), Hill (1993), Howell and Prevenier (2001), Jupp (1996), Lieberman (2010), Lustick (1996), Mahoney and Villegas (2007), Mariampolski and Hughes (1978), Markoff (2002), Milligan (1979), Moravcsik (2010), Prior (2003), Thies (2002), Trachtenberg (2006). For specific examples of how historical documentation can mislead, see Davenport and Ball (2002), Greenstein and Immerman (1992), Harrison (1992), Lieshout *et al.* (2004).

Data gathered in an obtrusive fashion (e.g., interviews or surveys) are subject to researcher bias. Subjects may tell the researcher what they think s/he wants to hear, or what they think is appropriate in a given context. Data gathered in an unobtrusive fashion are usually mediated by someone other than the researcher, so they may also be subject to these biases. In particular, if one is viewing an event through the eyes of later analysts, one must be aware of whatever lenses (or blinders) they may be wearing. Their interpretation of the activity might not be the only possible interpretation, or they may have made errors of a factual nature.

Even where primary sources are available, one must be wary of the data collection process. Consider that the main source of information about crime, rebellion, and political protest in previous historical eras comes from the official records of police investigations. Police and military authorities have a natural interest in suppressing unrest, so it is not surprising that they keep close records of this sort of activity. Thus, an extensive set of records accumulated by French authorities during and after the uprising of the Paris Commune, including interrogation of key actors in the rebellion, provide the most important primary source for our understanding of that key event (Bourgin and Henriot 1924); likewise, for other episodes of rebellion, protest, and crime throughout recorded history. Needless to say, one would not want to uncritically accept the authorities' interpretations of these events (though one would not want to reject them out of hand either).

A combination of primary and secondary sources should give one a more complete view of what is actually going on than could be garnered from either genre on its own. Just as one should be wary of relying solely on secondary sources, one should be equally wary of relying solely on primary sources. There may be secrets that later observers have uncovered that would help one interpret events occurring long ago or far away.

But the problem of interpretation stemming from source material is only partially captured by the hallowed distinction between primary and secondary sources. It is not simply a matter of getting closer to or further from the action, it is also a matter of the perspectives that each source brings to the subject under investigation. A contemporary example is offered by Christian Davenport and Patrick Ball (2002) in their research on state repression in Guatemala. As part of this research, conducted over the past few decades, they reviewed "17 newspapers within Guatemala, documents from four human rights organizations within as well as outside of the country, and 5,000 interviews conducted by the International Center for Human Rights Research within Guatemala." Sorting through this material, they find recurring patterns. Specifically, "newspapers tend to focus on urban environments and disappearances; human rights organizations highlight events in which large numbers of individuals were killed and when large numbers were being killed throughout the country in general; and ... interviews tend to highlight rural activity, perpetrators, and disappearances as well as those events that occurred most recently" (Davenport and Ball 2002: 428). In short, each source has a distinct window on the topic, which sheds light on some particular facet of the topic. None is wrong, but all are partial. And this, in turn, stems from the position each of these sources occupies. The authors summarize,

[N]ewspapers, tied to both urban locales/markets and authorities, tend to highlight events that occur within time periods of excessive state repression (i.e., within years in which the overall number of killings is highest). This identification/distribution occurs predominantly in an environment where the regime is not overly restrictive. These sources become useful in documenting obvious behavior or that which is deemed politically salient within a specified political-geographic context. At the same time, journalistic sources may be relatively weaker at identifying events in more remote areas that occur during periods of relatively less state repressiveness and that are relatively smaller in scale ... In contrast, human rights organizations in Guatemala tend to highlight violations where they are most frequent, most destructive (i.e., where they injure the most individuals at one time), and where the context is most dire (i.e., during historical periods when individuals are generally being killed in the greatest numbers and when political openness is limited). As a result, these sources are useful in comprehensively trying to document human rights abuses – especially those of a particularly destructive nature ... Finally, interviewees tied inexorably to their homes, loss, revenge, and/or healing tend to highlight events that took place in the area with which they are most familiar ... Interviewees also favor highlighting the perpetrator who abused the victim(s) and specifically what was done during the violation. As a result, such sources are useful for identifying what happened and who did it within particular locales. (Davenport and Ball 2002: 446)

Typically, diverse sources will reveal different aspects of a problem. These differences are "tied to where the observers are situated, how they collect information, and the objectives of the organization" (Davenport and Ball 2002: 446). If these sources can be combined, as Davenport and Ball endeavor to do, the researcher will usually be able to put together a more complete picture of the phenomenon under study – in this case, the location, extent, and type of human rights violations occurring within Guatemala.

Sometimes, however, observers have frankly discordant views of a phenomenon, which cannot therefore be pieced together to form a coherent whole. Occasionally, this is the product of a false document, i.e., a document written by someone other than who the author claims to be, or at some other time, or in a different set of circumstances. The authenticity of sources must be carefully monitored. This old piece of advice becomes truer still in the electronic age, as the provenance of an e-document is probably easier to forge or misrepresent, and harder to authenticate, than hard-copy documents.

More commonly, discordant views of the historical record are rooted in divergent interests or ideologies. Consider that the interests of state authorities must have come to bear in their collection of data on crime and disorder, as discussed in our previous example. The potential biases of sources must therefore be carefully judged whenever a researcher uses those sources to reach conclusions on a subject.

This is not to suppose that some sources are thoroughly biased, while others are thoroughly reliable. More typically, each source is reliable for *some* features of an event but not for others. It is the researcher's task to figure out who can be relied on, and for what sort of information. Figuring this out is a matter of understanding who they are, what they are likely to know (and not know), and what their stakes and preconceptions might be.

Sometimes, knowing the potential bias of a source is sufficient to establish an upper or lower bound for the information in question. For example, one might surmise that any human rights violations admitted by organs of the state, or organs closely affiliated with the state, would provide a lower bound. Likewise, estimates provided by zealous human rights advocacy organizations may be regarded as an upper bound. Somewhere in between these extremes (but not necessarily in the middle!), one might suppose, lies the true value.

Note that in searching for a "consensus view" on a particular question of fact or interpretation it is not sufficient to enumerate sources according to their views. Suppose that five sources take one view of a matter and three take another. This does not necessarily offer vindication of the first view. For one thing, it is never entirely clear when one has fully exhausted the sources on a subject. More important, some sources are probably in a better position to know the truth. Others may have no first-hand knowledge of the matter, and thus simply repeat what they have heard elsewhere. So, although it is good to keep tabs on who says what, do not imagine that all testimony can be weighted equally.

The issues raised in this section are often difficult to evaluate. How is one to know whether a source is biased, and in what ways? If you are having trouble reaching conclusions on these issues, consult someone who has worked intensively with the sources you are dealing with. This sort of source-expertise – even if they know little about your chosen topic – is immensely helpful, precisely because so much of the business of sourcing is context-specific. Someone with knowledge of one historical era may be unhelpful in elucidating another historical era, for example. Someone with experience working in a particular part of the world, or working with a particular sort of research subject (e.g., trial attorneys or wholesale merchandisers), may help you distinguish between reliable and unreliable sources.

Also, bear in mind that judgments about sources are rarely final or definitive. That is why every work of social science includes a long clarificatory section focused on the nature of its sources. It is long because it is complicated. And it is complicated because sources – through which we understand the world – do not speak for themselves. More precisely, they may speak for themselves but their speech requires interpretation.

Identifying a hypothesis/theory

Some case studies are intended to test an extant theory, either drawn from the literature or formulated ex ante by the researcher. Other case studies are intended to identify a factor that is missing or not well understood from extant theories – i.e., a new causal factor (X) or set of factors (where X is understood as a vector). Where the case study performs this exploratory function, the field of endeavor is less structured. Nonetheless, there are some guidelines that case study researchers may follow.

First, insofar as the researcher wishes to make an original contribution to a body of literature, one is well advised to focus on a causal factor that others have neglected, or which is poorly understood. A novel cause, or a novel interpretation of a well-established cause, is a good cause.

Second, insofar as a case study is generalizable it must center on causes that might conceivably apply elsewhere. Idiosyncratic causal factors should not be major protagonists in the narrative. The problem is that it is not always easy to discern which factors might be generalizable. Moreover, the same cause may be differently framed. "Cleopatra's nose" (which Pascal ventured might have motivated Roman imperial policy in Egypt) may be generalized as "beauty," and thus considered as part of a general theory of war. The assassination of Archduke Ferdinand (often regarded as a proximal cause of World War I) may be reframed as a "trigger," and thus considered as part of a general theory of war. In order to be considered as general causes, factors must be stated in a manner that has plausible application to other cases in a larger population.

Third, insofar as a cause seems to enhance the probability of an outcome (if binary) or explain variation in that outcome (if interval-level), it is non-trivial, and hence worthy of study. Do not focus on causes that have little explanatory power.

Fourth, insofar as a cause is independent of other factors – a prime mover – it is also worthy of study. By contrast, if X is entirely explained by Z, there may be little point in focusing on X. Of course, all generalizable features of the universe have causes, and these can in principle be traced backward in an endless regress. Nonetheless, if these prior causes are hard to specify, perhaps the product of many factors acting together, or are essentially random (unexplainable), then X is more likely to be regarded as *the* cause of Y.

Rival explanations

Once a hypothesis has been identified, it is important to canvas widely for rival explanations. This canvas should include extant work on the particular case under examination, general theoretical frameworks that might be brought to bear on the subject, as well as your own intuition. Think about rival explanations that critical readers of your work might construct.

When testing rival explanations, one must treat them fairly – not as "straw men." In order to dismiss a rival explanation, it must be given a good chance to succeed. For example, one should not dismiss a probabilistic theory with a single counter-example. More generally, the task of testing rival explanations involves thinking about each explanation as a proponent of that theory might think about it. This requires approaching a topic fresh, without all the baggage (preconceptions) one may have acquired in the process of developing one's own theory.

Of course, the goal is to generate a reasonably parsimonious explanation for a case. This does not mean that one must adopt a monocausal argument (cause X being the only cause of Y in Case A). But it is important to reduce the number of possible alternatives.

This call for parsimony stems from a distinguishing characteristic of case study analysis. While cross-case analysis with a large sample can accommodate virtually any number of causal factors as background factors (represented as covariates in a model or as parts of the error term), case study analysis is not very satisfactory if there are too many causal factors at work. It is hard enough to show that X_1 causes Y in Case A. If X_{2-10} are also at work, the too-many-variables problem becomes acute. Note that each of these alternative factors serves as a potential confounder. If Z can explain Y, it may also explain X. While this is a vexing aspect of cross-case work, it is debilitating in case-level analysis – unless, that is, some of these alternate explanations can be eliminated as causes in that particular case. (Do not assume, however, that the refutation of X_1 as a cause for Case A entails the refutation of X_1 as a cause for population B.)

Where rival causes can be (convincingly) eliminated as factors in a particular case, this elimination serves two important functions: (1) it eases concerns about potential confounders, and, for entirely different reasons, (2) it enhances the likelihood that X is the cause of Y.

The reasoning behind this second feature deserves clarification. First, one must assume that a limited number of causal factors are at work in generating Y within a single case. Second, one must assume that the outcome in question is not stochastic (i.e., an outcome with no identifiable explanation). With these assumptions in place, it becomes clear why the "logic of elimination" – if successful – enhances confidence in the favored explanation. Suppose vector Z contains all possible causes of Y, of which X is one. If Z_1 can be eliminated, the probability that X is a cause of Y increases (Gerring 2012b: Chapter 11).

The process of comparing diverse theoretical expectations with known facts of the case bears a strong resemblance to what Peirce (1931) called *abduction* and what later philosophers of science have called *inference to the best explanation* (Lipton 2004). There are many examples of this logic at work.

Consider the celebrated case of John Snow, who discovered the water-borne nature of cholera. Accounts of Snow's discovery suggest that his discovery began with his dissatisfaction with the reigning "miasma" theory – that cholera was air-borne (Johnson 2006). The miasma theory did a very poor job of explaining the pattern of infections in the neighborhood of Soho, London, where Snow lived. For example, confirmed cases of the disease were found in different neighborhoods, while among people living next to each other some contracted the disease and others did not. Presumably, if bad air caused cholera, then everyone living in the same area should be affected. Then there was the biological pattern of infection, which affected the small intestine but not the respiratory system. For a variety of reasons, the miasma theory seemed problematic – so problematic, in fact, that Snow was able to eliminate it as a possible cause of cholera. Having eliminated the only widely recognized explanation, Snow's alternative gained plausibility. With a plague whose arrival was so sudden, and symptoms so unique, it was pretty certain that there was a single cause. And with that assumption in place, the elimination of rival explanations is a powerful method of persuasion – even though it cannot, by itself, convince. (The proposed alternative must do a better job of making sense of the facts of the case, which, ultimately, Snow was able to show.)

Testable hypotheses

For a theory to be falsifiable, it must issue empirical predictions about the world. And these predictions, or hypotheses, must be applicable to the case under investigation if the case is to adjudicate among rival explanations.

One prediction is about the relationship of X to Y, the causal effect of theoretical interest. This is the centerpiece of large-C analysis, and it plays a role in case study analysis as well. Evidently, the observed covariation between X and Y must conform to theoretical expectations in order for the theory to be corroborated. Suppose one is evaluating the "power resource" theory of welfare state growth – that the development of redistributive programs are a product of the power and consolidation of the working class, as embodied in labor unions and left parties (Stephens 1979). Covariational evidence might take the form of showing, for the chosen case, that welfare state expansion occurs in periods when left parties are in power.

However, the intensive study of a case opens up many additional possibilities for theory testing. It is therefore vital to examine all relevant hypotheses suggested by a theory – your theory as well as alternate theories. What else (aside from the predicted covariation of X and Y) must be true about the world if the theory is true?

Often, these additional tests center on causal mechanisms (M) – what lies "inside the box" between X and Y. To test power resource theory, one might closely examine instances of welfare state expansion, critical junctures in which the shape of fiscal policy changed in fundamental ways, and with enduring consequences. In the United States, the most important juncture was probably the passage of the Social Security Act in 1935, which has been extensively studied by historians and social scientists (Quadagno 1984). Who agitated for the bill? Who wrote it? Who introduced it to Congress? Where did the initiative come from? Were the foremost proponents associated with left-wing parties, labor unions, and (more vaguely) the working class – or, alternatively, were they technocrats or members of the business community?

Empirical tests may also center on alternate outcomes. For example, if a theory suggests that X should affect Y_1 but not Y_2, then Y_2 serves as a placebo test (Gerring 2012b: Chapter 11; Glynn and Gerring 2015). For example, the power resource theory of the welfare state should apply to redistributive programs, but it should not (arguably) apply to other policy areas. If one finds an association between left party control and increased spending on the military, one might conclude that the association with welfare spending is spurious. Perhaps left parties are in favor of government spending across the board, regardless of whom it benefits.

Another sort of prediction involves actors at a lower level of analysis. If the theory centers on the behavior of governments, what does this imply about the beliefs and behavior of individual politicians? We have already discussed the role of elites in the context of "power resource" theory. How about the role of citizens? It might also be relevant whether low-income citizens are more supportive of the welfare state than middle- and upper-income citizens.

Ideally, a theory should be disaggregated down to the individual level; this enhances not only the possibility for testing but also the micro-foundations of the theory. Of course, one must be wary of the aggregation fallacy; what is true at one level may not be true at another level. Nonetheless, if within-case analysis is to proceed, it depends upon a certain concordance in causal relationships across levels of analysis.

At each level of analysis, we are testing theories against the available data, a process sometimes referred to as *pattern-matching, congruence analysis*, or *implication analysis* (Blatter and Blume 2008; Campbell 1966; George and Bennett 2005; Lieberson and Horwich 2008; Rogowski 1995; Trochim 1989). Let us consider a few examples drawn from other areas of research.

A frequently cited example is the first important empirical demonstration of the theory of relativity, which took the form of a single-event prediction on the occasion of the May 29, 1919, solar eclipse. Stephen Van Evera describes the impact of this prediction on the validation of Einstein's theory.

Einstein's theory predicted that gravity would bend the path of light toward a gravity source by a specific amount. Hence it predicted that during a solar eclipse stars near the sun would appear displaced – stars actually behind the sun would appear next to it, and stars lying next to the sun would appear farther from it – and it predicted the amount of apparent displacement. No other theory made these predictions. The passage of this one single-case-study test brought the theory wide acceptance because the tested predictions were unique – there was no plausible competing explanation for the predicted result – hence the passed test was very strong.[12]

The strength of this test is the extraordinary fit between the theory and a set of facts found in a single case, and the corresponding lack of fit between all other theories and this set of facts. Einstein offered an explanation of a particular set of anomalous findings that no other existing theory could make sense of. Of course, one must assume that there was no – or limited – measurement error. And one must assume that the phenomenon of interest is largely invariant; light does not bend differently at different times and places (except in ways that can be understood through the theory of relativity). And one must assume, finally, that the theory itself makes sense on other grounds (other than the case of special interest); it is a plausible general theory. If one is willing to accept these assumptions, then the 1919 "case study" provides a very strong confirmation of the theory. It is difficult to imagine a stronger proof of the theory from an observational (non-experimental) setting.

Theory testing is theory-dependent, as this example shows. It is useful insofar as a theory issues predictions that are specific (and therefore unlikely to exist by chance and unlikely to be confused with the predictions emanating from a rival theory), invariant (applying in the same fashion to all cases), and clearly scoped (with a well-defined population). Predictions of this sort may be described as "risky" since they offer many opportunities to fail, and their failure cannot easily be explained away, or accommodated by an ex post adjustment to the theory. Risky predictions such as Einstein's are common in natural-science fields such as physics.

In social science settings, by contrast, theories tend to be more generally pitched, with multiple possible causal mechanisms, and

---

[12] Van Evera (1997: 66–7). See also Eckstein (1975), Popper (1963).

therefore few risky predictions. There are many ways in which democracy might enhance growth (Gerring *et al.* 2005) or peace (Owen 1994). George and Bennett (2005: 209) point out that while the thesis of the democratic peace is as close to a "law" as social science has yet seen, it cannot be confirmed (or refuted) by looking at specific causal mechanisms because the causal pathways mandated by the theory are multiple and diverse. To take another much-discussed example, there are at least four ways in which natural resource wealth might affect the onset of civil war: (a) looting by rebels, (b) grievances among locals, (c) incentives for separatism, and (d) state weakness (Ross 2004: 39). Each of these is a matter of degrees, and most are rather hard to measure. This means that a case study will have a hard time identifying factors at work in a given case, and it will be even more problematic to try to generalize those findings to a larger population.

These are the limitations of theory testing in a case study format. Nonetheless, the opportunities for theory testing at a fine-grained level are one of the advantages that the case study offers over large-C studies of the same phenomenon.

Counterfactual thought experiments

Case studies delve into *singular* causality, the effect of X on Y for a single event. This is implicit in the notion of examining one case, or a small number of cases, in an intensive fashion. Singular causality runs into the (so-called) fundamental problem of causal inference (Holland 1986). One cannot travel back in time to replay the circumstances of Case A, changing only its value on X and leaving all else the same. The counterfactual for a particular outcome can only be imagined.

This philosophical problem should not be exaggerated, as singular causation is fairly easy to show in routine cases. Indeed, our legal system rests upon it. In criminal cases, one can rely on a large body of wisdom, direct clues, and other features that allow juries to convict or acquit with relative unanimity in most instances. There are few hung juries, and few verdicts are overturned upon appeal by higher courts. We take this as probative evidence that causal truth, beyond a reasonable doubt, has been attained.

Of course, social science case studies are generally a good deal more complex than criminal cases. Assumptions about normal behavior are problematic, precedents are scarce, and the people we are trying to understand may be removed from us in time, in space, and in other respects. They cannot usually be directly interrogated. And the factors of interest are often not directly observable, but rather latent.

Nonetheless, when understanding single events, case study researchers rely on the same technique used by jurists – the *counterfactual thought experiment*. This refers to the imaginative re-creation of an event under slightly different circumstances. Specifically, one is usually interested in ascertaining how and whether the value of Y would differ if the value of X had changed – while all else remained the same. It is an experiment in the mind (Fearon 1991; Lebow 2000; Levy 2008b, 2015; Tetlock and Belkin 1996).

To be clear, one cannot make any judgment about individual events without undertaking a counterfactual thought experiment. There is no way to claim that X is a cause of Y for a given event without imagining what the value of Y would be if X had been different. Thus, far from being an isolated technique it is ubiquitous – if not always explicitly acknowledged – in case-level analysis. Although one might also like to have evidence provided by a second case illustrating the "control" condition, this is not always possible, and, if possible, is always prone to confounding in a small-C setting.

Of course, counterfactual thought experiments are also subject to confounding. If one is imagining a change in X for a case observed over a certain period, it must be possible to imagine that background factors for that case (Z) hold constant during that period. Otherwise, it is impossible to envision the change in Y that X might produce. If background factors were in flux, they constitute confounders.

Temporality

To tease apart causal relations within a single case, clues derived from the temporal ordering of events are essential (Abbott 1990, 1992, 2001; Aminzade 1992; Buthe 2002; Griffin 1992, 1993; Grzymala-Busse 2011; Mahoney 2000; Pierson 2000, 2004; Thelen 2000). And to judge temporal relationships a chronological timeline, or *event history*, is indispensable. This may also be described as a graph of unit-level causal inference (Waldner 2015a, 2015b).

The chronology should begin *before* the causal factor of interest and extend all the way up to the outcome of interest, and perhaps beyond. Note that a qualitative analysis of X's relationship to Y is in some respects like a quantitative time-series analysis. The longer the temporal relationship can be observed, the greater our opportunities for gauging X's impact on Y, and identifying potential confounders. It is, however, unlike a time-series analysis insofar as one is unlikely to be able to observe X and Y throughout the whole period; or, it is irrelevant to observe them over a long period because they are not changing. In this setting, the relevant "covariational" features are the initial change of X (which might be understood in a binary fashion, as a move from $X = 0$ to $X = 1$) and the eventual change in the outcome (which might also be understood dichotomously). What is left to observe are the factors that may have contributed to ΔX and ΔY. So, look for things that preceded X and things that lie in between X and Y.

The latter are the essential features of what has come to be known as *process tracing*, represented by M in this book. A good chronology includes all relevant features of M. It is complete and continuous (Bennett and Checkel 2015; Waldner 2015b). Unfortunately, it is not always apparent how to judge completeness or continuity, i.e., which features are suitable for inclusion in a chronology and which features may be considered redundant. But one may assume that completeness exists when the connection between the events included in a chronology is tight – such that it is easy to see how a phenomenon evolved from step 1 to step 2, and step 2 to step 3, and difficult to see how any confounder could have disrupted that path.

The model of dominoes has served as a metaphor for this ideal. If one wishes to fully explain how the first domino is causally connected to the last domino, one would want to construct a chronology of dominoes that includes each domino's fall – the events leading up to, and causing, the outcome of interest. In this simple example, each domino serves a gateway function and there is only one pathway (flowing through all of these gates).

The chronology should serve to separate out relevant factors in terms of their temporal order. If this can be established, causal exogeneity/ endogeneity (what causes what) can often be inferred. Factors that seem to carry a "necessary" or "sufficient" quality should always be included in a chronology. When in doubt, the inclusion of ancillary details is not damaging, and certainly less damaging than the accidental exclusion of crucial details.

It is a short step from a chronology to a *causal diagram* that sets out all elements of the data-generating process in a clear and concise visual form. This includes X, Z, and M – with the understanding that each may be a vector of causal factors – along with Y. An excellent example is Mahoney's diagram of Skocpol's argument about the French revolution (see Figure 8.1).[13] While the diagram may be hard to follow, it is a useful simplification of a much lengthier argument, set forth in prose. Whatever the difficulties of constructing causal diagrams, if an argument cannot be diagramed, then it is not falsifiable. Insofar as falsifiability is a basic goal of science, we ought to embrace causal diagrams.[14]

---

[13] For additional examples of event-history diagrams of case study research, see Mahoney (2007), Schimmelfennig (2015), Waldner (2015b).

[14] Before quitting this subject, I should note that there is more than a passing resemblance between causal diagrams of the sort produced by Mahoney and causal graphs of the sort developed by Judea Pearl (2009) and other methodologists for purposes of causal analysis (Waldner 2015b). For present purposes, we view the diagram as a tool for clarification rather than a tool for laying out rules of causal inference.

Background assumptions

A final goal of case study research – whether undertaken on its own (a stand-alone case study) or in tandem with a large-C analysis (a multimethod study) – is to shed light on background assumptions. All causal models assume causal comparability. The expected value of Y must be the same for all observations in the sample, conditional on observables.

For large-C samples, this is understood in a probabilistic sense: P$(Y|X, Z)$ should be the same, on average, for all cases and for observations within a case (if the case is observed over time). For small-C samples, this is understood in a deterministic sense; it must be true for the cases studied. To be sure, one may regard the assumption of causal comparability more loosely if the hypothesis is posed in a vague fashion ("X has a positive effect on Y") rather than a precise fashion ("A one-unit change in X increases Y by two units"), and most case studies do not intend to measure precise causal effects, as observed in Chapter 5. Nonetheless, any threat to the assumption of causal comparability is potentially damaging for the inference that the researcher wishes to draw.

Special attention to the assignment mechanism is warranted, as this is a source of potential bias in all observational analyses. Wherever X is not intentionally randomized by the researcher, one must worry about assignment bias (or selection bias, as it is sometimes called). The blessing is that case studies are often especially insightful in providing insight into the assignment principle at work in a particular instance (Dunning 2008: Chapter 7).

Consider Jeremy Ferwerda and Nicholas Miller's (2014) argument that devolution of power by an occupying power reduces resistance to foreign rule. To prove this theory, the researchers focus on France during World War II, when the northern part of the country was ruled directly by German forces and the southern part was ruled indirectly by the "Vichy" regime headed by Marshall Petain. The key methodological assumption of their regression discontinuity design is that the line of demarcation was assigned in an as-if random fashion. For the authors, and for their critics (Kocher and Monteiro 2015), this assumption requires in-depth case study research – research that promises to uphold, or call into question, the author's entire analysis.

As a second example, we may consider Romer and Romer's (2010) analysis of the impact of tax changes on economic activity. Because tax changes are non-random, and likely to be correlated with the outcome of interest, anyone interested in this question must be concerned with bias arising from the assignment of the treatment. To deal with this threat, Romer and Romer make use of the narrative record provided by presidential speeches and congressional reports to elucidate the motivation of tax policy changes in the postwar era. This allows them to distinguish policy changes that might have been motivated by economic performance from those that may be considered as-if random. By focusing solely on the latter, they claim to provide an unbiased test of the theory that tax increases are contractionary.

8.5   Summary

The quantitative/qualitative divide besets any discussion of case study methods. My proposed definition hinges on two features. Quantitative analysis utilizes observations that are laid out in a matrix and assumed to be comparable to one another in whatever respects are relevant for the analysis. These are analyzed in a formal manner, e.g., logic/set theory, Bayesian statistics, frequentist statistics, or randomization inference.

Qualitative analysis utilizes observations that are non-comparable, which is to say they are drawn from different populations and typically address different aspects of an argument. These are analyzed in an informal fashion, using the tools provided by natural language.

Typically, quantitative analysis is large-*N* while qualitative analysis is small-*N*, although the *N* of a qualitative analysis is hard to determine precisely because observations are not well defined.

Quantitative and qualitative modes of inference are not separated by an epistemological divide. Any qualitative observation can be transformed into a set of quantitative observations. Indeed, most quantitative observations began life (one might say) as qualitative observations. The coding of rich, qualitative data, according to a systematic protocol provided by a survey questionnaire, may be viewed as the conversion of qualitative observations into quantitative observations.

Since quantitative analysis is well-trodden ground, this chapter has focused mostly on qualitative analysis. First, I offer illustrations of how non-matrix observations can contribute to causal inference, even when utilized in an informal manner. Next, I offer a series of "rules of thumb" for handling qualitative data in the context of case study research.

These rules of thumb may be summarized as follows:

- Analyze sources according to their relevance (to the question of theoretical interest), proximity (whether the source is in a position to know what s/he is claiming), authenticity (the source is not fake or reflecting the influence of someone else), validity (the source is not biased), and diversity (collectively, sources represent a diversity of viewpoints on the question at hand).
- When identifying a new causal factor or theory, look for one: (a) that is potentially generalizable to a larger population, (b) that is neglected in the extant literature on your subject, (c) that greatly enhances the probability of an outcome (if binary) or explains a lot of variation in that outcome (if interval-level), and (d) that is exogenous (not explained by other factors).
- Canvas widely for rival explanations, which may also be regarded as potential confounders. Treat them seriously (not as "straw men"), dismissing them only when warranted. Utilize this logic of elimination, where possible, to enhance the strength of the favored hypothesis.

- For each explanation, construct as many testable hypotheses as possible, paying close attention to within-case opportunities, e.g., causal mechanisms.
- Enlist counterfactual thought experiments in an explicit fashion, making clear which features of the world are being altered, and which are assumed to remain the same, in order to test the viability of a theory. Also, focus on periods when background features are stable (so they do not serve as confounders).
- Utilize chronologies and diagrams to clarify temporal and causal interrelationships among complex causal factors. Include as many features as possible so that the time-line is continuous, uninterrupted.
- Pay close attention to background assumptions implicit in causal inferences about the case(s) under study, with special reference to the (presumably non-random) assignment of the treatment.

Researchers should bear in mind that these tips are intended to shed light on causal inference for an individual case or a small set of cases. Inferences for a particular case may – *or may not* – be generalizable to a larger population, an issue taken up in Chapter 10.

Researchers should also bear in mind that these rules are intended to be employed in a flexible manner, contingent upon the researcher's theoretical aims and the empirical lay of the land. They require considerable judgment, and should not be applied in a mechanical fashion. The pliable nature of this art may be regarded as its biggest flaw or its most important virtue, as discussed in the concluding chapter of the book.

Part IV

Validity

9 Internal validity

Having surveyed and defined our subject (Part I), and discussed case selection (Part II) and case analysis (Part III), I turn now to the problem of validity (Part IV). In dividing up this complex topic, I follow the traditional distinction between internal validity (this chapter) and external validity (Chapter 10). Both chapters focus primarily on problems of causal inference, with sidelong glances at descriptive inference.

It should be clarified from the start that these are not the strongest legs of the case study research design, which is probably more useful for discovery than for establishing validity (see Chapter 11). Nonetheless, any case study must make some claims to validity, so the subject is by no means peripheral.

My goal in writing these chapters is to alert readers to some of the methodological obstacles that beset case studies, as commonly practiced. Some of these obstacles are inherent in the enterprise, others are surmountable, and I shall suggest ways of tackling them. However, some of the solutions entail sacrifices, e.g., a different choice of topics or a less ambitious theoretical agenda. We must reckon with the costs, as well as the benefits, of reforming case study research.

Internal validity, our subject in this chapter, refers to the validity of inferences about X's relationship to Y for the studied sample, which in case study research consists of a single case or a small number of cases. Our primary focus will be on inferences pertaining to causal effects (i.e., treatment effects) rather than on mechanisms, scope conditions, or other aspects of causality. Our understanding of *causal effect* is a loose one, as clarified in Chapter 5. It includes statements about the direction of a causal effect (positive or negative) as well as more specific estimates of how much Y changes with a given change in X.

To assess internal validity, we need a frame of reference. After all, the utility of the case study method can only be evaluated by contrast with other research designs that might be used in its stead. The book takes as its point of departure a core distinction between small- and large-C research (see Chapter 2). For some purposes, this is sufficient. But for other purposes, we need to disaggregate the catch-all category – large-C – into finer categories. In the present context, it is helpful to distinguish (a) experiments (where a treatment is randomized across groups), (b) natural experiments (where a treatment is assigned naturally but in an as-if random fashion across groups), and (c) messy, observational data (where there is no pretense of random assignment).

With these sub-categories of large-C analysis, we may now assess the strengths and weaknesses of case study research in a more nuanced fashion, focusing exclusively on questions of internal validity. Six methodological issues are of fundamental importance: (1) manipulable-in-principle causes, (2) causal comparability (extending to several sub-topics), (3) the plausibility of a front-door approach to causal inference, (4) transparency and replicability, (5) separation of theory and empirics, and (6) informative estimates of uncertainty. Summary comparisons and contrasts across the four research designs are noted in Table 9.1.

Readers can appreciate that these comparisons are "gross" in the sense that they attempt to aggregate together all work that falls into these four, rather crudely defined, categories and attempt to reach summary conclusions about methodological issues that are extremely complex. Nonetheless, the comparisons contained in Table 9.1 are essential if one wishes to arrive at a balanced assessment of the

Table 9.1 Archetypal research designs compared with respect to internal validity

Features	Large-C			Small-C
	Random treatment (Experiment)	As-if random treatment (Natural experiment)	Non-random treatment (Observational)	Non-random treatment (Case study)
Manipulable-in-principle causes	Yes	Yes	Maybe	Rarely
Causal comparability				
Pre-treatment equivalence	Yes	Ideally	Unlikely	Unlikely
Security from stochastic threats	High	High	High	Very low
Opportunity for statistical correction	Yes	Yes	Yes	No
Observability	Low	Low	Low	High
Plausibility of front-door approach	Low	Low	Low	High
Transparency, replicability	High	Medium	Medium	Medium
Separation of theory and empirics	High	Low	Low	Low
Informative estimate of uncertainty	Yes	Maybe	Somewhat	No

strengths and weaknesses of case study research. We shall now discuss each of these items in turn.

9.1   Manipulable causes

A key feature in causal inference is the nature of the cause itself, specifically whether it is manipulable, or at least manipulable in principle. With a manipulable cause, one can easily envision the counterfactual – what the world would have looked like if X had been assigned a different value. Specifically, one can envision ceteris paribus conditions, which underlie all causal arguments (Woodward 2005).

Consider the argument that a shift from a majoritarian to a proportional electoral system enhances ethnic harmony in a divided society

(Reilly and Reynolds 1999). This is a manipulable cause. There are plenty of examples of governments changing electoral rules – without changing other features of society or politics. So, even if the researcher cannot him/herself change the law, we can easily envision what such a change would look like. Ceteris paribus conditions are clear.

Now consider the argument that modernization enhances the probability of a democratic regime type (Lipset 1959). This is a non-manipulable cause. The problem is that the cause itself is holistic, involving a congeries of factors such as income, education, urbanization, secularization, individualism, and so forth. Even if one chooses one of these factors such as per capita GDP as a proxy for the concept, one must reckon with all the correlates of modernization since these are part-and-parcel of the same concept. Of course, one could narrow the argument – from modernization to income – with the idea that all other correlates of modernization are to be understood as background conditions (of no theoretical importance). However, this is a fundamental change in tack. Usually, scholars view these elements as cohering in an holistic fashion. If income affects education and education affects income, we cannot easily disentangle the disparate features of the theory. So, if modernization is the cause, it is exceedingly difficult to envision what the background (ceteris paribus) conditions of the argument might be, as virtually everything about a society is touched in some way by modernization, and all of these features may (plausibly) affect a country's regime type.

The point becomes clear if we imagine a specific research scenario, where we are trying to compare two countries, one of which is modernized and the other which is not, and where the two countries share other background characteristics. What would such a most-similar design look like? We might measure X with per capita GDP, but how would we measure Z? What are the background conditions against which a causal factor such as modernization can be assessed? It is not at all clear. This illustrates a generic problem affecting all causal arguments with non-manipulable causes.

Some believe that arguments with non-manipulable causes are not really causal (Holland 1986). I regard it as a matter of degree. Some treatments are manipulable in practice (e.g., any public policy). Others are manipulable in principle (e.g., changes in climate). And still others are hard to characterize. One can in principle manipulate the race or sex of an individual at birth; but this is not what most people have in mind when they say that "race matters for Y" or "sex matters for Y." Ideational features such as values, beliefs, or emotions cannot be directly manipulated; that is, one cannot change a person's ideas directly. One can of course provide information about a topic, or subject a person to a treatment calculated to change their ideas or values. Exposure is manipulable, and forms the basis for many experiments. But, again, this is not what many researchers mean when they invoke ideas as causes.[1] Holistic factors such as modernization are impossible to manipulate, though one may envision prior causes that are manipulable. For example, investment is widely viewed as a proximal cause of economic development, and we can easily imagine policies that spur (or retard) investment, thus affecting the course of modernization in a country. This brings the subject of modernization into the realm of manipulable causes. But we certainly cannot equate a particular policy (e.g., a change in tax policy) with modernization.

Suffice it to say, manipulability is not a cut-and-dried subject. Nonetheless, it is a critical issue for understanding internal validity. The more manipulable the cause, the easier it is to assess a set of findings – not to mention, to establish a strong research design. This, as much as anything else, distinguishes the different methodologies listed in Table 9.1.

Experiments have manipulable causes by definition (since the treatment must be manipulable by the researcher). Natural experiments feature manipulable-in-principle causes, though they have not been manipulated by the researcher. Observational research offers a varied

---

[1] For further discussion, see Jacobs (2015).

Table 9.2 Case studies with manipulable (in principle) treatments

Study	Causal factor
Epstein (1964) *A Comparative Study of Canadian Parties*	Directly elected executive
Friedman and Schwartz (1963) *A Monetary History of the United States*	Money supply
Hsieh and Romer (2001) *Was Federal Reserve Fettered?*	Money supply
Mondak (1995) *Newspapers and Political Awareness*	Local newspaper coverage
Romer and Romer (2010) *Macroeconomic Effects of Tax Changes*	Fiscal policy
Skendaj (2014) *International Insulation from Politics*	Foreign aid to government bureaucracies
Useem and Goldstone (2002) *Riot and Reform in US Prisons*	Prison reform
Walter (2002) *Committing to Peace*	Third-party commitment to peace agreement

terrain, and there is not much more we can say about it. Some studies feature manipulable causes (e.g., electoral laws) and others do not, or barely so (e.g., modernization).

Case study research also offers a diverse field of play. However, among our exemplars it is worth noting that very few satisfy a strong understanding of manipulability. Among the 148 studies in Table 1.2, I can identify only a small handful – listed in Table 9.2 – that clearly meet this criterion.

It seems that case studies *could* be enlisted in a fashion conducive to causal inference, but in the event often do not. Note that identifying a manipulable cause usually requires scoping down theoretical ambitions and perhaps also the units of analysis. The exemplars listed in Table 9.2 identify very specific causal factors – a directly elected executive, the money supply, local newspaper coverage, changes in tax policy, foreign aid, prison reform, and third-party commitment to peace agreements. Many of these factors operate at a level of analysis lower than the nation-state. Problems of internal validity often arise when a researcher chooses to work at a macro-societal level, i.e., when the units of interest are international systems, empires, nation-states, political parties, or social groups. By scoping down (to smaller units of analysis), one can usually identify manipulable causes and more satisfactory research designs (from the perspective of internal validity).

Case study researchers, however, are often drawn to larger, more diffuse causes that scarcely qualify as manipulable (by any interpretation). Following our discussion of modernization, let us consider Barrington Moore's (1966: 418) oft-cited argument that class relations account for the development of regime types – "no bourgeoisie, no democracy." The problem with this argument is that it is difficult to conceptualize a situation in which a bourgeois class is larger, stronger, or more coherent (or smaller, weaker, less coherent) while everything else remains the same in a country. Specifically, insofar as class structure (X) is closely tied to economic structure, and perhaps also to political structures (both of which may be represented as Z), it is hard to imagine a change in X that does not also involve a change in Z. And since Z may also influence the development of regimes (democracy or autocracy), it also serves as a potential confounder in any causal analysis. Thus, in Moore's study, and in others like it (e.g., Acemoglu and Robinson 2012), the causal factor of theoretical interest (X) is non-manipulable.

Likewise, case study work often deals in *causal frameworks* rather than specific causal hypotheses. For example, Graham Allison and Philip Zelikow's (1999) famed study of the Cuban missile crisis contrasts three models for understanding government behavior in foreign policy. The rational actor model focuses attention on "the goals and objectives of the nation or government," with the understanding that actions can be understood (in some rational sense) as a product of those goals (Zelikow, 1999: 4–5). The organizational behavior model focuses attention on "existing organizational components, their functions, and their standard operating procedures for acquiring information … defining feasible options …and implementation" (Zelikow, 1999: 5–6). The governmental politics model focuses attention on "bargaining games among players in the national government" (6). Evidently, it is not possible to verify or falsify an entire causal framework – and certainly not with a single case. Allison and Zelikow (1999: 385–6) remark:

What is … striking are the differences in the ways the analysts [informed by different models] conceive of problems, shape puzzles, unpack summary questions, and dig into the evidence in search of an answer. Why did the United States blockade Cuba? For [rational actor] analysts, this "why" asks for reasons that account for the American choice of the blockade as a solution to the strategic problem posed by the presence of Soviet missiles in Cuba. For [an organizational behavior] analyst, the challenge is to identify outputs of key organizations without which there would be no blockade. A [governmental politics] analyst understands the basic "why" as a question about the political bargaining among players with distinctive interests, quite disparate conceptions of what was to be done, and different views about the process by which competing preferences blended and blurred in the selected action.

A case study such as the *Essence of Decision* that is oriented around a framework – without a set of specific hypotheses (or with so many hypotheses that it would be impossible to pass or fail all of them) – is difficult to assess with respect to internal validity. In this respect, it illustrates a common theme in case study research.

9.2   Causal comparability

The core criterion of almost all research designs is *causal comparability*. Briefly, the expected value of Y, conditional on X (the causal factor of interest) and Z (a vector of observed background factors), should be equal for all units and all time periods under study. Otherwise stated, variation in X should not be correlated with un-conditioned factors that are also causes of Y, which might serve as confounders, generating a spurious (non-causal) relationship between X and Y.

Experiments achieve pre-treatment comparability (balance on background factors that might affect the outcome of interest) by randomizing the treatment across groups and by including a sufficient number of units in the experiment so that threats from stochastic background features can be minimized. So long as the randomization mechanism is properly administered, pre-treatment comparability is assured. Achieving post-treatment comparability is more complicated, and many experiments encounter difficulties in this respect, e.g., contamination across groups, interference across units, non-compliance, attrition, and so forth. Nonetheless, these are (usually) relatively minor problems relative to the core problem of pre-treatment comparability, and experimentalists have devised a number of strategies for dealing with them – including instrumental variables, conditioning on covariates, and re-descriptions of the treatment effect from average treatment effects (ATE) to average treatment effects on the treated (ATT) (Gerber and Green 2012; Shadish *et al.* 2002).

Natural experiments rely on as-if randomization to achieve pre-treatment comparability across groups, which are also assumed to contain a sufficient number of units to minimize stochastic threats to inference. However, it is often unclear whether, or to what extent, "nature" has faithfully achieved the ideal of randomization. Hence, natural experiments are only as plausible as the researcher's assumptions about the data-generating process. Natural experiments also encounter problems of post-treatment comparability – though, following the model of experimental designs, there are usually methods for dealing with this secondary problem (Dunning 2012).

Research with messy observational data, by definition, can assume neither pre- or post-treatment comparability. Statistical corrections are therefore required, and the believability of the finding is entirely dependent upon the plausibility of these corrections, a matter about which methodologists are rightly skeptical (Freedman 1991; Kittel 1999; Seawright 2010). At the very least, one might say that causal inferences drawn from messy observational data are assumption-laden.

Case study research, at its best, exemplifies a natural experiment with an extremely small sample. One can debate how common this circumstance is, just as one can debate the experimental qualities of natural experiments in a large-C setting. But we can agree that where it exists causal inference is greatly facilitated. And it stands to reason that this achievement is facilitated by the small scope of case study research. The logic inherent in case selection for case study research is an extension of the logic of matching – where background covariates are used to eliminate cases that are not well matched across treatment and control groups (Ho *et al.* 2007). The case study researcher looking for a best case, or best set of cases, continues this process of elimination by examining additional factors that might not be easily measured across the population, and therefore cannot be included as matching covariates. Note that these in-depth qualitative judgments cannot easily be incorporated into algorithmic methods of case selection, and it is for this reason that I advised case study researchers to use algorithms as a guide to selection rather than as a final determinant of selection (see Chapter 6). As with large-C matching, losses in external validity are traded off for gains in internal validity. By carefully selecting cases to study, one hopes to limit the number of potential confounders.

However, one must also bear in mind that because of the miniscule sample there is no opportunity to control for background factors that are not balanced across groups (or within the same group, observed through time). Random error in a large sample constitutes noise, and will not bias resulting estimates. But random error in a small sample is indistinguishable from bias. If, in a most-similar analysis, Cases A and B are not similar on all background factors, Z, it is impossible to arrive at an unbiased estimate of X's impact on Y. Case studies thus require a much stronger set of assumptions about causal comparability. Rather than assuming that cases are comparable to each other *on average* across treatment and control groups (or through time in a longitudinal study), one must assume that cases under study (or a single case observed before and after a treatment) are *exactly* comparable to each other and measured without error (George and McKeown 1985: 27; Glynn and Ichino 2016; Lieberson 1992, 1994; Sekhon 2004).

To be sure, the goal of most case studies is not to render a precise estimate of the causal effect, but rather to render a general verdict on whether X is a cause of Y and, if so, in which direction (positive or negative) the effect runs. As such, case studies can tolerate bias that runs in a "conservative" direction, i.e., against the hypothesis the researcher is attempting to prove. This sort of bias presumably attenuates the true causal effect, and thus allows the researcher to establish a lower bound.

For example, in his most-similar analysis of political parties in the United States and Canada, Leon Epstein describes both countries as possessing strong regional bases of power – a factor that is presumed to weaken the cohesion of political parties. In recent decades, this factor has become more significant in Canada than in the US. While this detracts from the similarity of background conditions, it biases the analysis *against* Epstein's argument. That is, greater regional bases of power should weaken political parties at national levels in Canada. The fact that strong party cohesion survives in the Canadian House of Commons suggests that this factor either does not serve as a confounder, or attenuates the true causal effect measured in Epstein's analysis. While the same calculations may be made in a large-C analysis, they are generally harder to assess by reason of the large number of units and settings that one must consider.

This leads to a more general point: causal processes in case studies are generally more *observable* than causal processes in large-C studies for the simple reason that the empirical material is limited. There is only one, or a small handful, of cases under investigation, and each case may therefore be studied intensively, drawing on data at the case level and at lower levels of analysis (within-case evidence), as discussed in Chapter 8. When cases are closely studied over a long period of time, enlisting both qualitative and quantitative evidence drawn from different levels of analysis and from many sources (e.g., ethnography, interviews, surveys, primary and secondary materials), the researcher has an opportunity to become intimate with the data-generating process. This means that she is more likely to be able to distinguish causal processes from spurious correlations. Consequently, she is less likely to be fooled. Specifically, the researcher is more likely to become aware of threats to inference – arising, e.g., from errors in measurement, non-random assignment, or post-treatment confounding.

By contrast, a researcher who ventures to incorporate hundreds or thousands of cases in an analysis is likely to be intimately acquainted with only a small handful of cases – or perhaps with none of them. Note that acquaintance with the empirical material is a prerequisite of case study research. The bona fides of a case study researcher with respect to his/her subject must be established, e.g., linguistic facility, access to sources and special archives, a list of interviews or participant-observation sites, and so forth. By contrast, the researcher working with a large-C dataset is under no obligation to demonstrate his/her familiarity with the material at hand.[2]

We must also bear in mind that the most serious threats of inference are those that are difficult to identify – the *unknown unknowns*, to quote Donald Rumsfeld's famous aphorism. This does not obviate the problem of stochastic threats to inference in case study research, but it surely reduces them since the researcher has ample opportunity to study the causal processes at work in a very specific setting.

9.3   Front-door approaches

Thus far, we have assumed that the main piece of evidence for causality arises from the pattern of covariation observed between X and Y. A different approach to causal inference arises from examining

---

[2] These advantages of case study research are discussed in Bowman, Lehoucq and Mahoney (2005), Brady and Collier (2004), Harding and Seefeldt (2013), Seawright (2016b).

the pathway (mechanism) from X and Y (Knight and Winship 2013; Waldner 2016). Judea Pearl (2009) refers to this as the "front-door" path from X to Y, using the example of the connection between smoking and lung cancer – which, he says, was confirmed not by $X \rightarrow Y$ covariational evidence but rather by evidence of the process by which smoking causes cancer. Specifically, if smoking (X) causes a build-up of tar (M) in the lungs, and tar is a cause of cancer (Y), then a causal connection between X and Y can be proven. That is, insofar as each of these connections is accepted – and not open to confounding – causal inference may be achieved by examining the path from X to Y through M.

Several assumptions are required in order for this method to achieve causal identification. These assumptions are easiest to understand when illustrated in a causal graph, as shown in Figure 9.1. In this graph, nodes represent variables and arrows represent (suspected) one-directional (acyclic) causal relationships. Unmeasured variables (which therefore cannot be conditioned in a causal analysis) are signaled by brackets. The confounder labeled Z_1 in the figure affects both X and Y. Its presence precludes the traditional approach to causal inference, resting on the covariation of X and Y, which in this instance is spurious. The secondary approach, through the front door, is signaled by the path from X to M and from M to Y. This is viable, however, only in the absence of confounding. As can be seen, there are three potential confounders, one affecting X and M (Z_2), the second affecting M and Y (Z_3), and the third affecting X, M, and Y (Z_4). The presence of any of these will torpedo the effort to reach causal inference through the front door. So, anyone using an investigation of causal mechanisms to reach causal inference must consider these possibilities carefully.

Naturally, the process becomes even more complicated if several paths from X to Y are at work. In this situation, each path must be isolatable from the rest. However, the goals of case study researchers are usually limited to ascertaining whether a single mechanism (M_1) is at work, leaving aside the more difficult task of ascertaining all the paths from X to Y and the relative strength of each (a precise estimate of

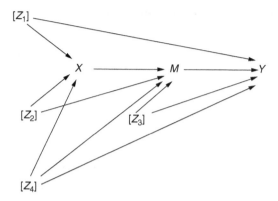

Figure 9.1   The front-door path with potential confounders
Notes: X = causal factor of theoretical interest. *M* = mechanism. *Y* = outcome. *Z* = unmeasured confounders.

causal effects registered through each causal pathway). If at least one path (M_1) can be confirmed, the generative force of X on Y is also confirmed (so long as M_1 is not canceled by additional unmeasured pathways, M_2).

To be sure, a front-door approach to causal inference is viable in both small- and large-C settings. However, insofar as the former offers greater opportunities to study causal mechanisms at work – see comments above on *observability* – it enjoys an elective affinity to this style of causal inference.

Ideally, the case study researcher is able to enlist both a traditional $X \to Y$ analysis and a front-door $X \to M \to Y$ analysis. This form of triangulation is especially helpful if the question of confounding in each analysis cannot be entirely dispensed with (as it generally cannot).

9.4   Transparency, replicability

Transparency refers to openness about the research process and how it unfolded over time. *Replicability*, in the narrow sense, means that someone other than the original researcher is able to access the data and repeat the procedures of the original analysis – qualitative and/or quantitative – working their way from the evidence to the author's conclusions. If this is not possible, i.e., if there is insufficient information to allow for this replication, then the value of a work is limited for it cannot be verified or falsified. One must simply take it on faith that the evidence gathered for a study supports the author's conclusions.[3] Transparency and replicability are closely related insofar as greater transparency enhances replicability. Thus, I treat them together as part of the same objective.

It is widely recognized that achieving transparency and replicability is harder to achieve in small-*C* studies than in large-*C* studies (Elman and Kapiszewski 2014). Certain characteristic features of the case study make it difficult to describe processes of data collection and analysis, to make data accessible, and then to replicate procedures after the fact. This has to do with the many ways in which a small number of cases can be "cased" (interpreted and given a broader significance), multiple and informal methods of case selection and analysis, and the ongoing interaction of theory and evidence – all of which characterize case study research. The informal nature of case study research seems to have encouraged a haphazard approach to transparency and replicability. As a result, case study research is in some ways more opaque than large-*C* research.

Fortunately, the problem is remediable (at least to some extent). Accordingly, and building on the work of many others, I propose that case study researchers adopt the following general protocol:

1. *Theory.* Clarify the theory or argument, e.g., whether it is descriptive or causal. If causal, the writers should specify the envisioned change

---

[3] For general discussions of replication, see Freese (2007), Dewald *et al.* (1986), *Journal of Human Resources* (1989), King (1995), Neuliep (1991). For discussion of replicability in the context of qualitative research, see Elman and Kapiszewski (2014), Lieberman (2010).

in X and its anticipated effect on Y, along with the suspected mechanism (M) and any relevant background conditions (Z). Whether descriptive or causal, the population (scope conditions) of the argument should also be specified. If different parts of the argument pertain to different populations, this should be clearly laid out.

2. *Case selection.* Clarify the method of case selection, including what was known about the case, or cases, prior to the selection and any changes in the sample that may have occurred during the research process.

3. *Evidence-gathering.* Clarify how within-case evidence was gathered in sufficient detail to allow someone to revisit the site and re-trace your steps, i.e., re-gather the same sort of evidence. For archival work, this may be facilitated by in-depth footnotes and appendices or by hypertext (Moravcsik 2010). For ethnographic work, it should be possible for someone else to revisit the original research site (even though relevant features may have changed in the interim). For work that relies on interviews, survey research, or original coding, all pertinent details of the data collection should be reported, e.g., sampling procedures, the questionnaire, initial contact with respondents, and so forth.

4. *Storage.* Once informant confidentiality is assured (e.g., by anonymizing sensitive data), data should be stored safely and made accessible to the public. Data in a matrix format can be stored on a secure server such as Dataverse (King 2007) or some other permanent archive. Qualitative data including "interview tapes, text files (transcripts from interviews, focus groups, and oral histories; case notes; meeting minutes; research diaries), scans of newspaper articles, images of official documents, and photographic, audio, and video materials" may be archived at the Qualitative Data Repository (US) or QUALIDATA (UK) (Elman *et al.* 2010).

5. *Analysis.* To allow for replication, it is necessary to state clearly how you analyzed your data. Quantitative analyses may be summarized in "do" files (software commands). Qualitative analysis is more

complicated, but not impossible. For an example of how to describe qualitative analysis so that subsequent readers can replicate each step, see Fairfield (2013). Of special importance to case study research are the following questions. Were there additional ("shadow") cases outside the formal case study that played a role in the analysis? What background assumptions are necessary in order to sustain the main argument?

6. *Sequence.* Of particular importance is the sequencing of each step of the research design. For example, with respect to case selection, did the researcher know the value of the outcome variable for the chosen case prior to its selection? If large-C analysis was utilized ("multimethod" research), did it precede or follow the case study portion of the study (or occur in tandem)? If the method of case selection is different from the method of subsequent analysis, is this distinction clear?

To achieve full transparency and replicability, all the procedures followed in a study must be scrupulously laid out in the order they were performed. I imagine that this might take the form of a short appendix, summarizing details contained in a longer research diary or laboratory notebook. In this fashion, processes that usually remain in the shadows would be brought into the open, allowing consumers of case studies to better understand the nature of the data and the probable strength of the findings, and also facilitating replication.

To this extent, problems of transparency and replicability commonly associated with case study research are remediable. Other aspects are likely to persist. However, before concluding that case study research is deficient relative to large-C research we must think seriously about the meaning of transparency and replicability.

In observational (non-experimental) settings, these terms often refer to the method of *analysis* rather than the method of *data collection*. This stems from the fact that observational research is often based on data collected by someone else. Anyone analyzing survey data drawn from the National Election Studies (NES) or the World Values Survey (WVS), or country-level data from repositories such as the World Development Indicators (WDI) or the Quality of Government dataset (QoG), is taking data "off the shelf," so to speak. As such, the researcher's obligation extends to listing the source of the data and whatever procedures were employed to analyze the data. That is it. Issues pertaining to data collection are swept under the rug because the researcher herself had nothing to do with it.

Some of the data drawn from these sources are undoubtedly excellent and others are flawed – and this judgment of course depends upon what one is using the data for. Some have well-structured codebooks explaining the origins of the data – and allowing for replication – and others do not. It all depends.

For present purposes, the point I want to emphasize is that potential problems of measurement error are typically off-loaded onto third parties if the author of a study is not responsible for the data that s/he analyzes. Perhaps it would be more precise to say that errors in measurement associated with third-party data collection are not considered under the rubric of transparency/replicability. Critics of a study employing data from the WVS might regard them as error-prone, but they would not accuse the study of being un-transparent or un-replicable.

Case study research invariably involves extensive *original* data collected from the chosen cases. This might be drawn from ethnography, interviews, surveys, primary sources, or secondary sources (reinterpreted by the researcher). Typically, it is a combination of the foregoing. As such, data collection and data analysis are interwoven in the same study. And this means that establishing transparency/replicability for case study research extends to the most intimate details of data collection. The consequence is that it imposes a much higher standard of transparency/replicability than is typically laid upon research with extant datasets. Our frustrations with transparency/replicability are thus, in part, a product of the somewhat arbitrary fashion in which these concepts are understood – with higher standards applying to case study research.

9.5   Separation of theory formation and testing

Problems of validity are posed when researchers develop a hypothesis using the same data that are subsequently used to test that hypothesis. The whole operation is evidently circular, leading to derogatory labels such as "curve-fitting" and "fishing." One might point out that this is not really testing at all but rather theory generation. One might also add that the exploratory quality of case study research constitutes one of its primary virtues. However, at present we are concerned with case studies as a confirmatory form of analysis, and hence with their validity.

Experiments, by contrast, provide a neat division between theory formation and theory testing insofar as the experimenter must devise the theory prior to testing it. Ex ante and ex post moments are precisely delineated in time. Of course, researchers may still engage in fishing by exploring myriad outcomes and interaction terms, or by repeating the same experiment until they "get it right." To mitigate these problems, many experimentalists now pre-register their main hypotheses and their proposed research design, including a plan of analysis, prior to conducting an experiment (Humphreys *et al.* 2013). With these expedients, validity can be more easily assessed.

In principle, the same mechanism could be adopted by researchers using observational data, including case studies. However, in order to be credible the claim to ex ante ignorance must be verifiable. Such an opportunity arises when there is a recognizably "prospective" element to the research. Specifically, wherever research involves site visits – to archives or to an ethnographic site – it is possible, in principle, to delineate a moment in time prior to the researcher's encounter with a body of data. Wherever new data are released to the public – e.g., the opening of a new archive, the discovery of a new data source, or the declassification of a new set of documents – it is similarly possible to establish prior ignorance.

These opportunities are as likely to occur for those employing large-C datasets as for those employing single cases. However, it may be more complicated for case study researchers relying primarily on qualitative analysis to identify falsifiable hypotheses since qualitative work lacks anything on the order of significance tests. Qualitative researchers would have to think hard, in advance, about what sort of evidence would decisively prove, or refute, their theory.

Yet, insofar as case study researchers wish to engage in hypothesis testing – and many seem to regard their own work in this fashion – this sort of exercise seems unavoidable. If it is not congenial, then case study researchers would be well advised to frame their work as exploratory rather than confirmatory.

The purpose of pre-registration, in any case, is not to discourage exploratory styles of research. Researchers who pre-register a study are as free to explore options as they would have been otherwise. The purpose of pre-registration is to allow end-users to distinguish theories arrived at ex ante from those arrived at ex post. Presumably, one would assign a higher probability to a hypothesis that was pre-registered than to a hypothesis that was developed after a researcher's encounter with the data.

For case study researchers who wish to engage in hypothesis testing, the option of pre-registration offers an opportunity to overcome prejudices among those in the academy who view *all* case study research as exploratory. Note that case study research is often regarded with suspicion, and this stems partly from a view that researchers have engaged in a circular process of theory formation and testing. If pre-registration is successful in overcoming some of this skepticism, it may allow case study researchers to present their work as they would like to have it perceived – as an effort to test theories. As such, it seems like a healthy addition to the toolkit of qualitative methods.

9.6   Informative estimates of uncertainty

All empirical studies are prone to error. It is a matter of utmost importance to be able to estimate that error in a realistic fashion. At a minimum, we want to be able to distinguish propositions that are very likely to be true from propositions that are unlikely to be true. Empirical truth being a matter of degrees, we would like to distinguish the probability of a proposition being true in as precise a fashion as possible, given the data at hand.

All large-*C* research designs produce, as a matter of routine, an estimate of uncertainty, expressed in a confidence interval, t-statistic, or p-value.[4] Unfortunately, these estimates do not usually provide an accurate estimate of uncertainty. They account for sampling error, but not for potential problems in the causal model (e.g., pre- or post-treatment confounders). Likewise, they do not incorporate features of the design such as the circular nature of theory formation and theory testing, selective reporting of results, and fishing. A lot remains hidden from the calculation of a p-value.

Experiments and natural experiments are less prone to problems stemming from a causal model, as discussed. Experiments, if accompanied by pre-registration, are less susceptible to problems stemming from fishing. But large-*C* observational data, as currently conducted, are generally subject to all of these problems.

Likewise, for case studies. Of course, case study researchers will certainly have considered sources of error and may discuss them in some detail. This is all to the good. However, there is no standard metric by which to present this information so we cannot compare uncertainty in one case study relative to uncertainty in another. In addition, case studies are utterly incapable of measuring stochastic error. Consequently, case studies receive the lowest score in this final measure of internal validity, as registered in the bottom row of Table 9.1.

A few additional points must be added to this discussion.

Note that the advantages accruing to case studies stem mostly from the in-depth knowledge that a researcher brings to the case(s) under study. However, this is his/her knowledge, not the reader's. So when

---

[4] Sometimes, as with randomization inference (Fischer's exact p-values) or sample average treatment effects (SATE) from a matching estimator, this measure of uncertainty is focused solely on internal validity. Elsewhere, the measure of uncertainty is intended to register sampling variance as well, which biases the estimate upward (under normal circumstances).

s/he reports that there are no confounders upsetting the relationship between X and Y, we have no way to dispute the contention – unless we happen to possess in-depth knowledge of that particular case.

Consider, as well, the informal nature of case selection and analysis, as discussed in Parts II and III of the book. Consider that many potential explanations usually beckon, all of which may be plausible to the outside observer. Consider the scope for researcher bias. This may occur in a calculated way, as researchers look for the case – and the within-case evidence – that proves their theory, i.e., cherry-picking.[5] It may also occur in an unconscious way, as researchers interact with participants in the study, influencing their responses and behavior through non-verbal cues. We have noted that case studies often derive theory from the evidence at hand, and in this respect are circular in their procedure. Typically, one visits a site (a place, an archive, a set of texts, a historical era) with a general research question, from which a specific argument is developed. That argument is then "tested" against evidence provided by the same case(s). As such, there is no effective separation between theory and evidence. Or testing is of a very loose sort.

For the sake of discussion, consider two archetypal research designs both of which attempt to ascertain the effect of X on Y. And suppose, for the moment, that we are concerned only with the internal validity of these two studies. The large-C study examines the relationship between X and Y across 200 municipalities using a regression analysis and a specification that includes background covariates that might serve as confounders (Z). The case study examines the relationship between X and Y in one municipality, relying on longitudinal evidence and evidence drawn from a lower level of analysis – much of it qualitative in nature. Without knowing anything further about these two studies, it is safe to say that the former will be easier to assess than the latter. That is, without any detailed knowledge of the research site, it will be possible to assess whether the stated results of the study are plausible or

---

[5] For discussion, see Skocpol and Somers (1980), Lustick (1996), Thies (2002).

implausible, basing one's judgment on generic features of the research design. Is the treatment as-if random? Is the estimator well chosen? Are plausible confounders included in the regression model? These are the sorts of questions that anyone with some methodological training is able to ask, and that any author is likely to address. By contrast, the number of questions that one would need to assess in order to reach a determination of the case study are innumerable. Moreover, assessing the answers to these questions would demand in-depth knowledge of the case, knowledge that persons other than the author are unlikely to be privy to, and would be difficult to verify.

There is no easy solution to the problem of assessment, especially as most of these problems stem from what I would regard as an intrinsic element of case study research – its informal nature.

All of that said, one ought to bear in mind that a case study without a p value is only marginally worse than a large-C observational data analysis with a p value that overlooks many of the factors that affect causal identification. The latter may mislead readers into believing that the hypothesis is true "with 95% confidence," while the case study offers no such totemic claims to virtue and is, in this sense, less likely to propagate false impressions about the true degree of uncertainty affecting a study.

9.7   Summary

In this chapter, we have assessed the role of case studies in achieving internal validity – unbiased estimates of a causal effect for a studied sample. To do so, we have compared three large-C designs – experiments, natural experiments, and observational data – with case studies. A summary of these comparisons and contrasts appears in Table 9.1.

By comparison with experimental and quasi-experimental studies, case studies appear to be deficient in most respects. However, one must appreciate that these exacting research designs will never be able to properly address many of the research questions that animate social science (Dunning 2012; Teele 2014).

As a consequence, most large-C analyses will likely continue to be based on "messy, observational" data, often analyzed with a regression model and bearing little resemblance to an experiment (natural or otherwise). This has caused considerable consternation among methodologists, who are acutely aware of the many assumptions required to reach causal inference with this sort of data.

Against this backdrop, case study research appears in a more favorable light. As Table 9.1 indicates, it is not easy to say whether studies based on large samples of observational data are superior to, or inferior to, case studies since these genres exhibit different strengths and weaknesses and since so much depends on how the particular study is implemented. There are strong-inferential large-C studies and strong-inferential small-C studies, and plenty that are weak in both genres.

I should also highlight a somewhat controversial claim advanced in this chapter. In two respects, I maintain, case study research is superior to large-C designs. First, case studies offer high observability – one can more readily "see" what is going in a causal field, including the presence of potential confounders. Second, one is more likely to satisfy the assumptions of a front-door approach to causal inference when the cases under study number one or several.

Before concluding, it is important to stress that internal validity is not the only criterion of importance. Considerations pertaining to external validity are introduced in the next chapter and additional desiderata are discussed briefly in Chapter 11.

10 External validity

A study must attempt to generalize from the chosen case(s) to a larger population of cases in order to qualify as a case study. Alternatively, this act of generalizing may occur after the fact, as a study is digested by a community of scholars who judge that it has some broader applicability.

Naturally, the breadth of a case study argument is always a matter of degrees. No case study denies the uniqueness of the case under special focus, and no case study (so-called) forswears the generalizing impulse altogether. So the particularizing/generalizing distinction is rightly understood as a continuum, not a dichotomy.

The point remains, if the study is not a case of something broader than itself, it is not a case study. In this chapter, I discuss various issues pertaining to external validity in case study research. This includes sample representativeness, the somewhat conflicting goals of internal and external validity, the task of establishing scope conditions for an argument, and the challenge of assessing claims to external validity.

Before entering this discussion, it is important to appreciate that the problem of external validity, or generalizability, is by no means unique to case studies. Experimental studies employ samples that, although large, are rarely chosen randomly – and for various reasons often cannot be chosen randomly – and thus face continual challenges in attempting to establish their external validity (Muller 2015). In this respect, case studies and experiments are kindred spirits.

10.1   Sample representativeness

When selecting cases, one aims for cases that are representative of a larger population. This is a core ("omnibus") goal of case selection, as discussed in Chapter 3. If a chosen case, or cases, is representative of the population – in whatever ways are relevant for the hypothesis at hand – then one has jumped the first hurdle to external validity.

Unfortunately, case study research is hard to generalize from because it includes, by definition, only a small number of cases of a more general phenomenon. Are the men chosen by Robert Lane (1962) typical of the American male, white, immigrant, working class? Is Middletown representative of other cities in America (Lynd and Lynd 1929/1956)? These sorts of questions forever haunt case study research.

If one wishes to represent a *distribution* of values present in a population, the problem of representativeness is even more extreme. One cannot adequately represent a whole distribution with one or several cases (so long as there is at least some variance along that distribution). We shall leave this problem aside, as case study researchers generally have a more modest goal – to represent typical values within a population.

Of all the problems besetting case study analysis, perhaps the most persistent – and the most persistently bemoaned – is the problem of sample bias.[1] Lisa Martin (1992: 5) finds that the over-emphasis of

---

[1] Achen and Snidal (1989), Collier and Mahoney (1996), Geddes (1990), King *et al.* (1994), Rohlfing (2004), Sekhon (2004). Some case study researchers appear to denigrate the importance of case representativeness. George and Bennett (2005: 30) write emphatically, "Case researchers do *not* aspire to select cases that are directly 'representative' of diverse populations and they usually do not and should not make claims that their findings are applicable to such populations except in contingent ways." However, it becomes clear that what the authors are inveighing against is not the goal of representativeness per se but rather the problem of a case study researcher who claims an inappropriately broad extension for her findings. "To the extent that

international relations scholars on a few well-known cases of economic sanctions – most of which failed to elicit any change in the sanctioned country – "has distorted analysts' view of the dynamics and characteristics of economic sanctions." Barbara Geddes (1990) charges that many analyses of industrial policy have focused exclusively on the most successful cases – primarily the East Asian NICs – leading to biased inferences. Anna Breman and Carolyn Shelton (2001) show that case study work on the question of structural adjustment is systematically biased insofar as researchers tend to focus on disaster cases – those where structural adjustment is associated with very poor health and human development outcomes. Case study work is particularly prone to problems of investigator bias since so much rides on the researcher's selection of one case (or a few).

Other biases, while not intentional, are worrisome nonetheless. For example, among nation-states some cases are well studied and others are scarcely studied at all. As a result, our knowledge of the world is heavily colored by a few "big" (populous, rich, powerful) countries. Indeed, a good deal of what we know (or think we know) about the world is built upon one country – the United States.[2] It could be that well-studied cases such as the US are not like less-studied cases with respect to outcomes of concern to researchers. If so, a serious problem of bias affects case study work in the social sciences.

The fundamental problem is that it is difficult to represent a larger population – in all ways relevant to the descriptive or causal claims of a study – with a sample of one or a few. That said, it may be possible for a researcher to minimize potential bias by avoiding cases that seem

there is a representativeness problem or a selection bias problem in a particular case study, it is often better described as the problem of 'overgeneralizing' findings to types or sub-classes of cases unlike those actually studied" (32).

[2] Wahlke (1979: 13) writes of the failings of the "behavioralist" mode of political science analysis. "It rarely aims at generalization; research efforts have been confined essentially to case studies of single political systems, most of them dealing . . . with the American system."

manifestly unrepresentative ("weird"). This is not trivial. However, one can never know for sure how representative one's case(s) is. This should not induce despair, but it should induce a healthy skepticism about claims to representativeness based solely on case study research.

When it comes to achieving external validity, the appropriate strategy is probably not to strain the credulity of extremely small samples, but rather to leave the issue of representativeness open-ended, or to combine case studies with large-C studies that can properly implement random sampling with a large sample – a multimethod approach to research (see Chapter 7).

10.2   A two-level game

While methodologists typically focus on problems of generalizability, it is important to bear in mind that the goal of a case study is not limited to developing and testing general theories. Case studies typically partake of two worlds. They are studies of something general, and of something particular. The particularizing/generalizing distinction thus helps us to understand different moments within the same case study. Part of the study is "idiographic" and another part "nomothetic."

This tension is apparent in Graham Allison's (1971) well-known study, whose subtitle, *Explaining the Cuban Missile Crisis*, invokes a narrow topic while the title, *Essence of Decision*, suggests a much larger topic (government decision-making). Evidently, different propositions within this same work apply to different subjects, a complication that is noted by the author.

With respect to the topic of social mobility, John Goldthorpe and Robert Erikson find that while some patterns are well explained by large-C models, others are resistant to those general explanations.

Our analyses pointed... to the far greater importance of historically formed cultural or institutional features or political circumstances which could not be expressed as variable values except in a quite artificial way. For example, levels of social fluidity were not highly responsive to the overall degree of educational inequality within nations, but patterns of fluidity did often reflect the distinctive, institutionally shaped character of such inequality in particular nations, such as Germany or Japan. Or again, fluidity was affected less by the presence of a state socialist regime per se than by the significantly differing policies actually pursued by the Polish, Hungarian or Czechoslovak regimes on such matters as the collectivization of agriculture or the recruitment of the intelligentsia. In such instances, then, it seemed to us that the retention of proper names and adjectives in our explanatory accounts was as unavoidable as it was desirable, and that little was to be gained in seeking to bring such historically specific effects within the scope of theory of any kind (Goldthorpe 1997: 17).

This empirical field offers a good example of how a single phenomenon (social mobility) may exhibit features that are both uniform and unique across a population.

A certain degree of ambiguity may be inherent in the enterprise, for it is difficult to write a study of a single case that does not also function as a case study, and vice-versa. Nor is it always easy to neatly separate each moment in a single work. The reason for this structural ambiguity is that the utility of the case study rests on its double function. One wishes to know both what is particular to that case *and* what is generalizable, and it may be difficult to cleanly distinguish one from the other.

Avner Greif (1998: 59) offers the following caveat at the conclusion of his study of late medieval Genoa:

This study demonstrates the complexity of investigating self-enforcing political systems. Such an investigation requires a detailed examination of the particularities of the time and place under consideration, utilizing a coherent, context-specific model. Thus, it may be premature to attempt to generalize based on this study regarding the sources and implications of self-enforcing political systems.

Here a researcher steeped in the nomothetic tradition of economics comes to terms with the fact that generalizations based on his case study are highly speculative.[3]

The dual functions of a case study – to explain the case and to shed light on a larger population – are addressed specifically by Lisa Martin (1992: 97) in her study of multilateral economic sanctions. Martin confesses,

although I have chosen the cases to allow testing the hypotheses [of theoretical interest], other factors inevitably appear that seem to have had a significant influence on cooperation in particular cases. Because few authors have focused on the question of cooperation in cases of economic sanctions, I devote some attention to these factors when they arise, rather than keeping my analysis within the bounds of the hypotheses outlined in [the theory chapter].

The rationale for following this dual approach may be briefly laid out. First, although idiosyncratic factors have no (apparent) generalizability, they may play an essential role in reconstructing causal relationships at the case level. Specifically, they may serve as antecedent causes (affecting treatment assignment), as mechanisms, as confounders, or as alternate outcomes (providing placebo tests for a theory). Insofar as factors specific to a case help to account for the data-generating process they play an important role in reaching causal inference at the case level – even if they have no utility in building general theory.

---

[3] George and Smoke (1974: 105) offer parallel reflections on their own case studies, focused on deterrence in international relations. "These case studies are of twofold value. First, they provide an empirical base for the theoretical analysis . . . But second, the case studies are intended to stand in their own right as historical explanations of the outcomes of many of the major deterrence efforts of the Cold War period. They are 'historical' in the sense that they are, of course, retrospective. However, they are also analytical in the sense that we employ a variety of tools and concepts in attempting to explain the *reasons* behind a particular outcome in terms of the inner logic of the deterrence process [a logic that is presumably extends across past, present, future]. They are therefore as much 'political science' as they are 'history.'"

Second, there is a practical consideration. Imagine that a researcher restricts herself only to elements of the case that are generalizable (i.e., she rigorously maintains a nomothetic mode of analysis). Such rigor clarifies the population of the primary inference, but also constitutes a considerable waste of scholarly resources. Consider a study of economic growth that focuses on Mauritius as a case study yet refuses to engage causal questions unless they are clearly applicable to other countries. No mention of factors specific to the Mauritian case is allowed; all proper nouns are converted into common nouns.[4] Imagine that the fruit of an anthropologist's ten-year study of a remote tribe, never heretofore visited, culminates in the analysis of a particular causal relationship deemed to be generalizable, but at the cost of ignoring all other features of tribal life in the resulting study. One may suppose that colleagues, mentors, and funding agencies would be unhappy with an economic history, or an ethnography, that is so tightly focused on a general causal issue. Studies of the foregoing sort do not exist precisely because they are unduly general.

Since it is often difficult to tell which of the many features of a given case are typical of a larger set of cases (and hence fodder for generalizable inferences), and which are particular to the case under study, the appropriate protocol is to report all facts and hypotheses that might be relevant – in short, to *over-report*. Much of the detail provided by the typical case study may be regarded as "field notes" of plausible utility for future researchers, perhaps with rather different agendas in mind.

In sum, it seems justifiable for case studies to function on two levels simultaneously, the case itself and some broader class of (perhaps difficult to specify) cases. The defining characteristic of the case study is its ability to infer a larger whole from a much smaller part. Yet, both the part and the whole retain some importance in the final product. All case studies are to a certain extent betwixt and between. They partake of two worlds: they are particularizing *and* generalizing.

---

[4] This is the advice rendered by Przeworski and Teune (1970).

As such, conducting a case study obliges one to play a two-level game that is not unlike the process of international negotiations (Putnam 1988). And this, in turn, helps to make sense of several ongoing issues in causal inference – between the cause-in-fact and the counterfactual cause, causes-of-effects and effects-of-causes – that pull the case study researcher in two directions.

Cause-in-fact versus counterfactual cause

In constructing causal explanations for individual cases, there is often ambiguity about whether the identified cause(s) should be understood as cause(s) *in fact* (token cause(s)) or *counterfactual* cause(s). The former refers to what actually caused a particular outcome in that particular case, and corresponds to our everyday notion of causation. The latter refers to factors that would have been necessary or sufficient to achieve an outcome (or degrees of variation in an outcome), given certain background conditions.

To distinguish these two types of explanation, we shall briefly consider the parable of a man wandering in the desert. This proverbial man relies on a leaky canteen for water and it is clear that there is insufficient water to keep him alive before he reaches his destination. The man dies. Knowing only this, one would be inclined to regard the leak in the canteen as the cause of his demise. However, it happens that the water in the canteen is poisoned, and it is this poison that actually kills him – which we can tell because there is still water in the canteen when his body is discovered, signifying he did not die of thirst. There is only one cause in fact (poison) while there are two counterfactual causes (poison and the leaky canteen). A leaky canteen is a sufficient cause of death – or, alternatively, a non-leaky canteen is a necessary cause of survival.

For legal purposes, one might regard only the poison as a cause (Hart and Honore 1959). But for purposes of generalizability, both seem relevant. That is, if we are trying to determine why people (occasionally) die in the desert, we should be concerned with poison as well as leaky canteens, both of which have causal power in the general sense. Since case studies are – by definition – aiming to generalize across a larger population of cases, it follows that causal analysis should focus on counterfactual causes rather than (or in addition to) token causes. However, token causes may be important – and impossible to avoid – as a way of making sense of causal relationships in an individual case. Thus, returning to our leitmotif, we can justify both modes of analysis, with the caveat that a counterfactual understanding of causality must guide whatever general theory arises from the case.

Causes-of-effects versus effects-of-causes

The analysis of a case may attempt to reconstruct all the causes of an outcome or may focus on a single causal factor, i.e., a specific $X \rightarrow Y$ hypothesis. The former has come to be known as a *causes-of-effects* argument and the latter as an *effects-of-causes* argument (Holland 1986).

It should be obvious that explaining all the causes of Y is a lot more difficult than explaining one cause of Y. Indeed, it is not even clear what a complete explanation might consist of, given the problem of endless causal regress. (How far back in time should one go?) Likewise, a causes-of-effects analysis is unlikely to be generalizable – at least not in a clear fashion. Many of the causes of Y in Case A may be particular to Case A. Or perhaps X_{1-3} are idiosyncratic, X_4 applies to one population, and X_5 to another. In any case, a causes-of-effects style of analysis is generally geared to a particular case, or small set of cases, that are under analysis – not to a larger population.

Because of the difficulties inherent in a causes-of-effects style of analysis, and because a case study's contribution to knowledge is based primarily on its generalizability, one might be inclined to favor an effects-of-causes style of analysis. However, when the researcher's focus is on a particular case, it may also make good sense to try to illuminate – at least in a provisional way – each contributing cause of an outcome.

Indeed, case studies usually work on two tracks, as we have shown: they attempt to explain the case under intensive investigation (which is often deemed to have some intrinsic importance) as well as to shed light on a larger population. Explaining an outcome for Case *A* means elucidating all the possible factors that contributed (or may have contributed) to an outcome in that case. This sort of analysis takes an exploratory form, since (as noted) the very notion of completeness is ambiguous and perhaps impossible to satisfy. One researcher's complete explanation of *Y* is bound to differ from another's, which is why no two historical accounts of the same event are identical. Even so, a great deal of effort is expended in the course of a case study and clues discovered during the course of that investigation should be preserved for later researchers, in some fashion. It could be that they will serve as fodder for some future study.

Thus, I conclude that in the context of case study research both styles of causal analysis have their uses. This does not preclude researchers from adopting a purely effects-of-causes approach – where the goal of case analysis is focused narrowly on a single hypothesis. But it does justify those who wish to work both sides of the street.

10.3   Establishing scope conditions

Given the structural conflict between the two moments of the case study – the particularizing and the generalizing – it is crucial that case study writers be as clear as possible about which of their propositions are intended to describe the case under intensive investigation and which are intended to apply to a broader set of cases. Each inference must have a clear breadth, domain, scope, or population (terms that I use interchangeably).

Regrettably, these matters are often left ambiguous. At the outset of an ethnographic account of life on a city sidewalk, Mitchell Duneier addresses the issue of generalizability. He acknowledges that the setting for his study – Greenwich Village, New York – is different from many other settings, but he does not say which settings are similar enough to warrant generalizable claims. "In the end," writes Duneier (1999: 11), "I must leave it to readers to test my observations against their own, and hope that the concepts I have developed to make sense of this neighborhood will prove useful in other venues." Responsibility for establishing scope conditions is thus abnegated, and the study is less useful – and certainly less falsifiable – as a result.

E.P. Thompson's (1963) renowned history *The Making of the English Working Class* provides a case study of class formation in one national setting (England). Thompson does not offer a specific theory of class formation, aside from the rather hazy notion of a working class participating in its own development. Thus, unless we intuit a great deal (creating general theory where there is only a suggestion of one) we can derive relatively little that might be applicable to a broader population of cases.

Many case studies examine a loosely defined general topic – war, revolution, gender relations – in a particular setting. The narrowest terrains sometimes claim the broadest extensions. Studies of a war are studies of war; studies of a farming community are studies of farming communities everywhere; studies of individuals are studies of leadership or of human nature; and so forth. However, such studies may not attempt to elucidate general theories of war, farming, leadership, or human nature. This would be true, for example, of most case study work in the interpretivist tradition.[5] Similarly, case studies with

---

[5] Clifford Geertz (1973: 26), echoing the suspicion of most historians, anthropologists – presumably of all those who hold an interpretivist view of the social science enterprise – describes generalizing across cases as *clinical inference*. "Rather than beginning with a set of observations, attempting to subsume them under a governing law, such inference begins with a set of (presumptive) signifiers, attempts to place them within an intelligible frame. Measures are matched to theoretical predictions, but symptoms (even when they are measured) are scanned for theoretical peculiarities – that is, they are diagnosed." For a brief overview of interpretivism, see Gerring (2004a). Indeed, this genre of case study, which I have

take-home messages like "Ideas matter," "Institutions matter," "Politics matters," or "Critical junctures matter" do not generally culminate in far-reaching predictions. They tell us about an instance in which one of these frameworks mattered ("Ideas mattered *here*"), but do not produce generalizable, testable propositions. They offer a framework, which may be used to shed light on a particular case, but not a falsifiable proposition that could be applied to other cases.

A more ambiguous example is provided by Elisabeth Wood's renowned study of democratization in South Africa and El Salvador. Summarizing one of the book's main arguments, Wood (2000: 5) writes,

> Democracy in both countries was forced from below by the sustained insurgency of lower-class actors. Once-unyielding elites in South Africa and El Salvador conceded democracy because popular insurgency, although containable militarily, could not be ended, and the persisting mobilization eventually made compromise preferable to continued resistance. In contrast to the transitions in many countries where mobilization by the poor played a lesser role ... in South Africa and El Salvador the timing of the transitions, the split among elite factions between those supporting and those opposing the transition, the political actors who negotiated the transition, and the nature of the compromises that led to democracy were all forced through insurgent mobilization. My central claim ... is that the transition to democracy would not have taken place in either country when it did, as it did, and with the same consequences in the absence of sustained popular mobilization.

It is difficult to see how these arguments, so narrowly focused, could be translated to a broader population. And yet, Wood also claims that the experience of these two countries can be generalized to other

called idiographic, may also be referred to as interpretivist (Lijphart 1971). Skocpol and Somers (1980) call it "contrast of contexts."

cases, a claim she explores (opaquely, in my view) in the concluding chapter.

Studies focused on some element of politics in the United States often frame their analysis as a study of politics – by implication, politics *in general* (everywhere and always). One is left to wonder whether the study pertains only to American politics, to all contemporary polities, or in varying degrees to both. Indeed, the slippage between study and case study may account for much of the confusion that we encounter when reading single-case analyses. Ongoing controversies over the validity of Theda Skocpol's analysis of social revolution, Michael Porter's analysis of industrial competitiveness, Alexander George and Richard Smoke's study of deterrence failure, as well as many other case-based studies, rest partly on the failure of these authors to clarify the scope of their inferences.[6] It is not clear what these studies are *about*. At any rate, it is open to dispute. If, at the end of a study, the population of the primary inference remains ambiguous, so does the hypothesis. It is not falsifiable. Clarifying an inference may involve some sacrifice in narrative flow, but it is rightly regarded as the entry price of social science.

What is the right scope?

Caution is evidently required when specifying the population of an inference. One does not wish to claim too much. Nor does one wish to claim too little. Mistakes can be made in either direction.

In this discussion, I shall emphasize the virtues of breadth, for it is my sense that many case study researchers lean towards narrow propositions – which seem more modest, more conservative – without realizing the costs of doing so. For example, Tasha Fairfield (2015: 298) describes her population as consisting of 54 proposed reforms

---

[6] Skocpol (1979), Porter (1990), George and Smoke (1974). See also discussion in Collier and Mahoney (1996), Geddes (1990), King *et al.* (1994).

occurring in Argentina, Bolivia, and Chile across several decades. Yet, her work suggests that she wishes to draw inferences about the reform process that extend across other countries and time periods. (Indeed, if her book had no relevance for other countries and time periods, it would be of little or no theoretical interest.)[7]

The case study researcher may feel that in light of the in-depth knowledge she has acquired about her case and her comparative ignorance of other cases it would be irresponsible to speculate on the latter. Misgivings are understandable. However, if properly framed – as a hunch rather than a conclusion – there is no need to refrain from a clear statement of scope conditions. These hunches are vital signposts for future research. They bring greater clarity to the inference of primary interest and point the way to a cumulative research agenda. No case study research should be allowed to conclude without at least a nod to how one's case might be situated in a broader universe of cases. Without this generalization, the case study sits alone. Its insights, regardless of their brilliance, cannot be integrated into a broader field of study.

In discussion of two extraordinarily influential works of comparative history – Barrington Moore's (1966) *Social Origins of Dictatorship and Democracy* and Theda Skocpol's (1979) *States and Social Revolutions* – Skocpol and Margaret Somers (1980) declare that these studies, and others like them, "cannot be readily generalized beyond the cases actually discussed," for they are inductive rather than deductive exercises in

---

[7] Jack Goldstone (1997: 108) argues that case studies are "aimed at providing explanations for particular cases, or groups of similar cases, rather than at providing general hypotheses that apply uniformly to *all* cases in a suspected case-Universe." Alexander George and Richard Smoke (1974: 96; see also George and Bennett 2005: 30–1) advise the use of case studies for the formulation of what they call "contingent generalizations" – "if circumstances *A* then outcome *O*." Like many case study researchers, they lean towards a style of analysis that investigates differences across cases or across sub-types, rather than commonalities. Harry Eckstein (1975), on the other hand, envisions case studies that confirm (or disconfirm) hypotheses as broad as those provided by cross-case studies.

causal analysis. Any attempt to project the arguments in these works onto future revolutions, or onto revolutions outside the class of specified outcomes, is foolhardy. The authors defend this limited scope by likening case-based research to a map. "No matter how good the maps were of, say, North America, the pilot could not use the same map to fly over other continents" (Skocpol and Somers 1980: 195).

The map metaphor is apt for some phenomena, but not for others. It betrays the authors' general assumption that most phenomena of interest to social science are highly variable across contexts, like the roadways and waterways of a continent. Consider the causes of revolutions, as explored by Skocpol (1979) in her path-breaking work. Skocpol carefully bounds her conclusions, which are said to apply only to states that are independent (through their history) of colonial rule – and hence exclude other revolutionary cases such as Mexico (1910), Bolivia (1952), and Cuba (1959) (Collier and Mahoney 1996: 81; George and Bennett 2005: 120). One's willingness to accept this scope-restriction is contingent upon accepting an important premise, namely that the causes of revolution in countries with colonial legacies are different from the causes of revolution in other countries. This is a plausible claim, but it is not beyond question. (Were the causes of revolution really so different in Cuba and Russia?)

When a researcher restricts an inference to a small population of cases, or to the population that s/he has studied (which may be large or small), s/he is open to the charge of gerrymandering – establishing a domain on no other basis than that certain cases seem to fit the inference under study. Donald Green and Ian Shapiro (1994) call this an "arbitrary domain restriction." The breadth of an inference must make sense; there must be an explicable reason for including some cases and excluding others. If the inference is about oranges, then all oranges – but no apples – should be included in the population. If it is about fruit, then both apples and oranges must be included. Defining the population – e.g., (a) oranges or (b) fruit – is thus critical to defining the inference.

The same goes for temporal boundaries. If an inference is limited to a specific time period, it is incumbent upon the writer to explain why that period is different from others. It will not do for writers to hide behind the presumption that social science cannot predict the future. Theoretical arguments cannot opt out of predicting future events if the future is like the present in ways that are relevant to the theory. Indeed, if future evidence were to be considered ineligible for judging the accuracy of already existing theories, then writers would have effectively side-stepped any out-of-sample tests (given that, in their construction, many social science theories have already exhausted all possible evidence that is currently available).

For a variety of reasons, social science gives preference to broad inferences over narrow inferences. First, the scope of an inference usually correlates directly with its theoretical significance. Broad empirical propositions are theory-building; narrow propositions usually have less theoretical significance (unless they are subsumable within some larger theoretical framework). Second, broad empirical propositions usually have greater policy relevance, particularly if they extend into the future. They help us to design effective institutions. Finally, the broader the inference, the greater its falsifiability; the relevant evidence that might be interrogated to establish the truth or falsehood of the inference is multiplied. For all these reasons, hypotheses should be extended as far as is logically justifiable.

Of course, no theory is infinitely extendable. Indeed, the notion of a "universal covering law" is deceptive since even the most far-reaching social-scientific theory has limits. The issue, then, is how to determine the *appropriate* boundaries of a given proposition. An arbitrary scope condition is one that cannot be rationally justified: there is no reason to suppose that the theory might extend to a specified temporal or spatial boundary, but not further – or nearer. A theory of revolution that pertains to the eighteenth, nineteenth, and twentieth centuries, but not to the twenty-first century, must justify this temporal exclusion. It must also justify the decision to lump three quite diverse centuries together in one single population. Similarly, a theory of revolution that pertains to Africa, but not to Asia, must justify this spatial exclusion. And a theory of revolution that pertains to the whole world must justify this spatial inclusion. It is not clear that the phenomenon of revolution is similar in all cultural and geo-political arenas.

Scope conditions may be arbitrarily large, as well as arbitrarily small. The researcher should not "define out," or "define in," temporal or spatial cases that do not fit the prescribed pattern unless she can think of good reasons why this might be so. Populations must not only be specified, but also justified. Upon this justification hinges the plausibility of the theory as well as the identification of a workable research design.

If, after much cogitation, the scope of an inference still seems ambiguous, the writer may adopt the following expedient. Usually, it is possible to specify a limited set of cases which the given proposition *must* cover if it is to make any sense at all – presumably the set of cases that are most-similar to the case(s) under study. At the same time, it is often possible to identify a larger population of cases that *may* be included in the circumference of the inference, though their inclusion is more speculative – presumably, because they share fewer character-istics with the case(s) under study. If the researcher distinguishes carefully between these two populations, readers will have a clear idea of the *manifest* scope, and the *potential* scope, of a given inference.

10.4   Assessing external validity

Claiming external validity is one thing; assessing it is another. The preferred approach to generalizing a hypothesis is to test it systematically across a large sample that is representative of a larger population. Case studies, however, are limited (by definition) to a small number of cases.

Nonetheless, there are several ways in which a study may establish its relevance for a larger population. This includes (a) subsequent replications of that study across other cases, (b) meta-analyses incorporating multiple case studies conducted in different settings, and (c) multimethod research.

One vision of how case studies can generalize to a broader population places the onus on a developing body of research. Rather than demanding external validity from each case study – a claim that will always be dubious – claims to generalizability may be tested, over time, as successive case studies of a subject cumulate. Jack Goldstone (2003: 43) contrasts case study cumulation with the large-C approach to generalization.

Let us say that explorers are surveying a large territory. If they took the large-N [large-C] statistical approach to developing knowledge of that territory, they would have to sample enough locations to provide reliable inferences regarding the territory as a whole. If the territory is fairly homogenous (or if its main characteristics are distributed in a statistically normal distribution across the territory), such sampling would produce a fairly quick, accurate, and reliable method of determining that territory's main characteristics. If, however, the territory has substantial local variations, and if the explorers are as interested in those variations as in any general characteristics, sampling will be useless. Moreover, as is commonly the case, if the territory has six or seven distinctive zones, then sampling may just produce confusing or inconclusive results, leading observers to imagine a fictitious "average" character that actually obtains nowhere.

By contrast, if the explorers spread out, and each surveys and seeks to understand the character of a different zone, they can put together a map of the entire territory with far greater accuracy than an overall sample would provide. Of course, it takes time, and none of the explorers by themselves would be able to make reliable inferences that extended beyond the zone that they had studied; but together, assembling their distinct maps, they cumulate genuine knowledge of the territory. Indeed, by comparing notes, they may find deep regularities, or relationships among or across different zones, that no statistical averages for the entire territory would reveal.

In Goldstone's view (see also Tilly 1984), case study researchers are explorers, each of whom provides in-depth knowledge about some portion of the world, current and past. In effect, case studies replicate, and in replicating they may cumulate to provide a more comprehensive vision of reality.

In a similar spirit, some writers have advocated the use of *meta-analysis* to aggregate results from case studies (Hoon 2013; Jensen and Rodgers 2001; Larsson 1993; Lucas 1974). Here, individual cases from diverse studies are pooled in a single dataset, with various weightings and restrictions, to provide a population-level estimate (Lipsey and Wilson 2001).

The tricky part is that in order to synthesize results from a range of studies, the studies must be similar enough to compare directly with each other. Unfortunately, social scientists tend to produce work that is highly idiosyncratic – in theory and/or operationalization. Even when the research design is large-*C* (either with observational or experimental designs), results do not easily cumulate (Briggs 2005; Gerring 2012b: Petitti 1993; Wachter 1988).

Case studies are especially resistant. To begin with, inputs and outputs tend to be highly contextual and thus do not travel easily across contexts. "Corruption" might mean something quite different in Uruguay and Uzbekistan, for example.

More importantly, case study researchers are supreme individualists, and their research often exhibits idiosyncratic features that are resistant to cumulation. George and McKeown (1985: 41–2) note,

one reason so many case studies in the past contributed unevenly and meagerly to theory development is that they lacked a clearly defined and common focus. Different investigators doing research on a phenomenon tended to bring diverse theoretical (and non-theoretical) interests to bear in their case studies. However interesting and well done in and of itself, each case study tended to pursue rather idiosyncratic research problems and to investigate a set of dependent and independent variables that often were correspondingly idiosyncratic. Moreover, many of these case studies lacked a clear focus, because the investigator was not guided by a well-defined theoretical objective and was drawn instead in directions dictated by the most readily available historical materials or by aspects of the case that were judged interesting on intuitive grounds. It is not surprising, therefore, that later researchers who did have a well-defined theoretical interest in certain historical cases found that earlier case studies often were of little value for their own purposes and had to be redone.

Problems of idiosyncrasy might be overcome (at least to the extent that it can ever be overcome) by mandating greater standardization of concepts and procedures. This is the goal of "structured, focused comparison," as articulated by Alex George and his collaborators (George 1979; George and Bennett 2005; George and McKeown 1985). However, this method is intended to embrace only the several cases in a case study. It is not clear, in other words, how one structured, focused comparison would fit together with a second structured, focused comparison, even if they were ostensibly focused on the same subject. The same problems of incommensurability to arise.

A final problem is sample representativeness. Assuming a sample of case studies could be assembled on a topic, one can anticipate that the sample would be radically unrepresentative, given that none of the cases was chosen in a random fashion, and many would share the same biases.

Perhaps there are settings such as public health, consumer behavior, and environmental change where case study meta-analyses can be successfully implemented.[8] And we can imagine other instances where some form of meta-analysis might make sense. For example, case studies of democratization might be subjected to a meta-analysis if the outcome (democratization) is defined in similar ways and the causal factors of interest are common across the studies. In doing so, non-representative elements of the resulting sample would need to be corrected (e.g., by weighting).

However, efforts to combine case studies are unlikely to be fruitful in most fields, for the reasons we have identified. The larger problem

---

[8] See Jensen and Rodgers (2001), Lucas (1974), Matarazzo and Nijkamp (1997), Paterson et al. (2001), Stall-Meadows and Hyle (2010), Rudel (2008).

is that the goal of case study research is often to discover new things rather than to confirm or disconfirm old things. As such, one is more or less obliged to *resist* efforts at standardization in the choice of research question and research design. And this, in turn, impedes cumulation.

A final approach to generalizability involves jettisoning the case study framework for a large-C framework that is amenable to random sampling or the inclusion of the entire population of theoretical interest (a census). This may be accomplished in a single study (multimethod research) or in successive studies (i.e., where a small-C study is followed by a large-C study, which may or may not be carried out by the same author). This, in my view, is the surest approach to the achievement of generalizability. It also serves as a segue to the concluding section of the book, where I argue that case studies, by themselves, should not be expected to satisfy all the methodological criteria of social science.

10.5   Summary

This chapter has taken up what many regard as the hardest challenge for case study research, demonstrating its relevance for a larger population of cases. External validity is difficult because of the extremely small sample of cases under study (perhaps limited to one) and the correspondingly large population of cases that is of theoretical interest. No method of case selection can overcome this problem of representativeness given the significant threat posed by stochastic error, as discussed in the first section of the chapter. To say that the external validity of case study research is tenuous, however, is not to say that case study research is irrelevant for larger theoretical concerns.

Next, we discussed the dual nature of case studies, which are concerned with a larger theoretical question but also with explaining the case under intensive investigation. This involves the researcher in a complex, two-level game – trying to please generalists (those who are interested in the larger population) as well as specialists (those who are interested in the case under study). While these might seem opposed, they are actually closely intertwined. One cannot attain internal validity without a close examination of the particulars of a case, and without establishing internal validity the question of external validity is more or less moot. Consequently, I argued that case study researchers must be concerned with various aspects of causality – causes-in-fact as well as counterfactual causes and causes-of-effects as well as effects-of-causes.

In reaching for external validity, case study researchers must wrestle with how to establish scope conditions for their argument. If there are several arguments, the researcher must clarify whether each applies to the same population, or to different populations. Characteristically, researchers are loath to claim more than they know. This is regarded as a "conservative" (i.e., judicious) bias. However, such a bias impairs the development of theory, not to mention the falsifiability of theories. If the reach of a theory extends only slightly beyond the case(s) under study, then it has very little chance of being proven wrong, and cannot be connected with research on similar topics conducted in other settings. Researchers must aim for a Goldilocks solution – a set of scope conditions that are neither too narrow nor too broad.

The final issue addressed in this chapter is how these claims to external validity might be assessed. One might, for example, depend upon later replications across other cases deemed to be part of the population. One might also conduct formal meta-analyses of case studies that are focused on the same hypothesis. Unfortunately, both of these potential solutions are vitiated by the lack of standardization that tends to characterize case study research. This, in turn, is a product of the case study's orientation toward developing new theories, rather than testing extant theories. Thus, I conclude that the best avenue toward assessing claims to external validity is the incorporation of large-C research in tandem with case study research, a *multimethod* approach.

Part V

Conclusions

11   Tradeoffs

Some of the methodological weaknesses of case study research reviewed in previous chapters are remediable. For example, there is no cost to clarifying arguments and scope conditions so that case study arguments can be more readily generalized across a broader set of cases.

A second class of problems is solvable, but not without sacrificing something of importance. For example, case studies could focus on manipulable causes, conforming to the potential-outcomes model of causal inference. However, doing so would mean eschewing large, diffuse institutional causes – inequality, class alliances, democracy, racism – in favor of smaller, more specific causes, entailing a fundamental shift of theoretical focus.

A third class of problems is inherent in the enterprise. Case studies are more useful for some research settings than for others. Like any method, the case study has its limits, and we should be cautious about employing it unless it really is the best available tool for the job. Also we should not stretch the limits of the method, forcing it to accomplish goals that it is not well designed for.

Throughout this book, I have contrasted small- and large-*C* research. In this final chapter, I will do so in a more systematic fashion, drawing together themes that have been articulated in the previous chapters.

My prosaic, but nonetheless crucial, thesis is that these two styles of research are good at different things. They have varying strengths and weaknesses. These tradeoffs, summarized in Table 11.1, are understood as affinities rather than invariant laws. Exceptions can be found to each one. Even so, these general tendencies are common in case study research and have been reproduced in multiple disciplines and sub-disciplines over the course of many decades.

Table 11.1 Summary of tradeoffs

	Small-C	Large-C
Validity	Internal	External
Research goal	Deep	Broad
Causal insight	Mechanisms	Effects
Population	Heterogeneous	Homogeneous
Variation in X and Y	Rare	Common
Data	Concentrated	Diffuse
Hypothesis	Generating	Testing

It should be stressed that each of these tradeoffs carries a ceteris paribus caveat. Case studies are more useful for generating new hypotheses, *all other things being equal*. The reader must bear in mind that additional factors also rightly influence a writer's choice of research design, and they may lean in the other direction. Ceteris is not always paribus. One should not jump to conclusions about the research design appropriate to a given setting without considering the entire set of criteria, some of which may be more important than others.

My concluding argument, at the end of the chapter, suggests that case studies are best approached in tandem with large-C studies, a solution which – whether achieved in a single (multimethod) study or across multiple studies within a field or sub-field – mitigates many of the problems commonly associated with the case study method. Tradeoffs can become synergies if small- and large-C approaches are combined.

11.1   Validity: internal versus external

The only way to overcome stochastic threats when inferring from a sample to a population is with a large sample obtained through random sampling. This is impossible in a research design focused on one or several cases. Even with a medium-sized sample, as advocated by Fearon and Laitin (see Chapter 6), stochastic threats to inference are considerable.

For this reason, external validity is never going to be the case study's strong suit, even if other problems of generalizability (reviewed in Chapter 10) are resolved. Case studies share this methodological feature with experimental and quasi-experimental research designs, where there are usually large samples but where cases are rarely chosen randomly from a known population.

By contrast, large-C observational research is more often able to make strong claims to external validity. That is to say, there is likely to be a large sample, which may be drawn randomly from a population or may even encompass the entire population. I do not wish to overstate the point, for surely one can find many biased samples in the annals of social science research. Nonetheless, when one seeks to generalize across large populations, one is apt to invoke large-C observational studies. This is their strong suit. The affinity to external validity seems clear.

11.2 Research goal: depth versus breadth

There is a persistent tradeoff between *depth* and *breadth* in social science. Researchers may choose to gather a broad range of information about a narrow range of cases or a narrow range of information about a broad range of cases. In a matrix format, this may be understood as a tradeoff between the number of variables (K) and the number of observations (N). Colloquially, one may either know a lot about a little or a little about a lot. Small-C studies prioritize the former while large-C studies prioritize the latter.

While the virtues of breadth are often extolled in social science texts, it may be worth pondering on the virtues of depth. One of the primary features of the case study method is the detail, richness, fullness, or completeness (there are many ways of expressing this idea) that is accounted for by an explanation. By contrast, "reductionist" large-C analysis often has little to say about individual cases. A study may aim only to explain the occurrence/non-occurrence of a revolution, while a case study would also strive to explain specific features of that event – why it occurred when it did and in the way that it did. Case studies are thus rightly identified with "holistic" analysis and with a "thick" description of events.[1] Narratives work handily in a case study format, while they strain the conventions of large-C analysis.

Arguments about the "contextual sensitivity" of case studies are perhaps more fairly understood as arguments about depth. The case study researcher who feels that large-C research on a topic is insensitive to context is not arguing that *nothing at all* is consistent across the chosen cases. Rather, the case study researcher's complaint is that much more could be said about the phenomenon in question with a reduction in inferential scope.[2]

Whether to strive for breadth or depth is not a question that can be answered in any definitive way. It is said that some researchers would prefer to explain 90% of the variance in a single case while others would rather explain 10% of the variance across 100 cases. There are lumpers (generalizers) and splitters (particularizers). Economists, political scientists, and sociologists are often more interested in generalizing than in particularizing, while anthropologists and historians are usually more interested in explaining particular contexts. But the cleavage does not always conform neatly to disciplinary lines. All we can safely conclude is that researchers face a choice. The case study method may be defended, as well as criticized, along these lines (Ragin 2000: 22).

---

[1] I am using the term "thick" in a somewhat different way than in Geertz (1973).
[2] Ragin (1987: Chapter 2). Herbert Blumer's (1969: Chapter 7) complaints, however, are more far-reaching.

11.3   Causal insight: mechanisms versus effects

Research on causal inference focuses primarily on the causal effect, $X \rightarrow Y$. For this purpose, large-C designs are generally optimal, and case studies generally sub-optimal. Indeed, case studies do not usually try to estimate a precise causal effect; instead, they attempt to ascertain whether X is a cause of Y and, if so, whether the effect is positive or negative. Thus, case studies are not as ambitious as large-C studies when it comes to evaluating causal effects.

But causal effects are not the only piece of information relevant to causal inference. Nowadays, the central role of causal mechanisms is also widely appreciated (Gerring 2007c). X must be connected to Y in a plausible fashion; otherwise, it is unclear whether a pattern of covariation is truly causal in nature. Without a clear understanding of the causal pathway at work, in a causal relationship it is impossible to interpret the results or to establish scope conditions.

It has become a common criticism of large-C research – e.g., into the causes of growth, democracy, civil war, and other macro-level outcomes – that such studies demonstrate correlations between inputs and outputs without clarifying the reasons for those correlations. We learn, for example, that infant mortality is strongly correlated with state failure (Goldstone *et al.* 2000); but it is quite another matter to interpret this finding, which is consistent with a number of different causal mechanisms. Sudden increases in infant mortality might be the product of famine, of social unrest, of new disease vectors, of government repression, and of countless other factors, some of which might be expected to impact the stability of states, and others which are more likely to be a result of state instability. Research on these topics reveals, in the words of one author, that large-C cross-national studies are "often right for the wrong reasons yet also wrong for the wrong reasons" (Sambanis 2004: 260; see also Dessler 1991; King 2004; Ward and Bakke 2005).

Case studies, if well constructed, may allow one to peer into the box of causality to the intermediate factors lying between some structural cause and its purported effect. Ideally, they allow one to "see" X and Y interact – Hume's billiard ball crossing the table and hitting a second ball.[3] Barney Glaser and Anselm Strauss (1967: 40) point out that in fieldwork "general relations are often discovered *in vivo*; that is, the field worker literally sees them occur." When studying decisional behavior, case study research may offer insight into the intentions, the reasoning capabilities, and the information-processing procedures of the actors involved in a given setting.

Bear in mind that explaining any social action usually (always?) involves understanding the perceptions of the actors who participated in that action. In many settings, actor-centered meanings are more or less self-evident. When people behave in apparently self-interested ways, the researcher may not feel compelled to investigate the intentions of the actors.[4] Buying low and selling high is intentional behavior, but it probably does not require detailed ethnographic research in situations where we know (or can intuit) what is going on. On the other hand, if one is interested in why markets work differently in different cultural contexts, or why persons in some cultures give away their accumulated goods, or why in some other circumstances people do *not* buy low and sell high (when it would appear to be their interest to do so), one is obliged to move beyond readily apprehensible ("obvious") motivations such as self-interest (Geertz 1978). Indeed, the concept of self-interest is,

---

[3] This has something to do with the existence of process-tracing evidence, a matter discussed below. But it is not necessarily predicated on this sort of evidence. Sensitive time-series data, another specialty of the case study, are also relevant to the question of causal mechanisms.

[4] To be sure, self-interested behavior (beyond the level of self-preservation) is also, on some level, socially constructed. Yet, if we are interested in understanding the role of pocket-book voting on election outcomes, there is little to be gained by investigating the origins of money as a motivating force in human behavior. Some things we can afford to take for granted. For useful discussion, see Abrami and Woodruff (2004).

to a significant degree, culturally conditioned. In these situations – encompassing many, if not most, of the events that social scientists have interested themselves in – careful attention to meaning, as understood by the actors themselves, is essential (Davidson 1963; Ferejohn 2004; Stoker 2003; Rabinow and Sullivan 1979; Taylor 1970; Weber 1968: 8). Howard Becker (1970: 64, quoted in Hamel 1993: 17) explains,

To understand an individual's behaviour, we must know how he perceives the situation, the obstacles he believed he had to face, the alternatives he saw opening up to him. We cannot understand the effects of the range of possibilities, delinquent subcultures, social norms and other explanations of behaviour which are commonly invoked, unless we consider them from the actor's point of view.

Because the case study format is focused and intensive, it facilitates the interpretivist's quest, to understand social action from the perspective of the actors themselves. Many types of evidence may be brought to bear on this question – e.g., archival, ethnographic, interview. An example of the latter is provided by Dennis Chong, who uses in-depth interviews with a very small sample of respondents in order to better understand the process by which people reach decisions about civil liberties issues. Chong (1993: 868) comments:

One of the advantages of the in-depth interview over the mass survey is that it records more fully how subjects arrive at their opinions. While we cannot actually observe the underlying mental process that gives rise to their responses, we can witness many of its outward manifestations. The way subjects ramble, hesitate, stumble, and meander as they formulate their answers tips us off to how they are thinking and reasoning through political issues.[5]

This sort of evidence would be very difficult to calibrate in a large-C format.

---

[5] For other examples of in-depth interviewing and ethnography, see Duneier (1999), Hochschild (1981), Lane (1962).

Case-based investigations of causal mechanisms occasionally call into question a general theoretical argument. Deterrence theory, as it was understood in the 1980s, presumed a number of key assumptions, namely that "actors have exogenously given preferences and choice options, and they seek to optimize preferences in light of other actors' preferences and options ... [that] variation in outcomes is to be explained by differences in actors' opportunities ... and [that] the state acts as if it were a unitary rational actor" (Achen and Snidal 1989: 150). A generation of case studies, however, suggested that, somewhat contrary to theory (a) international actors often employ "shortcuts" in their decision-making processes (i.e., they do not make decisions de novo, based purely on an analysis of preferences and possible consequences); (b) a strong cognitive bias exists because of "historical analogies to recent important cases that the person or his country has experienced firsthand" (e.g., "Somalia = Vietnam"); (c) "accidents and confusion" are often manifest in international crises; (d) a single important value or goal often trumps other values (in a hasty and ill-considered manner); and (e) actors' impressions of other actors are strongly influenced by their self-perceptions (information is highly imperfect). In addition to these cognitive biases, there are a series of psychological biases (Jervis 1989: 196-; see also George and Smoke 1974). In sum, while the theory of deterrence may still hold, the causal pathways of this theory seem to be considerably more variegated than previous work based on large-C research had led us to believe. In-depth studies of particular international incidents were helpful in uncovering these complexities.[6]

Dietrich Rueschemeyer and John Stephens (1997: 62) offer a second example of how an examination of causal mechanisms may call into question a general theory based on large-C evidence. The thesis of interest concerns the role of British colonialism in fostering democracy among post-colonial regimes. In particular, the authors

---

[6] George and Smoke (1974: 504). For another example of case study work that tests theories based upon predictions about causal mechanisms, see McKeown (1983).

investigate the diffusion hypothesis, that democracy was enhanced by "the transfer of British governmental and representative institutions and the tutoring of the colonial people in the ways of British government." On the basis of in-depth analysis of several cases, the authors report:

We did find evidence of this diffusion effect in the British settler colonies of North America and the Antipodes; but in the West Indies, the historical record points to a different connection between British rule and democracy. There the British colonial administration opposed suffrage extension, and only the white elites were "tutored" in the representative institutions. But, critically, we argued on the basis of the contrast with Central America, British colonialism did prevent the local plantation elites from controlling the local state and responding to the labor rebellion of the 1930s with massive repression. Against the adamant opposition of that elite, the British colonial rules responded with concessions which allowed for the growth of the party-union complexes rooted in the black middle and working classes, which formed the backbone of the later movement for democracy and independence. Thus, the narrative histories of these cases indicate that the robust statistical relation between British colonialism and democracy is produced only in part by diffusion. The interaction of class forces, state power, and colonial policy must be brought in to fully account for the statistical result.

Whether or not Rueschemeyer and Stephens are correct in their conclusions need not concern us here. What is critical, however, is that any attempt to deal with this question of causal mechanisms is heavily reliant on evidence drawn from case studies. In this instance, as in many others, the question of causal pathways is simply too difficult, requiring too many poorly measured or unmeasurable variables, to allow for accurate cross-sectional analysis.[7]

---

[7] A third example of case study analysis focused on causal mechanisms concerns policy delegation within coalition governments. Michael Thies (2001) tests two theories about how parties delegate power. The first, known as *ministerial government*, supposes that parties delegate ministerial portfolios in their entirety to one of their members (the party whose minister holds the portfolio). The second theory, dubbed *managed delegation*, supposes that members of a multiparty coalition delegate power,

To be sure, causal mechanisms do not always require explicit
attention. They may be quite obvious. And in other circumstances,
they may be amenable to large-C investigation. For example, a sizeable
literature addresses the causal relationship between trade openness
and the welfare state. The usual empirical finding is that economies
that are more open are associated with higher social welfare spending.
The question then becomes why such a robust correlation exists.
What are the plausible interconnections between trade openness and
social welfare spending? One possible causal path, suggested by David
Cameron (1978), is that increased trade openness leads to greater
domestic economic vulnerability to external shocks (due, for instance,
to changing terms of trade). If so, one should find a robust correlation
between annual variations in a country's terms of trade (a measure of
economic vulnerability) and social welfare spending. As it happens,
the correlation is not robust, and this leads some commentators to
doubt whether the putative causal mechanism proposed by David
Cameron and many others is actually at work (Alesina *et al.* 2001).
Thus, in instances where an intervening variable can be effectively
operationalized across a large sample of cases, it may be possible to
test causal mechanisms without resorting to case study investigation.[8]

---

but also actively monitor the activity of ministerial posts held by other parties. The
critical piece of evidence used to test these rival theories is the appointment of junior
ministers (JMs). If JMs are from the same party as the minister, we can assume that
the ministerial government model is in operation. If the JMs are from different
parties, Thies infers that a managed delegation model is in operation where the JM is
assumed to perform an oversight function over the activity of the bureau in question.
This empirical question is explored across four countries – Germany, Italy, Japan,
and the Netherlands – providing a series of case studies focused on the internal
workings of parliamentary government. (I have simplified the nature of the evidence
in this example, which extends not only to the simple presence or absence of cross-
partisan JMs, but also to a variety of additional process-tracing clues.) Other good
examples of within-case research that shed light on a broader theory can be found in
Canon (1999), Martin (1992), Martin and Swank (2004), Young (1999).

[8] For additional examples of this nature, see Feng (2003), Papyrakis and Gerlagh
(2003), Ross (2001).

Even so, the opportunities for investigating causal pathways are generally more apparent in a case study format. Consider the contrast between formulating a standardized survey for a large group of respondents and an in-depth interview with a single subject or a small set of subjects, such as is undertaken by Dennis Chong in a previous example. In the latter situation, the researcher can probe into details that would be impossible to delve into, let alone anticipate, in a standardized survey. S/he may also be in a better position to make judgments as to the veracity and reliability of the respondent. Tracing causal mechanisms is about cultivating sensitivity to a local context. Often, these local contexts are essential to large-C testing. Yet, the same factors that render case studies useful for micro-level investigation also make them less useful for measuring mean (average) causal effects. It is a classic tradeoff.

Moreover, the tradeoff has important consequences for perceptions of viability across small- and large-C designs. Note that causal effects are generally easier to ascertain than causal mechanisms (Gerring 2010; Imai *et al.* 2011). Since case studies often focus on mechanisms, this elective affinity may serve to reinforce the general impression that small-C studies are inferior to large-C studies when it comes to causal inference. The missing element in this discussion is that the difficulties posed by causal mechanisms are often best handled in a case study format – even if the result must be regarded as provisional. It is a hard job but an essential one, and much easier when attention is focused on a single case or a small number of cases.

11.4   Population: heterogeneous versus homogeneous

The logic of large-C analysis is premised on some degree of cross-unit comparability (unit homogeneity). Cases must be similar to each other in whatever respects might affect the causal relationship that the writer is investigating, or such differences must be controlled for.

Uncontrolled heterogeneity means that cases are "apples and oranges"; one cannot learn anything about underlying causal processes by comparing their histories. The underlying factors of interest mean different things in different contexts (conceptual stretching) or the $X \rightarrow Y$ relationship of interest is different in different contexts (unit heterogeneity).

Case study researchers are often suspicious of large-sample research, which, they suspect, contains heterogeneous cases whose differences cannot easily be modeled. "Variable-oriented" research is said to involve unrealistic "homogenizing assumptions."[9] In the field of international relations, it is common to classify cases according to whether they are deterrence failures or deterrence successes. However, Alexander George and Richard Smoke (1974: 514) point out that "the separation of the dependent variable into only two sub-classes, deterrence success and deterrence failure," neglects the great variety of ways in which deterrence can fail. Deterrence, in their view, has many independent causal paths (causal equifinality), and these paths may be obscured when a study lumps heterogeneous cases into the same sample.

Another example, drawn from clinical work in psychology, concerns heterogeneity among a sample of individuals. Michel Hersen and David Barlow (1976: 11) explain:

Descriptions of results from 50 cases provide a more convincing demonstration of the effectiveness of a given technique than separate descriptions of 50 individual cases. The major difficulty with this approach, however, is that the category in which these clients are classified most always becomes unmanageably heterogeneous. "Neurotics," [for example] … may have less in common than any group of people one would choose randomly. When cases are described individually, however, a clinician stands a better chance of gleaning some important information, since specific problems and specific

---

[9] Ragin (2000: 35). See also Abbott (1990), Bendix (1963), Meehl (1954), Przeworski and Teune (1970: 8–9), Ragin (1987; 2004: 124), Znaniecki (1934: 250–1).

procedures are usually described in more detail. When one lumps cases together in broadly defined categories, individual case descriptions are lost and the ensuing report of percentage success becomes meaningless.

One important aspect of heterogeneity across cases is generated by interaction effects. Although each case within a population may possess the same causal factors, these factors may not operate independently. Insofar as they interact with each other, they produce unique outcomes that are difficult to understand unless one has an holistic understanding of the case (Anderson *et al.* 2005). Consider ten binary causal factors, X_{1-10}. If these factors operate on Y independently of each other, they can be readily studied in a large-C setting. But if they interact with one another, there are 2^{10} (1,024) possible combinations. It would require an extremely large population – and a fairly even distribution of data across the possible cells – to test these many possibilities. By contrast, a single case, intensively studied, may allow one to gauge the impact of various factors on each other, solving the problem of causal complexity. (I certainly do not mean to suggest that it will always solve this problem, merely that in some circumstances – given sufficient within-case evidence – it may do so.)

Of course, the researcher's theoretical interests may be more focused, e.g., on a single causal factor. Even so, interactions pose a threat to inference. If appropriately matched cases do not exist in the larger population – or if there are only a very few of them – a large-C approach to inference is not very robust (Brady and Collier 2004; Glynn and Ichino 2016).

As a final example, consider the following two questions: (1) Why do social movements happen?, and (2) Why did the American civil rights movement happen? The first question is general, but its potential cases are extremely heterogeneous. Indeed, it is not even clear how one would construct a universe of comparable cases. The second question is narrow, but – I think – answerable. I hasten to add that quite a number of factors may provide plausible explanations for the American civil rights movement and the methodological grounds for distinguishing good from bad answers is not entirely clear. Even so, I find work on this topic more convincing than large-C work that attempts to encompass all social movements.[10]

Under circumstances of extreme case-heterogeneity, the researcher may decide that she is better off focusing on a single case or a small number of relatively homogeneous cases. Within-case evidence, or cross-case evidence drawn from a handful of most-similar cases, may be more useful than large-C evidence, even though the ultimate interest of the investigator is in a broader population of cases. Suppose one has a population of very heterogeneous cases, one or two of which undergo quasi-experimental transformations. Probably, one gains greater insight into causal patterns throughout the population by examining these cases in detail than by some large-C analysis.

By the same token, if the cases available for study are relatively homogeneous, then the methodological argument for large-C analysis is correspondingly strong. The inclusion of additional cases is unlikely to compromise the results of the investigation because these additional cases are sufficiently similar to provide useful information.

The issue of population heterogeneity/homogeneity may be understood, therefore, as a tradeoff between N (observations) and K (variables). If, in the quest to explain a particular phenomenon, each potential case offers only one observation and also requires one control variable (to neutralize heterogeneities in the resulting sample), the available degrees of freedom remain the same even while the sample expands. In this setting, there is no point in extending a two-case study to include additional cases. If, on the other hand, each additional case is relatively cheap – if no additional control variables are needed (following the regression model) or if the additional case offers more than one useful observation (through time) – then a cross-case research

---

[10] Contrast McAdam (1988) with McAdam, Tarrow and Tilly (2001). On this general point, see Davidson (1963).

design may be warranted (Shalev 1998). To put the matter more simply, when adjacent cases are unit-homogeneous, the addition of more cases is easy, for there is no (or very little) heterogeneity to worry about. When adjacent cases are heterogeneous, additional cases are expensive, for every added heterogeneous element must be correctly modeled, and each modeling adjustment requires a separate (and probably unverifiable) assumption – or, one must regard all heterogeneity as noise and pray that there are no systematic errors. The more background assumptions are required in order to make a causal inference, the more tenuous that inference is; it is not simply a question of attaining statistical significance. The ceteris paribus assumption at the core of all causal analysis is brought into play.

Before concluding this discussion, it is important to point out that researchers' judgments about case comparability are not, strictly speaking, matters that can be empirically verified. To be sure, one can look – and ought to look – for empirical patterns among potential cases. If those patterns are strong, then the assumption of case comparability seems reasonably secure, and if they are not, then there are grounds for doubt. However, debates about case comparability usually concern borderline instances. Consider that many phenomena of interest to social scientists are not rigidly bounded. If one is studying democracies, there is always the question of how to define a democracy, and therefore how high or low the threshold for inclusion in the sample should be. Researchers have different ideas about this, and these ideas can hardly be tested in a rigorous fashion. Similarly, there are longstanding disputes about whether it makes sense to lump poor and rich societies together in a single sample, or whether these constitute distinct populations. Again, the borderline between poor and rich (or "developed" and "undeveloped") is blurry, and the notion of hiving off one from the other for separate analysis is equally questionable, and equally unresolvable on purely empirical grounds. There is no safe (or "conservative") way to proceed. A final sticking point concerns the cultural/historical component of social phenomena. Many case study researchers feel that to compare societies with vastly different cultures and historical trajectories is meaningless. Yet, many large-*C* researchers feel that to restrict one's analytic focus to a single cultural or geographic region is highly arbitrary, and equally meaningless. In these situations, it is evidently the choice of the researcher how to understand case homogeneity/heterogeneity across the potential populations of an inference. Where do like cases end and un-like cases begin?

Because this issue is not, strictly speaking, empirical, it may be referred to as an *ontological* element of research design. An ontology is a vision of the world as it really is, a more or less coherent set of assumptions about how the world works, a research *Weltanschauung* analogous to a Kuhnian paradigm (Gutting 1980; Hall 2003; Kuhn 1962/1970; Wolin 1968). While it seems odd to bring ontological issues into a discussion of social science methodology, it may be granted that social science research is not a purely empirical endeavor. What one finds is contingent upon what one looks for, and what one looks for is to some extent contingent upon what one expects to find. Stereotypically, case study researchers tend to have a "lumpy" vision of the world; they see cases – e.g., countries, communities, and persons – as highly individualized phenomena. Cross-case researchers, by contrast, have a less differentiated vision of the world; they are more likely to believe that things are pretty much the same everywhere, at least as respects basic causal processes. These basic assumptions, or ontologies, drive many of the choices that these two sorts of researchers make when scoping out appropriate ground for research.

11.5   Variation in *X* and *Y*: rare versus common

When analyzing causal relationships, we must be concerned with the distribution of evidence across available cases. Specifically, we must be concerned with the distribution of *useful variation* – understood here as any sort of variation (temporal or spatial) in relevant parameters that might yield clues about a causal relationship. Where useful variation is rare – i.e., limited to a few cases – the case study format recommends itself. Where, on the other hand, useful variation is common, a large-*C* method of analysis may be more defensible.

Consider a phenomenon like revolution, an outcome that occurs very rarely. The empirical distribution on this variable, if we count each country-year as an observation, consists of thousands of non-revolutions (0) and just a few revolutions (1). Intuitively, it seems clear that these "revolutionary" cases are of great interest. We need to know as much as possible about them, for they exemplify all the variation that we have, temporally and spatially. In this circumstance, a case study mode of analysis is difficult to avoid, though it might be combined with a large-*C* analysis. As it happens, many outcomes of interest to social scientists are quite rare, so the issue is by no means trivial.[11]

By way of contrast, consider a phenomenon like turnover, understood as a situation where a ruling party or coalition is voted out of office. Turnover occurs within most democratic countries on a regular basis, so the distribution of observations on this variable (incumbency/turnover) is relatively even across the universe of country-years. There are lots of instances of both outcomes. Under these circumstances, a large-*C* research design seems plausible, for the variation across cases is regularly distributed.

Note that if the researcher is investigating a causal relationship (involving both *X* and *Y*), rather than an open-ended investigation of

---

[11] Consider the following topics and their – extremely rare – instances of variation: early industrialization (England, the Netherlands), fascism (Germany, Italy), the use of nuclear weapons (United States), world wars (WWI, WWII), single non-transferable vote electoral systems (Jordan, Taiwan, Vanuatu, pre-reform Japan), electoral system reforms within established democracies (France, Italy, Japan, New Zealand, Thailand). The problem of "rareness" is less common where parameters are scalar, rather than dichotomous. But there are still plenty of examples of phenomena whose distributions are skewed by a few outliers, e.g., population (China, India), personal wealth (Bill Gates, Warren Buffett), ethnic heterogeneity (Papua New Guinea).

a particular parameter (X or Y), then the relevant question is how the cases in a population vary across *all* parameters that might affect the outcome or a factor of particular interest. Here, we are interested in the degree to which a particular causal model is dominated by a few cases, understood as *influential* cases (Chapter 5). The intuition is that any case which affects the performance of a key independent variable or the entire causal model should be investigated in a more intensive fashion. If there are no such cases, then a large-C form of analysis may be sufficient.

Another sort of variation concerns that which might occur *within* a given case. Suppose that only one or two cases within a large population exhibit quasi-experimental qualities, the factor of special interest (X) varies, and there is no corresponding change in other factors that might affect the outcome (Z). Clearly, we are likely to learn a great deal from studying this particular case – perhaps a lot more than we might learn from studying hundreds of additional cases that deviate from the experimental ideal. But again, if many cases have this experimental quality, there is little point in restricting ourselves to a single example; a large-C research design may be justified.

The general point here is that the distribution of useful variation across a population of cases matters a great deal in the choice between small- and large-C research designs. (Many of the issues discussed in Chapters 5 and 6 are relevant to this discussion of what constitutes "useful variation." Thus, I have touched upon these issues only briefly in this section.) Indeed, this may be the most important factor militating towards one or the other research design.

11.6   Data: concentrated versus diffuse

Information is not free. Someone must define relevant concepts, gather data, collate them, and assure equivalence across units. Gathering data

across cases (especially if they are heterogeneous) is especially complicated, and often fraught. For a variety of reasons, evidence gathered
for a single case is often easier – easier to collect and to relate within a
common framework – than evidence gathered across cases. Within-
case evidence is often "cheaper" than cross-case evidence.

Likewise, the appeal of small- and large-C studies depends upon the
data that are at hand, or could be easily gathered. Sometimes, information about a topic is lumpy; it exists for a few cases, but not for others.
For example, across nation-states one generally finds that information
for a handful of Western European or European-offshoot societies is
plentiful, while information for the rest of the world is scarce.

Alternatively, information may be distributed evenly across many
cases, but its quality may be highly uneven. Large-C studies often suffer
from bad data. For this sort of situation, the old adage – garbage in,
garbage out – applies. No useful conclusions will result from an analysis
based on dubious ground-level data. Moreover, it will be difficult to
rectify this problem if one's cases number in the hundreds or thousands. One can spot-check the data for errors and thereby gain an
understanding of their reliability; but one cannot correct the data
without engaging in an in-depth study of every case in the dataset.
There are simply too many data points to allow for this.

A final possibility is that relevant information exists nowhere and has
to be collected by the researcher, de novo. This would be true for topics
that are new, under-explored, or where data collection has not been
carried out in a systematic, coordinated fashion.

These common situations militate toward a case study format. Here,
the researcher has an opportunity to collect original data, fact-check,
consult multiple sources, go back to primary materials, and overcome
whatever biases may affect the secondary literature. In their study of
social security spending, Mulligan *et al.* (2002: 13) note that

although our spending and design numbers are of good quality, there are some
missing observations and, even with all the observations, it is difficult to

reduce the variety of elderly subsidies to one or two numbers. For this reason, case studies are an important part of our analysis, since those studies do not require numbers that are comparable across a large number of countries. Our case study analysis utilizes data from a variety of country-specific sources, so we do not have to reduce "social security" or "democracy" to one single number.

The collection of original data is typically more difficult in large-C analysis than in case study analysis, involving greater expense, greater difficulties in identifying and coding cases, learning foreign languages, traveling, gaining access, and so forth. Whatever can be done for a set of cases can usually be done more easily and more reliably for a single case.

Case studies also lend themselves to a style of data collection that would be impossible in a large-C format. Consider the difficulty of studying deviants. Howard Becker (1963: 168) observes,

The student who would discover the facts about deviance has a substantial barrier to climb before he will be allowed to see the things he needs to see. Since deviant activity is activity that is likely to be punished if it comes to light, it tends to be kept hidden and not exhibited or bragged about to outsiders. The student of deviance must convince those he studies that he will not be dangerous to them, that they will not suffer for what they reveal to him. The researcher, therefore, must participate intensively and continuously with the deviants he wants to study so that they will get to know him well enough to be able to make some assessment of whether his activities will adversely affect theirs.

Certain topics require participant-observation, and ethnography is inherently case-based.

However, this point is easily turned on its head. Datasets are now available to study many cases of concern to the social sciences. In an era of "big data," where data are stored on the web or easily compiled from web-based sources, it may not be necessary to collect original information for one's book, article, or dissertation. In this context, in-depth single-case analysis is often more time-consuming than large-C analysis. Note that the case study format imposes hurdles of its own – e.g., travel to distant climes, risk of personal injury, expense, and so forth. It is interesting to note that some observers consider case studies to be "relatively *more* expensive in time and resources" (Stoecker 1991: 91). In these settings, there is no practical advantage to a case study format. Thus, much depends upon the lay of the land, i.e., the availability of evidence on a topic of interest to the researcher.

11.7   Hypothesis: generating versus testing

Of the various contrasts highlighted in Table 11.1, one stands out as especially crucial insofar as it affects virtually every methodological issue touched upon in this book. This concerns the tradeoff between exploration and verification/falsification, or theory generating and theory testing.

Social science research involves a quest for new theories as well as a testing of existing theories; it is comprised of both "conjectures" and "refutations" (Popper 1963). Regrettably, social science methodology has focused almost exclusively on the latter. The conjectural element of social science is usually dismissed as a matter of guesswork, inspiration, or luck – a leap of faith, and hence a poor subject for methodological reflection.[12] Yet, it will readily be granted that many works of social science, including most of the acknowledged classics, are seminal rather than definitive. Their classic status derives from the introduction of a new idea or a new perspective that is subsequently subjected to analysis that is more rigorous. Indeed, it is difficult to devise a program of falsification the first time a new theory is proposed. Pathbreaking research, almost by definition, is protean.

---

[12] Karl Popper (quoted in King, Keohane, and Verba 1994: 14) writes: "there is no such thing as a logical method of having new ideas . . . Discovery contains 'an irrational element,' or a 'creative intuition.'" One recent collection of essays and interviews takes new ideas as its special focus (Munck and Snyder 2006), though it may be doubted whether there are generalizable results.

Subsequent research on that topic tends to be more definitive insofar as its primary task is to verify or falsify a pre-existing hypothesis.

Thus, the world of social science may be usefully divided according to the predominant goal undertaken in a given study, either hypothesis generating (exploratory) or hypothesis testing (confirmatory). There are two moments of empirical research, a lightbulb moment and a skeptical moment, each of which is essential to the progress of a discipline.[13]

Case studies enjoy a natural advantage in research of an exploratory nature. Ignorance is bliss when it comes to case study research. The less we know about a subject, the more valuable a case study of that subject is likely to be.

Several millennia ago, Hippocrates reported what were, arguably, the first case studies ever conducted. They were 14 in number.[14] Darwin's insights into the process of human evolution came after his travels to a few select locations, notably Easter Island. Freud's revolutionary work on human psychology was constructed from a close observation of less than a dozen clinical cases. Piaget formulated his theory of human cognitive development while watching his own two children as they passed from childhood into adulthood. Levi-Strauss's structuralist theory of human cultures was built on the analysis of several North and South American tribes. Douglass North's neoinstitutionalist theory of economic development is constructed largely through a close analysis of a handful of early developing states – primarily England, the Netherlands, and the United States (North and Thomas 1973; North

---

[13] Reichenbach (1938) also distinguished between a "context of discovery" and a "context of justification." Likewise, Peirce's concept of *abduction* recognizes the importance of a generative component in science. For further discussion, see Feyerabend (1975), Hanson (1958), McLaughlin (1982), Nickles (1980), Popper (1965).

[14] Bonoma (1985: 199). Some of the following examples are discussed in Patton (2002: 245).

and Weingast 1989). Many other examples might be cited of seminal ideas that derived from the intensive study of a few key cases.[15]

Arguably, our knowledge of the world arises out of the understanding we have of one or several cases – persons, organizations, groups, or institutions that we know especially well. Insights into general theory arise from insights derived originally from specific cases. Proper nouns precede common nouns.

Evidently, the sheer number of examples of a given phenomenon does not, by itself, produce insight. It may only confuse. How many times did Newton observe apples fall before he recognized the nature of gravity? This is an apocryphal example, but it illustrates a central point: small-C studies may be more useful than large-C studies when a subject is being encountered for the first time or is being considered in a fundamentally new way. After reviewing the case study approach to medical research, one researcher finds that although case reports are commonly regarded as the lowest or weakest form of evidence, they are nonetheless understood to comprise "the first line of evidence." The hallmark of case reporting, according to Jan Vandenbroucke (2001: 331), "is to recognize the unexpected." This is where discovery begins.

Yet, the advantages that case studies offer in work of an exploratory nature may also serve as impediments in work of a confirmatory/disconfirmatory nature. Let us briefly explore why this might be so.[16]

Traditionally, scientific methodology has been defined by a segregation of conjecture (theory formation) and refutation (theory testing). One should not be allowed to contaminate the other.[17] Yet, in the real

---

[15] The tradeoff between discovery and testing is implicit in Achen and Snidal (1989), who criticize the case study for its deficits in the latter genre but also acknowledge the benefits of the case study along the former dimension (167–8). Indeed, most work on case study methods highlights its insight into theory development (e.g., George and Bennett 2005; Glaser and Strauss 1967).

[16] For discussion of this tradeoff in the context of economic growth theory, see Temple (1999: 120).

[17] Geddes (2003), King, Keohane, and Verba (1994), Popper (1934/1968).

world of social science, inspiration is often associated with perspiration. "Lightbulb" moments arise from a close engagement with the particular facts of a particular case. Inspiration is more likely to occur in the laboratory than in the shower.

The circular quality of conjecture and refutation is particularly apparent in case study research. Charles Ragin (1992b) notes that case study research is all about "casing" – defining the topic, including the hypothesis(es) of primary interest, the outcome, and the set of cases that offer relevant information *vis-à-vis* the hypothesis. A study of the French Revolution may be conceptualized as a study of revolution, of social revolution, of revolt, of political violence, and so forth. Each of these topics entails a different population and a different set of causal factors. A good deal of authorial intervention is necessary in the course of defining a case study topic, for there is a great deal of evidentiary leeway. Yet, the "subjectivity" of case study research allows for the generation of a great number of hypotheses, insights that might not be apparent to the large-C researcher who works with a thinner set of empirical data across a large number of cases and with a more determinate (fixed) definition of cases, variables, and outcomes. It is the very fuzziness of case studies that grants them a strong advantage in research at exploratory stages, for the single-case study allows one to test a multitude of hypotheses in a rough-and-ready way. Nor is this an entirely "conjectural" process. The covariational relationships discovered among different elements of a single case have a prima facie causal connection: they are all at the scene of the crime. This is revelatory when one is at an early stage of analysis, for there is no identifiable suspect and the crime itself may be difficult to discern. The fact that A, B, and C are present at the expected times and places (relative to some outcome of interest) is sufficient to establish them as independent variables. Proximal evidence is all that is required. Hence, the common identification of case studies as "plausibility probes," "pilot studies," "heuristic studies," "exploratory," and "theory-building" exercises.[18]

---

[18] Eckstein (1975), Ragin (1992a, 1997), Rueschemeyer and Stephens (1997).

A large-C study, by contrast, generally allows for the testing of only a few hypotheses, but does so with a somewhat greater degree of confidence, as is appropriate to work whose primary purpose is to test an extant theory. There is less room for authorial intervention because evidence gathered from a large-C research design can be interpreted in a limited number of ways. It is in this respect more reliable. One would not wish to overstate the point, as there is plenty of open-ended, exploratory work conducted in a large-C framework, as the accusation of "p hacking" (Head *et al.* 2015) suggests. Even so, there is less wiggle room in a large-C environment simply because there are fewer variables the researcher is at liberty to manipulate.

Another way of stating the point is to say that while case studies lean toward Type 1 errors (falsely rejecting the null hypothesis), large-C studies lean toward Type 2 errors (failing to reject the false null hypothesis). Those who regard the avoidance of Type 1 errors as the linchpin of science will greet this conclusion with alarm. However, Type 2 errors must also be reckoned with. Researchers may falsely accept a null hypothesis, missing a true causal relationship between X and Y. Here, the flexibility of case study research becomes an asset rather than a liability. And, from this angle, case study research may be vigorously defended as a method of exploration. This explains why case studies are more likely to be paradigm generating, while large-C studies toil in the prosaic but highly structured field of normal science.

I do not mean to suggest that case studies never serve to confirm or disconfirm hypotheses. Evidence drawn from a single case may falsify a necessary or sufficient hypothesis, as discussed earlier. Case studies are also often useful for the purpose of elucidating causal mechanisms, and this obviously affects the plausibility of an $X \rightarrow Y$ relationship. However, general theories rarely offer the kind of detailed and determinate predictions on within-case variation that would allow one to reject a hypothesis through pattern-matching (without additional large-C evidence). Theory testing is not the case study's strong suit.

Let us explore this tension in greater detail. Many problems of internal validity in case study research stem from the lack of a clear hypothesis. If one begins with a vague research question, or a poorly specified hypothesis, it will be difficult to identify the best-possible case to explore that question or hypothesis. Ambiguity in theory impedes case selection. This is what drives the changing status of a case as research develops, as discussed in Chapter 2. Likewise, a flaccid theory will impede theory testing – one does not know which causal mechanisms or other patterns in the data are stipulated by the theory; placebo tests are impossible.

At the same time, we must appreciate that if a researcher already has a very definite and detailed theory, there is probably less need for a case study, as large-C studies are more adept at hypothesis testing.

To make this point, let us contrast two settings.

1. A great deal is known about the relationship of X to Y, which is presumed to be causal based on large-C analysis and theoretical exposition.
2. Very little is known about the causes of Y, as large-C analyses have not been conducted (or are inconclusive) and theorizing is indeterminate.

In the first setting, a case study will be easy to design and we can use evidence drawn from the large-C study to select the most appropriate case and thus avoid researcher bias. However, case study research is not likely to add very much to what we already know about this particular research question. If the causal effect is already established, there is little point in using a case study to try to estimate the impact of X on Y. If the mechanism connecting X to Y is unclear, there may be good reasons to employ case study evidence to shed light on this aspect of the research question. This, of course, is generally a harder question to answer.

In the second setting, by contrast, it will be very difficult to design a good case study. There is no (or only very sketchy) large-C evidence at hand and no causal model that one might construct. Perhaps the outcome is not even measurable across cases. In this situation, case study research is just about the only practical avenue of investigation, and it is apt to be quite informative. Informative means that evidence gathered by the case study will allow us to update our priors about the causes of Y. It does not mean that a strong causal inference will be possible. This may or may not be forthcoming.

This, then, is the conundrum. Specifying a theory renders case selection and case analysis more fruitful, but also less informative. The more you know about your topic, the less you probably need to engage in an intensive, focused, and detailed (and *time-consuming*) form of analysis.

This may help to explain why many of the most prominent case studies – as listed in Table 1.2 – are not those with the highest apparent validity. Yet, they tell us things, albeit in a rather vague way, that we did not know. Likewise, those studies with the greatest internal validity are often not the most influential. They confirm things that we already (pretty much) know, or things that – while not trivial – are not exactly earth shaking.

Consider Richard Fenno's (1978: 251) frank discussion of how he began his project on Congressional "homestyles."

Like any other political scientist interested in representative-constituent relations, I had been teaching the received wisdom on the subject. Part of that wisdom tells us that the representative's perception of his or her constituency is an important variable. But, in the absence of much empirical exposition of such perceptions and in the presence of politicians who seemed less than cognizant of all segments of their "constituency," I had been telling students that the subject . . . deserved "further research." Someone, I kept saying, should address the perceptual question: What does a member of Congress see when he or she sees a constituency?

When Fenno (1978: 251) set out to follow members of Congress as they made the rounds among their constituents, conducting impromptu on-the-spot interviews,

I had no idea what kinds of answers I would get. I had no idea what questions to ask. I knew only that I wanted to get some number of House members to talk about their constituency perceptions – up and down and all around the subject ... My hope was that I might be able to piece together their perceptions, categorize them in some way, and generalize about them.

And so he did, producing one of the most influential studies of a much-studied subject (the US Congress). The main argument to arise from this research is contained in the idea of *concentric circles*. Members of Congress care about all their constituents but they do so in different ways and to different degrees, and they relate to them differently. The broadest circle encompasses everyone in the district. The next circle consists of supporters – those who are likely to turn out and vote for the member. The next circle consists of primary supporters – those who carry the burden of campaigning. Finally, the smallest circle consists of the representative's family, friends, and advisors. The sort of treatment a constituent receives, and the weight that is accorded to his or her opinion, depends upon which circle s/he falls into.

If the theory of concentric circles had been fully formulated prior to Fenno's fieldwork, he might have constructed a standardized survey to measure these features in a systematic fashion across a larger and more representative sample. He might also have devised unobtrusive measures (e.g., locations of visits) so that the results of the study were not subject to interviewer bias or respondent bias. (Respondents are not always entirely candid.) In this fashion, his arguments might have been more precise and could have claimed greater internal and external validity. However, Fenno did not know what he was going to find before he found it. Neither do most researchers whose work opens new paths.

The tradeoff between hypothesis generating and hypothesis testing helps us to reconcile the enthusiasm of case study researchers and the skepticism of case study critics. They are both right, for the looseness of case study research is a boon to new conceptualizations just as it is a bane to falsification.

11.8   From Tradeoffs to Synergies

Persistent tradeoffs between small- and large-C research are summarized in Table 11.1. To review, small-C studies prize internal validity while large-C studies prize external validity. Small-C studies prize depth while large-C studies prize breadth. Small-C studies often shed light on causal mechanisms while large-C studies are usually better at measuring causal effects. Small-C studies are useful when the population of interest is extremely heterogeneous while large-C studies are often more useful when the population is relatively homogeneous. Small-C studies are useful when X and Y exhibit variation only in a few cases, while large-C methods apply naturally when there is regular variation in the inputs and outputs of interest. Small-C studies are especially useful when available data are concentrated in a few cases, while large-C studies are useful when data are spread evenly across many cases. Finally, and perhaps most importantly, small-C studies are adept at generating new hypotheses while large-C studies are adept at testing extant hypotheses.[19]

It is not hard to see why these two genres are often perceived as being in conflict with each another, for they have very different sensibilities. Researchers are lumped into one or the other school; journals adopt one or the other profile. Not surprisingly, a degree of skepticism – and, occasionally, outright hostility – has crept into relations between these disparate approaches to the empirical world.

At various points in the narrative I have reminded the reader that this is to some extent a false dichotomy insofar as (a) case studies always integrate some degree of analysis across a broader set of cases, which may be informal (shadow cases) or formal (multimethod research). Likewise, case studies participate in an ongoing research

---

[19] Other evaluations of the strengths and weaknesses of case study research can be found in Flyvbjerg (2006), Levy (2002), Verschuren (2001).

tradition that includes large-C studies. These may be integrated in the introductory literature review, by way of summarizing what we know about a subject prior to considering the more focused evidence at hand. Case studies rarely, if ever, stand on their own.

It follows that the suspicion of case study work that one finds in the social sciences today may be the product of a too-literal interpretation of the case study method. A case study *tout court* is thought to mean a case study *tout seul*.

Yet rarely, if ever, does an author rest a large generalization on a single case or a small set of cases. By way of provocation, I shall insist there is no such thing as a case study existing outside a broader frame of (large-C) knowledge. To conduct a case study implies that one has also conducted large-C analysis or at least thought about a broader set of cases. Otherwise, it is impossible for an author to answer the defining question of all case study research: what is this a case *of*?

Likewise, I shall insist that there is no such thing as a large-C study existing outside knowledge of particular cases. In the social sciences, this is almost inconceivable, as knowledge about many cases is built – logically and logistically – upon knowledge of individual cases.

It follows that there is no situation in which small-C results cannot be synthesized with results gained from large-C analysis, and vice-versa. It follows, further, that small- and large-C studies should be viewed as partners in the iterative task of descriptive and causal investigation. Large-C arguments draw on within-case assumptions (i.e., about causal mechanisms) and within-case arguments draw on large-C assumptions. Neither works very well when isolated from the other.

In most circumstances, it is advisable to conduct both types of analysis. Each is made stronger by the other. Rather than thinking of these methodological options as opponents, we might do better to think of them as complements. This is the virtue of cross-level work, also known as triangulation. Researchers may do both and, arguably, *must* engage both styles of analysis.[20] In this fashion, problems of validity, uncertainty, replicability, and representativeness are generally mitigated.

I do not mean to imply that both styles of research need to be sandwiched into the same study. Sometimes, space considerations, technical demands, or limitations of background knowledge prevent one study from encompassing both approaches. Nonetheless, a multimethod approach to research may be integrated within a research stream, so long as authors are cognizant of each others' work, and mindful of framing their theories and research designs in ways that facilitate cumulation (Lieberman 2016).

---

[20] This distinction is drawn from Ragin (1987; 2004: 124). It is worth noting that Ragin's distinctive method (QCA) is also designed to overcome this traditional dichotomy.

References

Abadie, Alberto, Javier Gardeazabal. 2003. "The Economic Costs of Conflict: A Case Study of the Basque Country." *American Economic Review* 93:1, 113–32.

Abadie, Alberto, Alexis Diamond, Jens Hainmueller. 2015. "Comparative Politics and the Synthetic Control Method." *American Journal of Political Science* 59:2, 495–510.

Abbott, Andrew. 1990. "Conceptions of Time and Events in Social Science Methods: Causal and Narrative Approaches." *Historical Methods* 23:4, 140–50.

1992. "From Causes to Events: Notes on Narrative Positivism." *Sociological Methods and Research* 20:4, 428–55.

2001. *Time Matters: On Theory and Method.* Chicago, IL: University of Chicago Press.

Abell, Peter. 1987. *The Syntax of Social Life: The Theory and Method of Comparative Narratives.* Oxford: Clarendon.

2004. "Narrative Explanation: An Alternative to Variable-Centered Explanation?" *Annual Review of Sociology* 30, 287–310.

Abrami, Regina M., David M. Woodruff. 2004. "Toward a Manifesto: Interpretive Materialist Political Economy." Presented for delivery at the annual meeting of the American Political Science Association, Chicago, IL.

Acemoglu, Daron, James A. Robinson. 2005. *Economic Origins of Dictatorship and Democracy.* Cambridge: Cambridge University Press.

2012. *Why Nations Fail: The Origins of Power, Prosperity, and Poverty.* New York: Crown.

Acemoglu, Daron, Simon Johnson, James A. Robinson. 2003. "An African Success Story: Botswana." In Dani Rodrik (ed.), *In Search of Prosperity: Analytic Narratives on Economic Growth.* Princeton, NJ: Princeton University Press.

Achen, Christopher H., W. Phillips Shively. 1995. *Cross-Level Inference.* Chicago, IL: University of Chicago Press.

Achen, Christopher H., Duncan Snidal. 1989. "Rational Deterrence Theory and Comparative Case Studies." *World Politics* 41, 143–69.

Adamson, Fiona. 2001. "Democratization and the Domestic Sources of Foreign Policy: Turkey in the 1974 Cyprus Crisis." *Political Science Quarterly* 116, 277–303.

Adcock, Robert K. 2008. "The Curious Career of 'the Comparative Method': The Case of Mill's Methods." Presented at the annual meeting of the American Political Science Association, Boston, MA.

Ahmed, Amel, Rudra Sil. 2012. "When Multi-Method Research Subverts Methodological Pluralism – Or, Why We Still Need Single-Method Research." *Perspectives on Politics* 10:4, 935–53.

Alesina, Alberto, Arnaud Devleeschauwer, William Easterly, Sergio Kurlat, Romain Wacziarg. 2003. "Fractionalization." *Journal of Economic Growth* 8:2, 155–94.

Alesina, Alberto, Edward Glaeser, Bruce Sacerdote. 2001. "Why Doesn't the US Have a European-Style Welfare State?" *Brookings Papers on Economic Activity* 2, 187–277.

Alexander, J., B. Giesen, R. Munch, Neil Smelser (eds.). 1987. *The Micro-Macro Link.* Berkeley, CA: University of California Press.

Allen, William Sheridan. 1965. *The Nazi Seizure of Power: The Experience of a Single German Town, 1930–1935.* New York: Watts.

Allison, Graham T. 1971. *Essence of Decision: Explaining the Cuban Missile Crisis.* Boston, MA: Little, Brown.

Allison, Graham T., Philip Zelikow. 1999. *Essence of Decision: Explaining the Cuban Missile Crisis*, 2nd edn. Boston, MA: Little, Brown.

Almond, Gabriel A., Sidney Verba. 1963/1989. *The Civic Culture: Political Attitudes and Democracy in Five Nations.* Thousand Oaks, CA: Sage.

Alperovitz, Gar. 1996. *The Decision to Use the Atomic Bomb.* New York: Vintage.

Alston, Lee J. 2008. "The 'Case' for Case Studies in New Institutional Economics." In Éric Brousseau, Jean-Michel Glachant (eds.), *New Institutional Economics: A Guidebook.* Cambridge: Cambridge University Press, 103–21.

Alston, Lee J., Gary D. Libecap, Robert Schneider. 1996. "The Determinants and Impact of Property Rights: Land Titles on the Brazilian Frontier." *Journal of Law, Economics, and Organization* 12, 25–61.

Amenta, Edwin. 1991. "Making the Most of a Case Study: Theories of the Welfare State and the American Experience." In Charles C. Ragin (ed.), *Issues and Alternatives in Comparative Social Research*, Leiden: E.J. Brill, 172–94.

Aminzade, Ronald. 1992. "Historical Sociology and Time." *Sociological Methods and Research* 20, 456–80.

Andersen, Robert. 2008. *Modern Methods for Robust Regression*. Thousand Oaks, CA: Sage.

Anderson, Perry. 1974. *Lineages of the Absolutist State*. London: New Left Books.

Anderson, R.A., B.F. Crabtree, D. J. Steele, R.R. McDaniel. 2005. "Case Study Research: The View from Complexity Science." *Qualitative Health Research* 15:5, 669–85.

Angrist, Joshua D., Jorn-Steffen Pischke. 2009. *Mostly Harmless Econometrics: An Empiricist's Companion*. Princeton, NJ: Princeton University Press.

2015. *Mastering Metrics: The Path from Cause to Effect*. Princeton, NJ: Princeton University Press.

Ankeny, Rachel A. 2011. "Using Cases to Establish Novel Diagnoses: Creating Generic Facts by Making Particular Facts Travel Together." In Peter Howlett, Mary S. Morgan (eds.), *How Well Do Facts Travel? The Dissemination of Reliable Knowledge*. Cambridge: Cambridge University Press, 252–72.

2012. "Detecting Themes and Variations: The Use of Cases in Developmental Biology." *Philosophy of Science* 79, 644–54.

2014. "The Overlooked Role of Cases in Causal Attribution in Medicine." *Philosophy of Science* 81, 999–1011.

Arceneaux, Kevin, David W. Nickerson. 2009. "Modeling Certainty with Clustered Data: A Comparison of Methods." *Political Analysis* 17:2, 177–90.

Aronson, Jeffrey K., Manfred Hauben. 2006. "Drug Safety: Anecdotes that Provide Definitive Evidence." *British Medical Journal* 333:7581, 1267–9.

Aymard, Maurice. 1982. "From Feudalism to Capitalism in Italy: The Case that Doesn't Fit." *Review* 6, 131–208.

Bailey, Mary Timney. 1992. "Do Physicists Use Case Studies? Thoughts on Public Administration Research." *Public Administration Review* 52:1, 47–54.

Banfield, Edward C. 1958. *The Moral Basis of a Backward Society*. Glencoe, IL: Free Press.

Bassey, Michael. 1999. *Case Study Research in Educational Settings*. Buckingham: Open University Press.

Bates, Robert H., Avner Greif, Margaret Levi, Jean-Laurent Rosenthal, Barry Weingast. 1998. *Analytic Narratives*. Princeton, NJ: Princeton University Press.

Beach, Derek, Rasmus Brun Pedersen. 2013. *Process-Tracing Methods: Foundations and Guidelines*. Ann Arbor, MI: University of Michigan Press.

Beck, Nathaniel. 2010. "Causal Process 'Observation': Oxymoron or (Fine) Old Wine." *Political Analysis* 18, 499–505.

Becker, Howard Saul. 1961. *Boys in White: Student Culture in Medical School*. Chicago, IL: University of Chicago Press.

    1963. *Outsiders: Studies in the Sociology of Deviance*. New York: Free Press of Glencoe.

    1970. "Life History and the Scientific Mosaic." In *Sociological Work: Method and Substance*. Chicago, IL: Aldine, 63–73.

Belich, James. 2010. "Exploding Wests: Boom and Bust in Nineteenth-Century Settler Societies." In Jared Diamond, James A. Robinson (eds.), *Natural Experiments in History*. Cambridge, MA: Harvard University Press.

Belsey, David A., Edwin Kuh, Roy E. Welsch. 2004. *Regression Diagnostics: Identifying Influential Data and Sources of Collinearity*. New York: Wiley.

Benbasat, Izak, David K. Goldstein, Melissa Mead. 1987. "The Case Research Strategy in Studies of Information Systems." *MIT Quarterly* 11:3, 369–86.

Bendix, Reinhard. 1963. "Concepts and Generalizations in Comparative Sociological Studies." *American Sociological Review* 28:4, 532–9.

1978. *Kings or People: Power and the Mandate to Rule*. Berkeley, CA: University of California Press.

Benedict, Ruth. 1934. *Patterns of Culture*. Boston, MA: Houghton Mifflin.

Benjamin, Ludy T. 2006. *A Brief History of Modern Psychology*. New York: Wiley.

Bennett, Andrew. 2008. "Process Tracing: A Bayesian Approach." In Janet Box-Steffensmeier, Henry Brady, David Collier (eds.), *Oxford Handbook of Political Methodology*. Oxford: Oxford University Press, 702–21.

2015. "Disciplining Our Conjectures: Systematizing Process Tracing with Bayesian Analysis." In Andrew Bennett, Jeffrey T. Checkel (eds.), *Process Tracing: From Metaphor to Analytic Tool*. Cambridge: Cambridge University Press, 276–98.

Bennett, Andrew, Jeffrey T. Checkel (eds.). 2015. *Process Tracing: From Metaphor to Analytic Tool*. Cambridge: Cambridge University Press.

Bennett, Andrew, Colin Elman. 2007. "Case Study Methods in the International Relations Subfield." *Comparative Political Studies* 40:2, 170–95.

Bennett, Andrew, Joseph Lepgold, Danny Unger. 1994. "Burden-Sharing in the Persian Gulf War." *International Organization* 48:1, 39–75.

Berg, Bruce L., Howard Lune. 2011. *Qualitative Research Methods for the Social Sciences*, 8th edn. Englewood Cliffs: Prentice Hall.

Bernard, H. Russell. 1988. *Research Methods in Cultural Anthropology*. Thousand Oaks, CA: Sage.

2001. *Research Methods in Anthropology: Qualitative and Quantitative Approaches*. Lanham, MD: Rowman & Littlefield.

Bernard, L.L. 1928. "The Development of Method in Sociology." *The Monist* 38, 292–320.

Blatter, Joachim, Till Blume. 2008. "In Search of Co-Variance, Causal Mechanisms or Congruence? Towards a Plural Understanding of Case Studies." *Swiss Political Science Review* 14, 315–55.

Blatter, Joachim, Markus Haverland. 2012. *Designing Case Studies: Explanatory Approaches in Small-N Research*. Basingstoke: Palgrave Macmillan.

Blumer, Herbert. 1969. *Symbolic Interactionism: Perspective and Method.* Berkeley, CA: University of California Press.

Bock, Edwin A. (ed.) 1962. *Essays on the Case Method.* New York: Inter-University Case Program.

Boix, Carles. 1999. "Setting the Rules of the Game: The Choice of Electoral Systems in Advanced Democracies." *American Political Science Review* 93:3, 609–24.

Boix, Carles, Susan C. Stokes (eds.). 2007. *Oxford Handbook of Comparative Politics.* Oxford: Oxford University Press.

Bolgar, Hedda. 1965. "The Case Study Method." In B.B. Wolman (ed.), *Handbook of Clinical Psychology.* New York: McGraw-Hill, 28–39.

Bollen, Kenneth A., Robert W. Jackman. 1985. "Regression Diagnostics: An Expository Treatment of Outliers and Influential Cases," *Sociological Methods and Research* 13, 510–42.

Bonoma, Thomas V. 1985. "Case Research in Marketing: Opportunities, Problems, and a Process." *Journal of Marketing Research* 22:2, 199–208.

Bourgin, Georges, Gabriel Henriot. 1924. *Procès-verbaux de la Commune de 1871*, vols. 1–2. Paris: E. Leroux.

Bowman, Kirk, Fabrice Lehoucq, James Mahoney. 2005. "Measuring Political Democracy: Case Expertise, Data Adequacy, and Central America." *Comparative Political Studies* 38:8, 939–70.

Brady, Henry E. 2004. "Data-Set Observations v. Causal-Process Observations: The 2000 US Presidential Election." In Henry E. Brady and David Collier (eds.), *Rethinking Social Inquiry: Diverse Tools, Shared Standards.* Lanham, MD: Rowman & Littlefield.

Brady, Henry E., David Collier (eds.). 2004. *Rethinking Social Inquiry: Diverse Tools, Shared Standards.* Lanham, MD: Rowman & Littlefield.

Breman, Anna, Carolyn Shelton. 2001. "Structural Adjustment and Health: A Literature Review of the Debate, Its Role-Players and Presented Empirical Evidence." CMH Working Paper Series, Paper No. WG6:6. WHO, Commission on Macroeconomics and Health.

Bremer, Stuart A. 1992. "Dangerous Dyads: Conditions Affecting the Likelihood of Interstate War, 1816–1965." *Journal of Conflict Resolution* 36:2, 309–41.

1993. "Democracy and Militarized Interstate Conflict, 1816–1965." *International Interactions* 18:3, 231–49.

Briggs, Derek C. 2005. "Meta-Analysis: A Case Study." *Evaluation Review* 29:2, 87–127.

Brinkerhoff, Robert O. 2002. *The Success Case Method.* San Francisco, CA: Berrett-Koehler.

Bromley, D.B. 1986. *The Case Study Method in Psychology and Related Disciplines.* New York: John Wiley & Sons.

Brooke, M. 1970. *Le Play: Engineer and Social Scientist.* London: Longman.

Brown, Christine, Keith Lloyd. 2001. "Qualitative Methods in Psychiatric Research." *Advances in Psychiatric Treatment* 7, 350–6.

Brown, Michael E., Sean M. Lynn-Jones, Steven E. Miller (eds.). 1996. *Debating the Democratic Peace.* Cambridge, MA: MIT Press.

Buchbinder, S., E. Vittinghoff. 1999. "HIV-infected Long-Term Nonprogressors: Epidemiology, Mechanisms of Delayed Progression, and Clinical and Research Implications." *Microbes Infect.* 1:13, 1113–20.

Bulmer, Martin. 1984. *The Chicago School of Sociology: Institutionalization, Diversity and the Rise of Sociological Research.* Chicago, IL: University of Chicago Press.

Bunce, Valerie. 1981. *Do New Leaders Make a Difference? Executive Succession and Public Policy under Capitalism and Socialism.* Princeton, NJ: Princeton University Press.

Burawoy, Michael. 1998. "The Extended Case Method." *Sociological Theory* 16:1, 4–33.

Burawoy, Michael, Joshua Gamson, Alice Burton. 1991. *Ethnography Unbound: Power and Resistance in the Modern Metropolis.* Berkeley, CA: University of California Press.

Burgess, Ernest W. 1927. "Statistics and Case Studies as Methods of Social Research." *Sociology and Social Research* 12, 103–20.

Burian, Richard M. 2001. "The Dilemma of Case Studies Resolved: The Virtues of Using Case Studies in the History and Philosophy of Science." *Perspectives on Science* 9, 383–404.

Buthe, Tim. 2002. "Taking Temporality Seriously: Modeling History and the Use of Narratives as Evidence." *American Political Science Review* 96:3, 481–93.

Caldwell, John C. 1986. "Routes to Low Mortality in Poor Countries." *Population and Development Review* 12:2, 171–220.

Cameron, David. 1978. "The Expansion of the Public Economy: A Comparative Analysis." *American Political Science Review* 72:4, 1243–61.

Campbell, Donald T. 1966. "Pattern Matching as an Essential in Distal Knowing." In K.R. Hammond (ed.), *The Psychology of Egon Brunswick*. New York: Holt, Rinehart & Winston.

   1968/1988. "'The Connecticut Crackdown on Speeding: Time-Series Data in Quasi-Experimental Analysis." In E. Samuel Overman (ed.), *Methodology and Epistemology for Social Science*. Chicago, IL: University of Chicago Press.

   1975/1988. "'Degrees of Freedom' and the Case Study." In E. Samuel Overman (ed.), *Methodology and Epistemology for Social Science*. Chicago, IL: University of Chicago Press.

Canon, David T. 1999. *Race, Redistricting, and Representation: The Unintended Consequences of Black Majority Districts*. Chicago, IL: University of Chicago Press.

Carey, John M. 2007. "Competing Principals, Political Institutions, and Party Unity in Legislative Voting." *American Journal of Political Science* 51, 92–107.

Carter, Lief H., Thomas F. Burke. 2015. *Reason in Law*, 8th edn. Chicago, IL: University of Chicago Press.

Chandler, Alfred D. 1962. *Strategy and Structure: Chapters in the History of the American Industrial Enterprise*. Cambridge, MA: Harvard University Press.

Chandler, James, Harry Harootunian, Arnold Davidson (eds.). 1994. *Questions of Evidence: Proof, Practice, and Persuasion across the Disciplines*. Chicago, IL: University of Chicago Press.

Childs, Geoff, Melvyn C. Goldstein, Ben Jiao, Cynthia M. Beall. 2005. "Tibetan Fertility Transitions in China and South Asia." *Population and Development Review* 31:2, 337–49.

Chong, Dennis. 1993. "How People Think, Reason, and Feel about Rights and Liberties." *American Journal of Political Science* 37:3, 867–99.

Cipolla, C. M. 1991. *Between History and Economics: An Introduction to Economic History*. Oxford: Blackwell.

Coase, Ronald H. 1959. "The Federal Communications Commission." *The Journal of Law and Economics* 2, 1–40.

2000. "The Acquisition of Fisher Body by General Motors." *The Journal of Law and Economics* 43:1, 15–31.

Cohen, Morris R., Ernest Nagel. 1934. *An Introduction to Logic and Scientific Method*. New York: Harcourt, Brace & Company.

Collier, David. 1993. "The Comparative Method." In Ada W. Finifter (ed.), *Political Science: The State of the Discipline II*. Washington, DC: American Political Science Association.

2011. "Understanding Process Tracing." *PS: Political Science and Politics* 44:4, 823–30.

Collier, David, James Mahoney. 1996. "Insights and Pitfalls: Selection Bias in Qualitative Research." *World Politics* 49, 56–91.

Collier, Paul, Anke Hoeffler. 2001. "Greed and Grievance in Civil War." World Bank Policy Research Working Paper No. 2355.

Collier, Paul, Nicholas Sambanis (eds.). 2005a. *Understanding Civil War: Evidence and Analysis, Vol. 1 – Africa*. Washington, DC: World Bank.

(eds.). 2005b. *Understanding Civil War: Evidence and Analysis, Vol. 2 – Europe, Central Asia, and Other Regions*. Washington, DC: World Bank.

Collier, Ruth Berins, David Collier. 1991/2002. *Shaping the Political Arena: Critical Junctures, the Labor Movement, and Regime Dynamics in Latin America*. Notre Dame, IN: University of Notre Dame Press.

Converse, Philip E., G. Dupeux. 1962. "Politicization of the Electorate in France and the United States." *Public Opinion Quarterly* 26, 1–23.

Coppedge, Michael, John Gerring, Staffan I. Lindberg, Daniel Pemstein, Svend-Erik Skaaning, Jan Teorell, Eitan Tzelgov, Yi-ting Wang, David Altman, Michael Bernhard, M. Steven Fish, Adam Glynn, Allen Hicken, Carl Henrik Knutsen, Kelly McMann, Megan Reif, Jeffrey Staton, Brigitte Zimmerman. 2015. "Varieties of Democracy: Methodology v4." Varieties of Democracy (V-Dem) Project.

Cornell, Svante E. 2002. "Autonomy as a Source of Conflict: Caucasian Conflicts in Theoretical Perspective." *World Politics* 54, 245–76.

Corsini, Raymond J. 2004. *Case Studies in Psychotherapy*. Thomson Learning.

Cousin, Glynis. 2005. "Case Study Research." *Journal of Geography in Higher Education* 29:3, 421–7.

Crandell, Jamie L., Corrine I. Voils, YunKyung Chang, Margarete Sandelowski. 2011. "Bayesian Data Augmentation Methods for the

Synthesis of Qualitative and Quantitative Research Findings." *Quality and Quantity* 45, 653–69.

Crossley, Michael, Graham Vulliamy. 1984. "Case-Study Research Methods and Comparative Education." *Comparative Education* 20:2, 193–207.

Curtiss, Susan. 1977. *Genie: A Psycholinguistic Study of a Modern-Day "Wild Child."* Boston, MA: Academic Press.

Dafoe, Allan, Nina Kelsey. 2014. "Observing the Capitalist Peace: Examining Market-Mediated Signaling and Other Mechanisms." *Journal of Peace Research* 51:5, 619–33.

Dahl, Robert A. 1961. *Who Governs? Democracy and Power in an American City.* New Haven: Yale University Press.

Daniels, Peter T., William Bright (eds.). 1996. *The World's Writing Systems.* Oxford: Oxford University Press.

Davenport, Christian, Patrick Ball. 2002. "Views to a Kill: Exploring the Implications of Source Selection in the Case of Guatemalan State Terror, 1977–1995." *Journal of Conflict Resolution* 46, 427–50.

David, Matthew (ed.). 2005. *Case Study Research*, 4 vols. Thousand Oaks, CA: Sage.

David, Paul. 1985. "Clio and the Economics of QWERTY." *American Economic Review* 75, 332–37.

Davidson, Donald. 1963. "Actions, Reasons, and Causes." *The Journal of Philosophy* 60:23, 685–700.

Davidson, P. O., C. G. Costello (eds.). 1969. *N = 1: Experimental Studies of Single Cases.* New York: Van Nostrand Reinhold.

DeFelice, Gene E. 1986. "Causal Inference and Comparative Methods." *Comparative Political Studies* 19:3, 415–437.

Delamont, S. 1992. *Fieldwork in Educational Settings – Methods, Pitfalls and Perspectives.* London: Falmer Press.

Denzin, Norman K., Yvonna S. Lincoln (eds.). 2000. *Handbook of Qualitative Research*, 2nd edn. Thousand Oaks, CA : Sage.

Dessler, David. 1991. "Beyond Correlations: Toward a Causal Theory of War." *International Studies Quarterly* 35, 337–55.

Dewald, William G., Jerry G. Thursby, Richard G. Anderson. 1986. "Replication in Empirical Economics: The Journal of Money, Credit, and Banking Project." *American Economic Review* 76:4, 587–603.

Diamond, Jared. 1992. *Guns, Germs, and Steel: The Fates of Human Societies.* New York: Norton.

Diamond, Jared, James A. Robinson (eds.). 2010. *Natural Experiments in History.* Cambridge, MA: Harvard University Press.

Diamond, Larry, Marc Plattner (eds.). 1994. *Nationalism, Ethnic Conflict, and Democracy.* Baltimore, MD: Johns Hopkins University Press.

Dion, Douglas. 1998. "Evidence and Inference in the Comparative Case Study." *Comparative Politics* 30, 127–45.

Dobbin, Frank. 1994. *Forging Industrial Policy: The United States, Britain and France in the Railway Age.* New York: Cambridge University Press

Downing, Brian M. 1992. *The Military Revolution and Political Change: Origins of Democracy and Autocracy in Early Modern Europe.* Princeton, NJ: Princeton University Press.

Dreze, Jean, Amartya Sen. 1989. "China and India." In Jean Dreze, Amartya Sen (eds.), *Hunger and Public Action.* Oxford: Oxford: Clarendon Press, 204–225.

Duff, Patricia. 2007. *Case Study Research in Applied Linguistics.* Routledge.

Dufour, Stephane, Dominic Fortin. 1992. "Annotated Bibliography on Case Study Method." *Current Sociology* 40:1, 167–200.

Dul, Jan, Tony Hak. 2007. *Case Study Methodology in Business Research.* Amsterdam: Elsevier.

Duneier, Mitchell. 1999. *Sidewalk.* New York: Farrar, Straus, Giroux.

Dunlavy, Colleen. 1994. *Politics and Industrialization: Early Railroads in the US and Prussia.* Princeton, NJ: Princeton University Press

Dunning, Thad. 2008. *Crude Democracy: Natural Resource Wealth and Political Regimes.* Cambridge: Cambridge University Press.

   2012. *Natural Experiments in the Social Sciences: A Design-Based Approach.* Cambridge: Cambridge University Press.

Eckstein, Harry. 1975. "Case Studies and Theory in Political Science." In Fred I. Greenstein, Nelson W. Polsby (eds.), *Handbook of Political Science, vol. 7. Political Science: Scope and Theory.* Reading, MA: Addison-Wesley, 79–138.

Eggan, Fred. 1954. "Social Anthropology and the Method of Controlled Comparison." *American Anthropologist* 56, 743–63.

Eichengreen, Barry. 1992. *Golden Fetters: The Gold Standard and the Great Depression, 1919–1939.* New York: Oxford University Press.

Eisenhardt, K. M. 1989. "Building Theories from Case Study Research." *Academy of Management Review* 14:4, 532–50.

Ellram, L. M. 1996. "The Use of the Case Study Method in Logistics Research." *Journal of Business Logistics* 17:2.

Elman, Colin. 2005. "Explanatory Typologies in Qualitative Studies of International Politics." *International Organization* 59:2, 293–326.

Elman, Colin, Miriam Fendius Elman (eds.). 2001. *Bridges and Boundaries: Historians, Political Scientists, and the Study of International Relations.* Cambridge, MA: MIT Press.

2002. "How Not to Be Lakatos Intolerant: Appraising Progress in IR Research." *International Studies Quarterly* 46:2, 231–62.

Elman, Colin, Diana Kapiszewski. 2014. "Data Access and Research Transparency in the Qualitative Tradition." *PS: Political Science and Politics* 47/1: 43–7.

Elman, Colin, Diana Kapiszewski, Lorena Vinuela. 2010. "Qualitative Data Archiving: Rewards and Challenges." *PS: Political Science and Politics* 43, 23–27.

Elman, Miriam Fendius (ed.). 1997. *Paths to Peace: Is Democracy the Answer?* Cambridge: Cambridge University Press.

Emigh, Rebecca. 1997. "The Power of Negative Thinking: The Use of Negative Case Methodology in the Development of Sociological Theory." *Theory and Society* 26, 649–84.

Epstein, Leon D. 1964. "A Comparative Study of Canadian Parties." *American Political Science Review* 58, 46–59.

Eriksen, Thomas Hylland, Finn Sivert Nielsen. 2001. *A History of Anthropology.* Pluto Press.

Ertman, Thomas. 1997. *The Birth of Leviathan: Building States and Regimes in Medieval and Early Modern Europe.* Cambridge: Cambridge University Press.

Evans, Peter B. 1995. *Embedded Autonomy: States and Industrial Transformation.* Princeton, NJ: Princeton University Press.

Everitt, Brian S., Sabine Landau, Morven Leese, Daniel Stahl. 2011. *Cluster Analysis*, 5th edn. New York: Wiley.

Fabrigar, Leandre R., Duane T. Wegener. 2011. *Exploratory Factor Analysis.* Oxford: Oxford University Press.

Fairfield, Tasha. 2013. "Going Where the Money Is: Strategies for Taxing Economic Elites in Unequal Democracies." *World Development* 47, 42–57.

2015. *Private Wealth and Public Revenue in Latin America: Business Power and Tax Politics.* Cambridge: Cambridge University Press.

Feagin, Joe R., Anthony M. Orum, Gideon Sjoberg. 1991. *A Case for the Case Study.* Chapel Hill: University of North Carolina Press.

Fearon, James D. 1991. "Counter Factuals and Hypothesis Testing in Political Science." *World Politics* 43, 169–95.

Fearon, James D., David D. Laitin. 2003. "Ethnicity, Insurgency, and Civil War." *American Political Science Review* 97:1, 75–90.

2008. "Integrating Qualitative and Quantitative Methods." In Janet M. Box-Steffensmeier, Henry E. Brady, David Collier (eds.),*The Oxford Handbook of Political Methodology.* Oxford: Oxford University Press.

2014. "Civil War Non-Onsets: The Case of Japan." *Journal of Civilization Studies* 1:1, 67–90.

2015. "Random Narratives." Unpublished manuscript, Department of Political Science, Stanford University. http://web.stanford.edu/group/ethnic/Random%20Narratives/random%20narratives.htm

Feng, Yi. 2003. *Democracy, Governance, and Economic Performance: Theory and Evidence.* Cambridge, MA: MIT Press.

Fenno, Richard F., Jr. 1977. "US House Members in Their Constituencies: An Exploration." *American Political Science Review* 71:3, 883–917.

1978. *Home Style: House Members in Their Districts.* Boston, MA: Little, Brown.

Ferejohn, John. 2004. "External and Internal Explanation." In Ian Shapiro, Rogers M. Smith, Tarek E. Masoud (eds.), *Problems and Methods in the Study of Politics.* Cambridge: Cambridge University Press.

Ferwerda, Jeremy, Nicholas Miller. 2014. "Political Devolution and Resistance to Foreign Rule: A Natural Experiment." *American Political Science Review* 108:3, 642–60.

Feyerabend, Paul. 1975. *Against Method.* London: New Left Books.

Finer, Samuel E. 1997. *The History of Government,* vols. 1–3. Cambridge: Cambridge University Press.

Fiorina, Morris P. 1977. *Congress: Keystone of the Washington Establishment.* New Haven: Yale University Press.

Fischer, David Hackett. 1970. *Historians' Fallacies: Toward a Logic of Historical Thought.* New York: Harper and Row.

Fishman, D.B. 1999. *The Case for Pragmatic Psychology*. New York: New York University Press.

Flyvbjerg, Bent. 2006. "Five Misunderstandings about Case Study Research." *Qualitative Inquiry* 12:2, 219–245.

2011. "Case Study." In Norman K. Denzin, Yvonna S. Lincoln (eds.), *The Sage Handbook of Qualitative Research*, 4th edn. Thousand Oaks, CA: Sage, 301–16.

Forrester, John. 1996. "If p, Then What? Thinking in Cases." *History of the Human Sciences* 9:3, 1–25.

Foucault, Michel. 1977. *Discipline and Punish*. London: Allen Lane.

Franzosi, Roberto, Sophie Doyle, Laura E. McClelland, Caddie Putnam Rankin, Stefania Vicari. 2013. "Quantitative Narrative Analysis Software Options Compared: PC-ACE and CAQDAS (ATLAS.ti, MAXqda, and NVivo)." *Quality and Quantity* 47:6, 3219–47.

Freedman, David A. 1991. "Statistical Models and Shoe Leather." *Sociological Methodology* 21, 291–313.

Freese, Jeremy. 2007. "Replication Standards for Quantitative Social Science: Why Not Sociology?" *Sociological Methods and Research* 36:2, 153–62.

Friedman, Milton, Anna Jacobson Schwartz. 1963. *A Monetary History of the United States, 1867–1960*. Princeton, NJ: Princeton University Press.

Gast, David L., Jennifer R. Ledford (eds.). 2009. *Single Subject Research Methodology in Behavioral Sciences*. Routledge.

Geddes, Barbara. 1990. "How the Cases You Choose Affect the Answers You Get: Selection Bias in Comparative Politics." In James A. Stimson (ed.), *Political Analysis*, Vol. 2, Ann Arbor, MI: University of Michigan Press).

2003. *Paradigms and Sand Castles: Theory Building and Research Design in Comparative Politics*. Ann Arbor, MI: University of Michigan Press.

Geertz, Clifford. 1963. *Peddlers and Princes: Social Change and Economic Modernization in Two Indonesian Towns*. Chicago, IL: University of Chicago Press.

1973. "Thick Description: Toward an Interpretive Theory of Culture." In *The Interpretation of Cultures*. New York: Basic Books.

1978. "The Bazaar Economy: Information and Search in Peasant Marketing." *American Economic Review* 68:2, 28–32.

George, Alexander L. 1979. "Case Studies and Theory Development: The Method of Structured, Focused Comparison." In Paul Gordon Lauren (ed.), *Diplomacy: New Approaches in History, Theory, and Policy*. New York: The Free Press.

George, Alexander L., Andrew Bennett. 2005. *Case Studies and Theory Development*. Cambridge, MA: MIT Press.

George, Alexander L., Timothy J. McKeown. 1985. "Case Studies and Theories of Organizational Decision-Making." In Robert F. Coulam, Richard A. Smith (eds.), *Advances in Information Processing in Organizations*. Greenwich, CT.: JAI Press, 21–58.

George, Alexander L., Richard Smoke. 1974. *Deterrence in American Foreign Policy: Theory and Practice*. New York: Columbia University Press.

Gerber, Alan S., Donald P. Green. 2012. *Field Experiments: Design, Analysis, and Interpretation*. New York: W.W. Norton.

Gerring, John. 2004a. "Interpretations of Interpretivism." *Qualitative Methods: Newsletter of the American Political Science Association Organized Section on Qualitative Methods* 1:2, 2–6.

2004b. "What Is a Case Study and What Is It Good For?" *American Political Science Review* 98:2, 341–54.

2006a. "The Case Study: What It Is and What It Does." In Carles Boix, Susan Stokes (eds.), *Oxford Handbook of Comparative Politics*. Oxford: Oxford University Press.

2006b. "Idiographic Studies: A Methodological Primer." *International Sociology* 21:5, 707–34.

2007a. *Case Study Research: Principles and Practices*. Cambridge: Cambridge University Press.

2007b. "Is There a (Viable) Crucial-Case Method?" *Comparative Political Studies* 40:3, 231–53.

2007c. "The Mechanismic Worldview: Thinking Inside the Box." *British Journal of Political Science* 38:1, 161–79.

2010. "Causal Mechanisms: Yes, But. . ." *Comparative Political Studies* 43:11, 1499–526.

2012a. "Mere Description." *British Journal of Political Science* 42:4, 721–46.

2012b. *Social Science Methodology: A Unified Framework*, 2nd edn. Cambridge: Cambridge University Press.

2017. "Qualitative Methods." *Annual Review of Political Science* 20 (May/June).

Gerring, John, Craig Thomas. 2005. "What is 'Qualitative' Evidence? When Counting Doesn't Add Up." Unpublished manuscript, Department of Political Science, Boston University.

Gerring, John, Dino Christenson. 2017. *Applied Social Science Methodology: An Introductory Guide*. Cambridge: Cambridge University Press.

Gerring, John, Lee Cojocaru. 2016. "Selecting Cases for Intensive Analysis: A Diversity of Goals and Methods." *Sociological Methods and Research* 45:3, 392–423.

Gerring, John, Rose McDermott. 2007. "An Experimental Template for Case-Study Research." *American Journal of Political Science* 51:3, 688–701.

Gerring, John, Philip Bond, William Barndt, Carola Moreno. 2005. "Democracy and Growth: A Historical Perspective." *World Politics* 57(3): 323–64.

Gerschenkron, Alexander. 1962. *Economic Backwardness in Historical Perspective*. Cambridge, MA: Harvard University Press.

Giddings, Franklin Henry. 1924. *The Scientific Study of Human Soceity*. Chapel Hill: University of North Carolina Press.

Gilgun, J. F. 1994. "A Case for Case Studies in Social Work Research." *Social Work* 39:4, 371–81.

Gill, Christopher J, Lora Sabin, Christopher H. Schmid. 2005. "Why Clinicians are Natural Bayesians." *British Medical Journal* 330:1080–3 (May 7).

Gilovich, Thomas. 1993. *How We Know What Isn't So*. New York: Free Press.

Ginzburg, Carlo. 1983. "Morelli, Freud and Sherlock Holmes: Clues and Scientific Method." In Umberto Eco, Thomas A. Sebeok (eds.), *The Sign of Three: Dupin, Holmes, Peirce*. Bloomington: Indiana University Press, 81–118.

1991. "Checking the Evidence: The Judge and the Historian." *Critical Inquiry* 18, 79–92.

2007. "Latitude, Slaves, and the Bible: An Experiment in Microhistory." In Angela N.H. Creager, Elizabeth Lunbeck, M. Norton Wise (eds.), *Science without Laws: Model Systems, Cases, Exemplary Narratives*. Durham: Duke University Press, 243–63.

Gisselquist, Rachel M. 2014. "Paired Comparison and Theory Development: Considerations for Case Selection." *PS: Political Science and Politics* 47:2, 477–84.

Glaser, Barney G., Anselm L. Strauss. 1967. *The Discovery of Grounded Theory: Strategies for Qualitative Research*. New York: Aldine de Gruyter.

Gleditsch, Nils P. 1992. "Democracy and Peace." *Journal of Peace Research* 29:4, 369–376.

Gluckman, Max. 1961. "Ethnographic Data in British Social Anthropology." *Sociological Review* 9:1, 5–17.

Glynn, Adam N., John Gerring. 2015. "Strategies of Research Design with Confounding: A Graphical Description." Unpublished manuscript, Department of Political Science, Emory University.

Glynn, Adam N., Nahomi Ichino. 2015. "Using Qualitative Information to Improve Causal Inference." *American Journal of Political Science* 59: 1055–71.

2016. "Increasing Inferential Leverage in the Comparative Method: Placebo Tests in Small-N Research." *Sociological Methods and Research* (forthcoming).

Goemans, Hein E., W. Spaniel. 2016. "Multi-Method Research: The Case for Formal Theory." *Security Studies* 25:1, 25–33.

Goemans, Hein E., Kristian Skrede Gleditsch, Giacomo Chiozza. 2009. "ARCHIGOS: A Data Set on Leaders 1875–2004, Version 2.9." Unpublished manuscript, Rochester University.

Goertz, Gary. 2016. "Multimethod Research." *Security Studies* 25, 3–24.

2017. *Multimethod Research, Causal Mechanisms, and Selecting Cases: The Research Triad*. Princeton, NJ: Princeton University Press.

Goertz, Gary, Jack Levy (eds.). 2007. *Explaining War and Peace: Case Studies and Necessary Condition Counterfactuals*. Routledge.

Goertz, Gary, James Mahoney. 2012. *A Tale of Two Cultures: Qualitative and Quantitative Research in the Social Sciences*. Princeton, NJ: Princeton University Press.

Goertz, Gary, Harvey Starr (eds.). 2003. *Necessary Conditions: Theory, Methodology and Applications*. New York: Rowman & Littlefield.

Goldstone, Jack A. 1991. *Revolution and Rebellion in the Early Modern World*. Berkeley, CA: University of California Press.

1997. "Methodological Issues in Comparative Macrosociology." *Comparative Social Research* 16, 107–20.

2003. "Comparative Historical Analysis and Knowledge Accumulation in the Study of Revolutions." In James Mahoney and Dietrich Rueschemeyer (eds.), *Comparative Historical Analysis in the Social Sciences*. Cambridge: Cambridge University Press.

Goldstone, Jack A. *et al.* 2000. "State Failure Task Force Report: Phase III Findings." http://www.cidcm.umd.edu/inscr/stfail/SFTF%20Phase%20III%20Report%20Final.pdf]

Goldthorpe, John H. 1997. "Current Issues in Comparative Macrosociology: A Debate on Methodological Issues." *Comparative Social Research* 16, 121–32.

Gordon, Sanford C., Alastair Smith. 2004. "Quantitative Leverage Through Qualitative Knowledge: Augmenting the Statistical Analysis of Complex Causes." *Political Analysis* 12, 233–55.

Gottschalk, Louis. 1969. *Understanding History*. New York: Knopf.

Gouldner, Alvin W. 1954. *Patterns of Industrial Bureaucracy*. New York: Free Press.

Gourevitch, Peter. 1986. *Politics in Hard Times: Comparative Responses to International Economic Crises*. Ithaca, NY: Cornell University Press.

Grass, N.S.B., Henrietta M. Larson. 1939. *Casebook in American Business History*. F.S. Crofts & Co.

Green, Donald P., Ian Shapiro. 1994. *Pathologies of Rational Choice Theory: A Critique of Applications in Political Science*. New Haven: Yale University Press.

Greenstein, Fred I., Richard H. Immerman. 1992. "What Did Eisenhower Tell Kennedy About Indochina? The Politics of Misperception." *Journal of American History* 79:2, 568–87.

Greif, Avner. 1998. "Self-Enforcing Political Systems and Economic Growth: Late Medieval Genoa." In Robert H. Bates, Avner Greif, Margaret Levi, Jean-Laurent Rosenthal, Barry Weingast (eds.), *Analytic Narratives*. Princeton, NJ: Princeton University Press, 23–63.

Griffin, Larry J. 1992. "Temporality, Events, and Explanation in Historical Sociology: An Introduction." *Sociological Methods and Research* 20:4, 403–27.

1993. "Narrative, Event-Structure Analysis, and Causal Interpretation in Historical Sociology." *American Journal of Sociology* 98, 1094–1133.

Grzymala-Busse, Anna. 2011. "Time Will Tell? Temporality and the Analysis of Causal Mechanisms and Processes." *Comparative Political Studies* 44:9, 1267–97.

Gutting, Gary (ed.). 1980. *Paradigms and Revolutions: Appraisals and Applications of Thomas Kuhn's Philosophy of Science*. Notre Dame, IN: University of Notre Dame Press.

Haber, Stephen. 2010. "Politics, Banking, and Economic Development: Evidence from New World Economies." In Jared Diamond,

James A. Robinson (eds.), *Natural Experiments in History*. Cambridge, MA: Harvard University Press.

Haggard, Stephan, Robert Kaufman. 2012. "Inequality and Regime Change: Democratic Transitions and the Stability of Democratic Rule." *American Political Science Review* 106:1–22.

Hall, Peter A. 2003. "Aligning Ontology and Methodology in Comparative Politics." In James Mahoney, Dietrich Rueschemeyer (eds.), *Comparative Historical Analysis in the Social Sciences*. Cambridge: Cambridge University Press.

2006. "Systematic Process Analysis: When and How to Use It." *European Management Review* 3, 24–31

Hamel, Jacques. 1993. *Case Study Methods*. Thousand Oaks, CA: Sage.

Hamilton, James D. 1994. *Time Series Analysis*. Princeton, NJ: Princeton University Press.

Hammersley, Martyn. 1989. *The Dilemma of Qualitative Method: Blumer, Herbert and the Chicago School*. London: Routledge & Kegan Paul.

Hancke, Bob. 2009. *Intelligent Research Design: A Guide for Beginning Researchers in the Social Sciences*. Oxford: Oxford University Press.

Hancock, Dawson R., Bob Algozzine. 2011. *Doing Case Study Research: A Practical Guide for Beginning Researchers*, 2nd edn. Teacher's College Press.

Handlin, Oscar. 1941. *Boston's Immigrants*. Cambridge, MA: Harvard University Press.

Hanson, Norwood Russell. 1958. *Patterns of Discovery*. Cambridge: Cambridge University Press.

Harding, David, K. Seefeldt. 2013. "Mixed Methods and Causal Analysis." In Stephen Morgan (ed.), *Handbook of Causal Analysis*. New York: Springer Verlag.

Harding, David J., Cybelle Fox, Jal D. Mehta. 2002. "Studying Rare Events Through Qualitative Case Studies: Lessons from a Study of Rampage School Shootings." *Sociological Methods and Research* 11:31, 174–217.

Harrison, Hope. M. 1992. "Inside the SED Archives: A Researcher's Diary." *Bulletin of the Cold War International History Project*. 2.

Hart, H.L.A., A.M. Honore. 1959. *Causality in the Law*. Oxford: Oxford University Press.

Hartley, J. F. 1994. "Case Studies in Organizational Research." In C. Cassell, G. Symon (eds.), *Qualitative Methods in Organizational Research: A Practical Guide*. London: Sage, 209–29.

Hartz, Louis. 1955. *The Liberal Tradition in America*. New York: Harcourt, Brace & World.

Harvey, Frank P., Michael Brecher (eds.). 2002. *Evaluating Methodology in International Studies*. Ann Arbor, MI: University of Michigan Press.

Harzing, A.W. 2002. "Are Our Referencing Errors Undermining Our Scholarship and Credibility? The Case of Expatriate Failure Rates." *Journal of Organizational Behavior* 23, 127–48.

Haynes, B.F., G. Pantaleo, A.S. Fauci. 1996. "Toward an Understanding of the Correlates of Protective Immunity to HIV Infection." *Science* 271, 324–8.

Head, M.L., L. Holman, R. Lanfear, A.T. Kahn, M.D. Jennions. 2015. "The Extent and Consequences of p-Hacking in Science." *PLoS Biology* 13:3, e1002106.

Healy, William. 1923. "The Contributions of Case Studies to American Sociology." *Publications of the American Sociological Society* 18, 147–55.

Heclo, Hugh. 1974. *Modern Social Policies in Britain and Sweden: From Relief to Income Maintenance*. New Haven: Yale University Press.

Hempel, Sandra. 2007. *The Strange Case of the Broad Street Pump: John Snow and the Mystery of Cholera*. Berkeley, CA: University of California Press.

Henry, Gary T. 1990. *Practical Sampling*. Thousand Oaks, CA: Sage.

Hernan, Miguel A., James M. Robins. In process. *Causal Inference*.

Herron, Michael C., Kevin M. Quinn. 2016. "A Careful Look at Modern Case Selection Methods." *Sociological Methods and Research* (forthcoming).

Hersen, Michel, David H. Barlow. 1976. *Single-Case Experimental Designs: Strategies for Studying Behavior Change*. Oxford: Pergamon Press.

Hill, Michael R. 1993. *Archival Strategies and Techniques*. Thousand Oaks, CA: Sage.

Hirschman, Albert O. 1967. *Development Projects Observed*. Washington, DC: Brookings Institution.

Ho, Daniel E., Kosuke Imai, Gary King, Elizabeth A. Stuart. 2007. "Matching as Nonparametric Preprocessing for Reducing Model Dependence in Parametric Causal Inference." *Political Analysis* 15:3, 199–236.

Hochschild, Jennifer L. 1981. *What's Fair? American Beliefs about Distributive Justice*. Cambridge, MA: Harvard University Press.

Holland, Paul W. 1986. "Statistics and Causal Inference." *Journal of the American Statistical Association* 81, 945–60.

Homans, George C. 1951. *The Human Group*. New York: Routledge & Kegan Paul.

Hoon, Christina. 2013. "Meta-Synthesis of Qualitative Case Studies: An Approach to Theory Building." *Organizational Research Methods* 16:4, 522–556.

Howard, Marc Morjé. 2003. *The Weakness of Civil Society in Post-Communist Europe*. Cambridge: Cambridge University Press.

Howell, Martha, Walter Prevenier. 2001. *From Reliable Sources: An Introduction to Historical Methods*. Ithaca: Cornell University Press.

Hsieh, Chang-Tai, Christina D. Romer. 2001. "Was the Federal Reserve Fettered? Devaluation Expectations in the 1932 Monetary Expansion." NBER Working Paper No. W8113 (February).

Humphreys, Macartan. 2005. "Natural Resources, Conflict, and Conflict Resolution: Uncovering the Mechanisms." *Journal of Conflict Resolution* 49:4: 508–37.

Humphreys, Macartan, Alan M. Jacobs. 2015. "Mixing Methods: A Bayesian Approach." *American Political Science Review* 109, 653–73.

Humphreys, Macartan, Raul Sanchez de la Sierra, Peter van der Windt. 2013. "Fishing, Commitment, and Communication: A Proposal for Comprehensive Nonbinding Research Registration." *Political Analysis* 21:1, 1–20.

Hunter, Floyd. 1953. *Community Power Structure*. Chapel Hill: University of North Carolina Press.

Hunter, Katherine Montgomery. 1991. *Doctors' Stories: The Narrative Structure of Medical Knowledge*. Princeton, NJ: Princeton University Press.

Huntington, Samuel P. 1968. *Political Order in Changing Societies*. New Haven: Yale University Press.

Imai, Kosuke, Luke Keele, Dustin Tingley. 2010. "A General Approach to Causal Mediation Analysis." *Psychological Methods* 15:4, 309–34.

Imai, Kosuke, Luke Keele, Dustin Tingley, Teppei Yamamoto. 2011. "Unpacking the Black Box of Causality: Learning about Causal Mechanisms from Experimental and Observational Studies." *American Political Science Review* 105:4, 765–89.

Imbens, Guido W., Donald B Rubin. 2015. *Causal Inference for Statistics, Social, and Biomedical Sciences: An Introduction*. Cambridge: Cambridge University Press.

Immergut, Ellen M. 1992. *Health Politics: Interests and Institutions in Western Europe*. Cambridge: Cambridge University Press.

Jacobs, Alan. 2015. "Process Tracing the Effects of Ideas." In Andrew Bennett, Jeffrey T. Checkel (eds.), *Process Tracing: From Metaphor to Analytic Tool*. Cambridge: Cambridge University Press, 41–73.

Jenicek, Milos. 2001. *Clinical Case Reporting in Evidence-Based Medicine*, 2nd edn. Oxford: Oxford University Press.

Jensen, Jason L., Robert Rodgers. 2001. "Cumulating the Intellectual Gold of Case Study Research." *Public Administration Review* 61:2, 235–46.

Jervis, Robert. 1989. "Rational Deterrence: Theory and Evidence." *World Politics* 41:2, 183–207.

Jocher, Katharine. 1928. "The Case Study Method in Social Research." *Social Forces* 7, 203–15.

Johnson, Chalmers. 1983. *MITI and the Japanese Miracle: The Growth of Industrial Policy, 1925–1975*. Stanford, CA: Stanford University Press.

Johnson, Steven. 2006. *The Ghost Map: The Story of London's Most Terrifying Epidemic – and How It Changed Science, Cities, and the Modern World*. New York: Riverhead Books.

Jones, Geoffrey, Jonathan Zeitlin (eds.). 2010. *The Oxford Handbook of Business History*. Oxford: Oxford University Press.

Journal of Human Resources. 1989. "JHR Policy on Replication and Data Availability." http://www.ssc.wisc.edu/jhr/replication.html

Jupp, Victor. 1996. "Documents and Critical Research." In Roger Sapsford, Victor Jupp (eds.), *Data Collection and Analysis*. Thousand Oaks, CA: Sage, 298–316.

Kaarbo, Juliet, Ryan K. Beasley. 1999. "A Practical Guide to the Comparative Case Study Method in Political Psychology." *Political Psychology* 20:2, 369–91.

Kalyvas, Stathis N. 1996. *Christian Democracy in Europe*. Ithaca: Cornell University Press.

Kanter, Rosabeth Moss. 1977. *Men and Women of the Corporation*. New York: Basic Books.

Kapiszewski, Diana, Lauren M. MacLean, Benjamin L. Read. 2015. *Field Research in Political Science: Practices and Principles*. Cambridge: Cambridge University Press.

Karl, Terry Lynn. 1997. *The Paradox of Plenty: Oil Booms and Petro-States*. Berkeley, CA: University of California Press.

Kauffman, Craig. 2012. "More Than the Sum of the Parts: Nested Analysis in Action." *Qualitative and Multimethod Research* 10:2, 26–30.

Kaufman, Herbert. 1960. *The Forest Ranger: A Study in Administrative Behavior*. Baltimore: Johns Hopkins University Press.

Kazancigil, Ali. 1994. "The Deviant Case in Comparative Analysis: High Stateness in Comparative Analysis." In Mattei Dogan, Ali Kazancigil (eds.), *Comparing Nations: Concepts, Strategies, Substance*. Cambridge: Blackwell, 213–38.

Kazdin, Alan E. 1982. *Single Case Research Designs*. Oxford: Oxford University Press.

Keen, Justin, Tim Packwood. 1995. "Qualitative Research: Case Study Evaluation." *British Medical Journal* (August 12), 444–6.

Kemp, Kathleen A. 1986. "Race, Ethnicity, Class and Urban Spatial Conflict: Chicago as a Crucial Case." *Urban Studies* 23:3, 197–208.

Kendall, Patricia L., Katherine M. Wolf. 1949/1955. "The Analysis of Deviant Cases in Communications Research." In Paul F. Lazarsfeld, Frank N. Stanton (eds.), *Communications Research, 1948–1949*. New York: Harper and Brothers, 1949. Reprinted in Paul F. Lazarsfeld, Morris Rosenberg (eds.), *The Language of Social Research*. New York: Free Press, 1995, 167–70.

Kennedy, Craig H. 2005. *Single-Case Designs for Educational Research*. Allyn and Bacon.

Kennedy, Paul. 1989. *The Rise and Fall of the Great Powers*. New York: Vintage.

Key, V.O., Jr. 1949. *Southern Politics in State and Nation*. New York: Vintage.

Khong, Yuen Foong. 1992. *Analogies at War: Korea, Munich, Dien Bien Phu, and the Vietnam Decisions of 1965*. Princeton, NJ: Princeton University Press.

Kindleberger, Charles P. 1990. *Historical Economics: Art or Science?* Berkeley, CA: University of California Press.

1996. *World Economic Primacy 1500–1990*. Oxford: Oxford University Press.

King, Charles. 2004. "The Micropolitics of Social Violence." *World Politics* 56:3, 431–55.

King, Gary. 1989. *Unifying Political Methodology: The Likelihood Theory of Statistical Inference*. New York: Cambridge University Press.

1995. "Replication, Replication." *PS: Political Science and Politics* 28: 443–99.

2007. "An Introduction to the Dataverse Network as an Infrastructure for Data Sharing." *Sociological Methods and Research* 36: 173–99.

King, Gary, Robert O. Keohane, Sidney Verba. 1994. *Designing Social Inquiry: Scientific Inference in Qualitative Research*. Princeton, NJ: Princeton University Press.

Kitschelt, Herbert. 1986. "Political Opportunity Structures and Political Protest: Anti-Nuclear Movements in Four Democracies." *British Journal of Political Science* 16:1, 57–85.

Kittel, Bernhard. 1999. "Sense and Sensitivity in Pooled Analysis of Political Data." *European Journal of Political Research* 35, 225–53.

Knack, Stephen, Philip Keefer. 1997. "Does Social Capital Have an Economic Payoff? A Cross-Country Investigation." *Quarterly Journal of Economics* 112, 1251–88.

Knaub, James R., Jr. 2008. "Finite Population Correction (FPC) Factor." In Paul J. Lavrakas (ed.), *Encyclopedia of Survey Research Methods*. Thousand Oaks, CA: Sage.

Knight, Carly R., Christopher Winship. 2013. "The Causal Implications of Mechanistic Thinking: Identification Using Directed Acyclic Graphs (DAGs)." In Stephen L. Morgan (ed.), *Handbook of Causal Analysis for Social Research*. Berlin: Springer, 297–300.

Kocher, Matthew, Nuno Monteiro. 2015. "What's in a Line? Natural Experiments and the Line of Demarcation in WWII Occupied France." Unpublished manuscript, Department of Political Science, Yale University.

Kohli, Atul. 2004. *State-Directed Development: Political Power and Industrialization in the Global Periphery*. Cambridge: Cambridge University Press.

Kratochwill, T.R. (ed.). 1978. *Single Subject Research*. New York: Academic Press.

Kreuzer, Markus. 2010. "Historical Knowledge and Quantitative Analysis: The Case of the Origins of Proportional Representation." *American Political Science Review* 104:369–92.

Kuehn, David. 2013. "Combining Game Theory Models and Process Tracing: Potential and Limits." *European Political Science* 12/1, 52–63.

Kuhn, Thomas S. 1962/1970. *The Structure of Scientific Revolutions*. Chicago, IL: University of Chicago Press.

Lakatos, Imre. 1978. *The Methodology of Scientific Research Programmes*. Cambridge: Cambridge University Press.

Lane, Robert. 1962. *Political Ideology: Why the American Common Man Believes What He Does*. New York: The Free Press.

Lange, Matthew. 2009. *Lineages of Despotism and Development*. Chicago, IL: University of Chicago Press.

2012. *Comparative-Historical Methods*. Thousand Oaks, CA: Sage.

Larsson, Rikard. 1993. "Case Survey Methodology: Quantitative Analysis of Patterns across Case Studies." *The Academy of Management Journal* 36:6, 1515–46.

Lawrence, Robert Z., Charan Devereaux, Michael Watkins. 2005. *Making the Rules: Case Studies on US Trade Negotiation*. Washington, DC: Institute for International Economics.

Lazarsfeld, Paul F., Allen H. Barton. 1951. "Qualitative Measurement in the Social Sciences: Classification, Typologies, and Indices." In Daniel Lerner, Harold D. Lasswell (eds.), *The Policy Sciences*. Stanford, CA: Stanford University Press, 155–192.

Lazarsfeld, Paul F., W.S. Robinson. 1940. "The Quantification of Case Studies." *Journal of Applied Psychology* 24, 817–25.

Le Roy Ladurie, Emmanuel. 1978. *Montaillou: The Promised Land of Error*. New York: G. Braziller.

Lebow, Richard Ned. 2000. "What's So Different about a Counterfactual?" *World Politics* 52, 550–85.

LeCroy, Craig W. 2014. *Case Studies in Social Work Practice*, 3rd edn. New York: Wiley.

Lerner, Daniel. 1958. *The Passing of Traditional Society: Modernizing the Middle East*. Glencoe, IL: Free Press.

Levi, Margaret. 1988. *Of Rule and Revenue*. Berkeley, CA: University of California Press.

Levy, Jack S. 2002. "Qualitative Methods in International Relations." In Frank P. Harvey , Michael Brecher (eds.), *Evaluating Methodology in International Studies*. Ann Arbor, MI: University of Michigan Press.

2008a. "Case Studies: Types, Designs, and Logics of Inference." *Conflict Management and Peace Science* 25:1–18.

2008b. "Counterfactuals and Case Studies." In Janet M. Box-Steffensmeier, Henry E. Brady, David Collier (eds.), *Oxford Handbook of Political Methodology*. Oxford: Oxford University Press, 627–44.

2015. "Counterfactuals, Causal Inference, and Historical Analysis." *Security Studies* 24:3, 378–402.

Lewis, Oscar. 1959. *Five Families: Mexican Case Studies in the Culture of Poverty*. New York: Basic Books.

Lieberman, Evan S. 2003. *Race and Regionalism in the Politics of Taxation in Brazil and South Africa*. Cambridge: Cambridge University Press.

2005. "Nested Analysis as a Mixed-Method Strategy for Comparative Research." *American Political Science Review* 99:3, 435–52.

2010. "Bridging the Qualitative-Quantitative Divide: Best Practices in the Development of Historically Oriented Replication Databases." *Annual Review of Political Science* 13, 37–59.

2015. "Nested Analysis: Toward the Integration of Comparative-Historical Analysis with Other Social Science Methods." In James Mahoney, Kathleen Thelen (eds.), *Advances in Comparative-Historical Analysis*. Cambridge: Cambridge University Press, 240–63.

2016. "Improving Causal Inference through Non-Causal Research: Can the Bio-Medical Research Cycle Provide a Model for Political Science?" Unpublished paper, Department of Political Science, MIT.

Lieberson, Stanley. 1985. *Making It Count: The Improvement of Social Research and Theory*. Berkeley, CA: University of California Press.

1992. "Small N's and Big Conclusions: An Examination of the Reasoning in Comparative Studies Based on a Small Number of Cases." In Charles C. Ragin, Howard S. Becker (eds.), *What Is a Case? Exploring the Foundations of Social Inquiry*. Cambridge: Cambridge University Press.

1994. "More on the Uneasy Case for Using Mill-Type Methods in Small-N Comparative Studies." *Social Forces* 72:4, 1225–37.

Lieberson, Stanley, Joel Horwich. 2008. "Implication Analysis: A Pragmatic Proposal for Linking Theory and Data in the Social Sciences." *Sociological Methodology* 38, 1–50.

Lieshout, Robert H., Mathieu L.L. Segers, Anna M. van der Vleuten. 2004. "De Gaulle, Moravcsik, and the Choice for Europe." *Journal of Cold War Studies* 6:4, 89–139.

Lijphart, Arend. 1968. *The Politics of Accommodation: Pluralism and Democracy in the Netherlands*. Berkeley, CA: University of California Press.

1971. "Comparative Politics and the Comparative Method." *American Political Science Review* 65, 682–93.

1975. "The Comparable Cases Strategy in Comparative Research." *Comparative Political Studies* 8:2, 158–77.

Linz, Juan J., Alfred Stepan (eds.). 1978a. *The Breakdown of Democratic Regimes: Europe.* Baltimore: Johns Hopkins University Press.

(eds.). 1978b. *The Breakdown of Democratic Regimes: Latin America.* Baltimore: Johns Hopkins University Press.

Lipset, Seymour Martin. 1959. "Some Social Requisites of Democracy: Economic Development and Political Legitimacy." *American Political Science Review* 53:1, 69–105.

Lipset, Seymour Martin, Martin A. Trow, James S. Coleman. 1956. *Union Democracy: The Internal Politics of the International Typographical Union.* New York: Free Press.

Lipsey, Mark W., David B. Wilson. 2001. *Practical Meta-Analysis.* Thousand Oaks, CA: Sage.

Lipton, Peter. 2004. *Inference to the Best Explanation*, 2nd edn. Oxford: Routledge.

Lorentzen, Peter, M. Taylor Fravel, Jack Paine. 2015. "Using Process Tracing to Evaluate Formal Models." Unpublished paper, Department of Political Science, University of California at Berkeley.

Lucas, Samuel R., Alisa Szatrowski. 2014. "Qualitative Comparative Analysis in Critical Perspective." *Sociological Methodology* 44:1, 1–79.

Lucas, W. 1974. *The Case Survey Method: Aggregating Case Experience.* Santa Monica, CA: Rand.

Luebbert, Gregory M. 1991. *Liberalism, Fascism, or Social Democracy: Social Classes and the Political Origins of Regimes in Interwar Europe.* Berkeley, CA: University of California Press.

Lustick, Ian S. 1996. "History, Historiography, and Political Science: Multiple Historical Records and the Problem of Selection Bias." *American Political Science Review* 90:3, 605–18.

Lutfey, Karen, Jeremy Freese. 2005. "Toward Some Fundamentals of Fundamental Causality: Socioeconomic Status and Health in the Routine Clinic Visit for Diabetes." *American Journal of Sociology* 110:5, 1326–72.

Lynd, Robert Staughton, Helen Merrell Lynd. 1929/1956. *Middletown: A Study in American Culture.* New York: Harcourt, Brace.

Madrigal, Róger, Francisco Alpízar, Achim Schlüter. 2011. "Determinants of Performance of Community-Based Drinking Water Organizations." *World Development* 39, 1663–1675.

Mahoney, James. 1999. "Nominal, Ordinal, and Narrative Appraisal in Macro-Causal Analysis." *American Journal of Sociology* 104:4, 1154–96.

2000. "Path Dependence in Historical Sociology." *History and Theory* 29:4, 507–48.

2002. *The Legacies of Liberalism: Path Dependence and Political Regimes in Central America*. Baltimore: Johns Hopkins University Press.

2007. "The Elaboration Model and Necessary Causes." In Gary Goertz, Jack Levy (eds.), *Explaining War and Peace: Case Studies and Necessary Condition Counterfactuals*. Routledge, 281–306.

2012. "The Logic of Process Tracing Tests in the Social Sciences." *Sociological Methods and Research* 41:4, 566–590.

Mahoney, James, Dietrich Rueschemeyer (eds.). 2003. *Comparative Historical Analysis in the Social Sciences*. Cambridge: Cambridge University Press.

Mahoney, James, Kathleen Thelen (eds.). 2015. *Advances in Comparative-Historical Analysis*. Cambridge: Cambridge University Press.

Mahoney, James, Rachel Sweet Vanderpoel. 2015. "Set Diagrams and Qualitative Research." *Comparative Political Studies* 48:1, 65–100.

Mahoney, James, Celso M. Villegas. 2007. "Historical Enquiry and Comparative Politics." In Carles Boix, Susan C. Stokes (eds.), *Oxford Handbook of Comparative Politics*. Oxford: Oxford University Press.

Mainwaring, Scott, Aníbal Pérez-Liñán. 2014. *Democracies and Dictatorships in Latin America: Emergence, Survival, and Fall*. Cambridge: Cambridge University Press.

Mann, Michael. 1986. *The Sources of Social Power, Volume I: A History of Power from the Beginnings to 1760 AD*. Cambridge: Cambridge University Press.

Mansfield, Edward D., Jack Snyder. 2005. *Electing to Fight: Why Emerging Democracies go to War*. Cambridge, MA: MIT Press.

Maoz, Zeev. 2002. "Case Study Methodology in International Studies: From Storytelling to Hypothesis Testing." In Frank P. Harvey, Michael Brecher (eds.), *Evaluating Methodology in International Studies: Millennial Reflections on International Studies*. Ann Arbor, MI: University of Michigan Press.

Maoz, Zeev, Alex Mintz, T. Clifton Morgan, Glenn Palmer, Richard J. Stoll (eds.). 2004. *Multiple Paths to Knowledge in International Politics: Methodology in the Study of Conflict Management and Conflict Resolution.* Lexington, MA: Lexington Books.

Mariampolski, Hyman, Dana C. Hughes. 1978. "The Use of Personal Documents in Historical Sociology." *The American Sociologist* 13, 104–13.

Markoff, John. 2002. "Archival Methods." In Neil Smelser, P. Baltes (eds.), *International Encyclopedia of the Social and Behavioral Sciences.* Oxford: Elsevier, 637–42.

Martin, Cathie Jo, Duane Swank. 2004. "Does the Organization of Capital Matter? Employers and Active Labor Market Policy at the National and Firm Levels." *American Political Science Review* 98:4, 593–612.

Martin, Isaac William. 2008. *The Permanent Tax Revolt: How the Property Tax Transformed American Politics.* Stanford, CA: Stanford University Press.

Martin, Lisa L. 1992. *Coercive Cooperation: Explaining Multilateral Economic Sanctions.* Princeton, NJ: Princeton University Press.

Matarazzo, Benedetto, Peter Nijkamp. 1997. "Meta-Analysis for Comparative Environmental Case Studies: Methodological Issues." *International Journal of Social Economics* 24:7/8/9, 799–811.

Mays, Nicolas, Catherine Pope. 1995. "Qualitative Research: Observational Methods in Health Care Settings." *British Medical Journal* (July 15), 182–4.

McAdam, Doug. 1982. *Political Process and the Development of Black Insurgency, 1930–1970.* Chicago, IL: University of Chicago Press.
  1988. *Freedom Summer.* New York: Oxford University Press.

McAdam, Doug, Sidney Tarrow, Charles Tilly. 2001. *Dynamics of Contention.* Cambridge: Cambridge University Press.

McKeown, Timothy J. 1983. "Hegemonic Stability Theory and Nineteenth-Century Tariff Levels." *International Organization* 37:1, 73–91.
  1999. "Case Studies and the Statistical World View." *International Organization* 53, 161–90.

McLaughlin, Robert. 1982. "Invention and Induction: Laudan, Simon and the Logic of Discovery," *Philosophy of Science* 49:2, 198–211.

McLeod, John. 2010. *Case Study Research in Counselling and Psychotherapy.* London: Sage.

McNeill, William Hardy. 1963. *The Rise of the West: A History of the Human Community.* Chicago, IL: University of Chicago Press.

Meckstroth, Theodore. 1975. "'Most Different Systems' and 'Most Similar Systems': A Study in the Logic of Comparative Inquiry." *Comparative Political Studies* 8:2, 133–77.

Meehl, Paul E. 1954. *Clinical v. Statistical Predictions: A Theoretical Analysis and a Review of the Evidence*. Minneapolis, MN: University of Minnesota Press.

Michels, Roberto. 1911. *Political Parties*. New York: Collier Books.

Miguel, Edward. 2004. "Tribe or Nation: Nation-Building and Public Goods in Kenya v. Tanzania." *World Politics* 56:3, 327–62.

Mill, John Stuart. 1843/1872. *The System of Logic*, 8th edn. London: Longmans, Green.

Milligan, John D. 1979. "The Treatment of an Historical Source." *History and Theory* 18:2, 177–96.

Mills, Albert J., Gabrielle Durepos, Elden Wiebe (eds.). 2010. *Encyclopedia of Case Study Research*. Thousand Oaks, CA: Sage.

Miron, Jeffrey A. 1994. "Empirical Methodology in Macroeconomics: Explaining the Success of Friedman and Schwartz's 'A Monetary History of the United States, 1867–1960.'" *Journal of Monetary Economics* 34, 17–25.

Mitchell, J. Clyde. 1983. "Case and Situation Analysis." *Sociological Review* 31:2, 187–211.

Mokyr, Joel (ed.) 2003. *The Oxford Encyclopedia of Economic History*, 5 vols. Oxford: Oxford University Press.

Mondak, Jeffery J. 1995. "Newspapers and Political Awareness." *American Journal of Political Science* 39:2, 513–27.

Monroe, Kristen Renwick. 1996. *The Heart of Altruism*. Princeton, NJ: Princeton University Press.

Moore, Barrington, Jr. 1966. *Social Origins of Dictatorship and Democracy: Lord and Peasant in the Making of the Modern World*. Boston, MA: Beacon Press.

Moore, Fiona. 2010. "Case Study Research in Anthropology." In Albert J. Mills, Gabrielle Durepos, Elden Wiebe (eds.), *Encyclopedia of Case Study Research*. Thousand Oaks, CA: Sage.

Moravcsik, Andrew. 2010. "Active Citation: A Precondition for Replicable Qualitative Research." *PS: Political Science and Politics* 43:1, 29–35.

Morgan, Stephen L. (ed.). 2013. *Handbook of Causal Analysis for Social Research*. Berlin: Springer.

Morgan, Stephen L., Christopher Winship. 2014. *Counterfactuals and Causal Inference: Methods and Principles for Social Research*. Cambridge: Cambridge University Press.

Muller, Seán M. 2015. "Causal Interaction and External Validity: Obstacles to the Policy Relevance of Randomized Evaluations." *World Bank Economic Review*.

Mulligan, Casey, Ricard Gil, Xavier Sala-i-Martin. 2002. "Social Security and Democracy." University of Chicago and Columbia University.

Munck, Gerardo L. 2004. "Tools for Qualitative Research." In Henry E. Brady and David Collier (eds.), *Rethinking Social Inquiry: Diverse Tools, Shared Standards*. Lanham: Rowman & Littlefield, 105–21.

Munck, Gerardo L., Richard Snyder (eds.). 2006. *Passion, Craft, and Method in Comparative Politics*. Baltimore: Johns Hopkins University Press.

Nagel, Ernest. 1961. *The Structure of Science: Problems in the Logic of Scientific Explanation*. New York: Harcourt.

Narang, Vipin, Rebecca M. Nelson. 2009. "Who Are These Belligerent Democratizers? Reassessing the Impact of Democratization on War." *International Organization* 63:357–79.

Neuliep, James W. (ed.). 1991. *Replication Research in the Social Sciences*. Thousand Oaks, CA: Sage.

Nicholson-Crotty, Sean, Kenneth J. Meier. 2002. "Size Doesn't Matter: In Defense of Single-State Studies." *State Politics and Policy Quarterly* 2:4, 411–22.

Nickles, Thomas (ed.). 1980. *Scientific Discovery, Logic and Rationality*. Dordrecht: D. Reidel.

Nielsen, Richard A. 2016. "Case Selection via Matching." *Sociological Methods and Research* (forthcoming).

Nissen, Sylke. 1998. "The Case of Case Studies: On the Methodological Discussion in Comparative Political Science." *Quality and Quantity* 32, 339–418.

North, Douglass C., Robert Paul Thomas. 1973. *The Rise of the Western World*. Cambridge: Cambridge University Press.

North, Douglass C., Barry R. Weingast. 1989. "Constitutions and Commitment: The Evolution of Institutions Governing Public Choice in Seventeenth-Century England." *Journal of Economic History* 49, 803–32.

Odell, John S. 2004. "Case Study Methods in International Political Economy." In Detlef F. Sprinz, Yael Wolinsky-Nahmias (eds.), *Models, Numbers and*

Cases: Methods for Studying International Relations. Ann Arbor, MI: University of Michigan, 56–80.

Olken, Benjamin A. 2007. "Monitoring Corruption: Evidence from a Field Experiment in Indonesia." *Journal of Political Economy* 115:2, 200–49.

Oltmanns, Thomas F., Michele T. Martin, John M. Neale, Gerald C. Davison. 2014. *Case Studies in Abnormal Psychology*, 10th edn. New York: Wiley.

O'Neill, A. M. 1968. "The Bases of Clinical Inference." *Journal of Clinical Psychology* 24, 366–72.

Ostrom, Elinor. 1990. *Governing the Commons: The Evolution of Institutions for Collective Action.* Cambridge: Cambridge University Press.

Owen, John. 1994. "How Liberalism Produces Democratic Peace." *International Security* 19, 87–125.

Pahre, Robert. 2005. "Formal Theory and Case-Study Methods in EU Studies." *European Union Politics* 6:1, 113–46.

Papyrakis, Elissaios, Reyer Gerlagh. 2003. "The Resource Curse Hypothesis and Its Transmission Channels." *Journal of Comparative Economics* 32, 181–93.

Paterson, B., S. Thorne, C. Canam, C. Jillings. 2001. *Meta-Study of Qualitative Health Research.* Thousand Oaks, CA: Sage.

Patton, Michael Quinn. 2002. *Qualitative Evaluation and Research Methods.* Thousand Oaks, CA: Sage.

Pearce, Lisa D. 2002. "Integrating Survey and Ethnographic Methods for Systematic Anomalous Case Analysis." *Sociological Methodology* 32, 103–32.

Pearl, Judea. 2009. *Causality: Models, Reasoning, and Inference*, 2nd edn. Cambridge: Cambridge University Press.

Peirce, C.S. 1931. *Collected Papers*, C. Hartshorn, P. Weiss (eds.), Cambridge, MA: Harvard University Press.

Peters, T. J., R. H. Waterman. 1982. *In Search of Excellence: Lessons from America's Best-Run Companies.* New York: Harper & Row.

Petitti, D. E. 1993. *Meta-Analysis, Decision Analysis, Cost-Effectiveness*, 2nd edn. New York: Oxford University Press.

Piekkari, Rebecca, Catherine Welch, Eriikka Paavilainen. 2009. "The Case Study as Disciplinary Convention: Evidence from International Business Journals." *Organizational Research Methods* 12: 567

Pierson, Paul. 2000. "Increasing Returns, Path Dependence, and the Study of Politics." *American Political Science Review* 94:2, 251–67.

2004. *Politics in Time: History, Institutions, and Social Analysis*. Princeton, NJ: Princeton University Press.

Pincus, Steve. 2011. *1688: The First Modern Revolution*. New Haven: Yale University Press.

Pinfari, Marco. 2012. *Peace Negotiations and Time: Deadline Diplomacy in Territorial Disputes*. Abington: Routledge.

Platt, Jennifer. 1992. "'Case Study' in American Methodological Thought." *Current Sociology* 40:1, 17–48.

2007. "Case Study." In William Outhwaite, Stephen P. Turner (eds.), *Sage Handbook of Social Science Methodology*. London: Sage, 100–18.

Polanyi, Karl. 1944/1957. *The Great Transformation*. Boston, MA: Beacon Press.

Popper, Karl. 1934/1968. *The Logic of Scientific Discovery*. New York: Harper & Row.

1963. *Conjectures and Refutations*. London: Routledge & Kegan Paul.

1965. *Conjectures and Refutations*. New York: Harper & Row.

Porter, Michael. 1990. *The Competitive Advantage of Nations*. New York: Free Press.

Posner, Daniel. 2004. "The Political Salience of Cultural Difference: Why Chewas and Tumbukas are Allies in Zambia and Adversaries in Malawi." *American Political Science Review* 98:4, 529–46.

Poteete, Amy R., Elinor Ostrom. 2005. "Bridging the Qualitative-Quantitative Divide: Strategies for Building Large-N Databases Based on Qualitative Research." Prepared for the annual meeting of the American Political Science Association, Washington, DC.

Prior, Lindsay. 2003. *Using Documents in Social Research*. Thousand Oaks, CA: Sage.

Proust, Marcel. 1992. *The Guermantes Way, Vol. 3, In Search of Lost Time*, D.J. Enright (ed.), C.K. Scott Moncrieff, Terence Kilmartin (trans.), New York: Chatto & Windus.

Przeworski, Adam, Henry Teune. 1970. *The Logic of Comparative Social Inquiry*. New York: John Wiley.

Przeworski, Adam, Michael Alvarez, Jose Antonio Cheibub, Fernando Limongi. 2000. *Democracy and Development: Political Institutions and Material Well-Being in the World, 1950–1990*. Cambridge: Cambridge University Press.

Putnam, Robert D. 1988. "Diplomacy and Domestic Politics: The Logic of Two-Level Games." *International Organization* 42, 427–60.

Putnam, Robert D., with Robert Leonardi, Raffaella Y. Nanetti. 1993. *Making Democracy Work: Civic Traditions in Modern Italy*. Princeton, NJ: Princeton University Press.

Quadagno, Jill S. 1984. "Welfare Capitalism and the Social Security Act of 1935." *American Sociological Review* 49:5, 632–47.

Raaflaub, Kurt A., Josiah Ober, Robert W. Wallace. 2007. *Origins of Democracy in Ancient Greece*. Berkeley, CA: University of California Press.

Rabinow, Paul, William M. Sullivan (eds.). 1979. *Interpretive Social Science: A Reader*. Berkeley, CA: University of California Press.

Radley, Alan, Kerry Chamberlain. 2012. "The Study of the Case: Conceptualising Case Study Research." *Journal of Community and Applied Social Psychology* 22:5, 390–9.

Ragin, Charles C. 1987. *The Comparative Method: Moving Beyond Qualitative and Quantitative Strategies*. Berkeley, CA: University of California.

1992a. "Cases of 'What Is a Case?'" In Charles C. Ragin, Howard S. Becker (eds.), *What Is a Case? Exploring the Foundations of Social Inquiry*. Cambridge: Cambridge University Press.

1992b. "'Casing' and the Process of Social Inquiry.'" In Charles C. Ragin, Howard S. Becker (eds.), *What Is a Case? Exploring the Foundations of Social Inquiry*. Cambridge: Cambridge University Press.

1997. "Turning the Tables: How Case-Oriented Research Challenges Variable-Oriented Research." *Comparative Social Research* 16: 27–42.

2000. *Fuzzy-Set Social Science*. Chicago, IL: University of Chicago Press.

2004. "Turning the Tables." In Henry E. Brady, David Collier (eds.), *Rethinking Social Inquiry: Diverse Tools, Shared Standards*. Lanham, MD: Rowman & Littlefield, 123–38.

Ragin, Charles C., Howard S. Becker (eds.). 1992. *What Is a Case? Exploring the Foundations of Social Inquiry*. Cambridge: Cambridge University Press.

Rapport, Aaron. 2015. "Hard Thinking about Hard and Easy Cases in Security Studies." *Security Studies* 24:3, 431–65.

Ray, James Lee. 1993. "Wars between Democracies: Rare or Nonexistent?" *International Interactions* 18:251–76.

Reichenbach, Hans. 1938. *Experience and Prediction: An Analysis of the Foundations and the Structure of Knowledge*. Chicago, IL: University of Chicago Press.

Reilly, Ben. 2000/2001. "Democracy, Ethnic Fragmentation, and Internal Conflict: Confused Theories, Faulty Data, and the 'Crucial Case' of Papua New Guinea." *International Security* 25:3, 162–85.

Reilly, Ben, Andrew Reynolds. 1999. *Electoral Systems and Conflict in Divided Societies*. National Academies Press.

Rice, Stuart A. 1928. *Quantitative Methods in Politics*. New York: Alfred A. Knopf.

Richards, Paul. 2011. "A Systematic Approach to Cultural Explanations of War: Tracing Causal Processes in Two West African Insurgencies." *World Development* 39:2. 212–20.

Roberts, Clayton. 1996. *The Logic of Historical Explanation*. University Park: Pennsylvania State University Press.

Robinson, Denise L. 2001. *Clinical Decision Making: A Case Study Approach*. Lippincott Williams & Wilkins.

Rodrik, Dani (ed.). 2003. *In Search of Prosperity: Analytic Narratives on Economic Growth*. Princeton, NJ: Princeton University Press.

Rogowski, Ronald. 1995. "The Role of Theory and Anomaly in Social-Scientific Inference." *American Political Science Review* 89:2, 467–70.

Rohlfing, Ingo. 2004. "Have You Chosen the Right Case? Uncertainty in Case Selection for Single Case Studies." Working paper, International University, Bremen, Germany.

  2008. "What You See and What You Get: Pitfalls and Principles of Nested Analysis in Comparative Research." *Comparative Political Studies* 41:11, 1492–514.

  2012. *Case Studies and Causal Inference: An Integrative Framework*. Basingstoke: Palgrave Macmillan.

Rohlfing, Ingo, Carsten Q. Schneider. 2013. "Improving Research on Necessary Conditions: Formalized Case Selection for Process Tracing after QCA." *Political Research Quarterly* 66:1, 220–35.

Romer, Christina D., David H. Romer. 2010. "The Macroeconomic Effects of Tax Changes: Estimates Based on a New Measure of Fiscal Shocks." *American Economic Review* 100, 763–801.

Rosenbaum, Paul R., Jeffrey H. Silber. 2001. "Matching and Thick Description in an Observational Study of Mortality after Surgery." *Biostatistics* 2, 217–32.

Rosenberg, Gerald. 1991. *The Hollow Hope: Can Courts Bring about Social Change?* Chicago, IL: University of Chicago Press.

Rosenblatt, Paul C. 1981. "Ethnographic Case Studies." In Marilynn B. Brewer, Barry E. Collins (eds.), *Scientific Inquiry and the Social Sciences.* San Francisco: Jossey-Bass, 194–225.

Ross, Michael L. 2001. "Does Oil Hinder Democracy?" *World Politics* 53, 325–61.

2004. "How Do Natural Resources Influence Civil War? Evidence from Thirteen Cases." *International Organization* 58, 35–67.

2013. *The Oil Curse: How Petroleum Wealth Shapes the Development of Nations.* Princeton, NJ: Princeton University Press.

Rossman, Gretchen B., Sharon F. Rallis. 1998. *Learning in the Field: An Introduction to Qualitative Research.* Thousand Oaks, CA: Sage.

Roth, Paul A. 1994. "Narrative Explanations: The Case of History." In Michael Martin, Lee C. McIntyre (eds.), *Readings in the Philosophy of Social Science.* Cambridge, MA: MIT Press.

Rubin, Donald B. 1974. "Estimating Causal Effects of Treatments in Randomized and Nonrandomized Studies." *Journal of Educational Psychology* 66, 688–701.

Rudel, Thomas K. 2008. "Meta-Analyses of Case Studies: A Method for Studying Regional and Global Environmental Change." *Global Environmental Change* 18, 18–25.

Rueschemeyer, Dietrich. 2003. "Can One or a Few Cases Yield Theoretical Gains?" In James Mahoney, Dietrich Rueschemeyer (eds.), *Comparative Historical Analysis in the Social Sciences.* Cambridge: Cambridge University Press.

2009. *Usable Theory: Analytic Tools for Social and Political Research.* Princeton, NJ: Princeton University Press.

Rueschemeyer, Dietrich, John D. Stephens. 1997. "Comparing Historical Sequences: A Powerful Tool for Causal Analysis." *Comparative Social Research* 16, 55–72.

Rueschemeyer, Dietrich, Evelyne Huber Stephens, John D. Stephens. 1992. *Capitalist Development and Democracy.* Chicago, IL: University of Chicago Press.

Rumsfeld, Donald H. 2002. News Transcript, United States Department of Defense. http://www.defense.gov/transcripts/2002/t05222002_t522sdma.html

Sagan, Scott. 1993. *The Limits of Safety: Organizations, Accidents, and Nuclear Weapons*. Princeton, NJ: Princeton University Press.

Sahlins, Marshall. 1958. *Social Stratification in Polynesia*. Seattle: University of Washington Press.

Sambanis, Nicholas. 2004. "Using Case Studies to Expand Economic Models of Civil War." *Perspectives on Politics* 2, 259–79.

Sarbin, Theodore R. 1943. "A Contribution to the Study of Actuarial and Individual Methods of Prediction." *American Journal of Sociology* 48, 593–602.

1944. "The Logic of Prediction in Psychology." *Psychological Review* 51, 210–28.

Schattschneider, E.E. 1935. *Politics, Pressures and the Tariff*. Englewood Cliffs, NJ: Prentice Hall.

Scheper-Hughes, Nancy. 1992. *Death without Weeping: The Violence of Everyday Life in Brazil*. Berkeley, CA: University of California Press.

Schimmelfennig, Frank. 2015. "Efficient Process Tracing: Analyzing the Causal Mechanisms of European Integration." In Andrew Bennett, Jeffrey T. Checkel (eds.), *Process Tracing: From Metaphor to Analytic Tool*. Cambridge: Cambridge University Press, 98–125.

Schmidt, R. 1983. "Interaction, Acculturation and the Acquisition of Communicative Competence." In N. Wolfson, E. Judd (eds.), *Sociolinguistics and Language Acquisition*. Rowley, MA: Newbury House, 137–74.

Schneider, Carsten Q., Ingo Rohlfing. 2013. "Combining QCA and Process Tracing in Set-Theoretic Multimethod Research." *Sociological Methods and Research* 42, 559–97.

2016. "Case Studies Nested in Fuzzy-Set QCA on Sufficiency: Formalizing Case Selection and Causal Inference." *Sociological Methods and Research* (forthcoming).

Scholz, Roland W., Olaf Tietje. 2002. *Embedded Case Study Methods: Integrating Quantitative and Qualitative Knowledge*. Thousand Oaks, CA: Sage.

Schultz, Kenneth. 2001. *Democracy and Coercive Diplomacy*. Cambridge: Cambridge University Press.

Scott, James C. 1998. *Seeing Like a State: How Certain Schemes to Improve the Human Condition Have Failed*. New Haven: Yale University Press.

Sealey, Anne. 2011. "The Strange Case of the Freudian Case History: The Role of Long Case Histories in the Development of Psychoanalysis." *History of the Human Sciences* 24:1, 36–50.

Seawright, Jason. 2010. "Regression-Based Inference: A Case Study in Failed Causal Assessment." In Henry E. Brady, David Collier (eds.), *Rethinking Social Inquiry: Diverse Tools, Shared Standards*, 2nd edn., Lanham, MD: Rowman & Littlefield, 247–71.

2016a. "The Case for Selecting Cases That Are Deviant or Extreme on the Independent Variable." *Sociological Methods and Research* (forthcoming).

2016b. *Multimethod Social Science: Combining Qualitative and Quantitative Tools*. Cambridge: Cambridge University Press.

Seawright, Jason, John Gerring. 2008. "Case-Selection Techniques in Case Study Research: A Menu of Qualitative and Quantitative Options." *Political Research Quarterly* 61:2, 294–308.

Sekhon, Jasjeet S. 2004. "Quality Meets Quantity: Case Studies, Conditional Probability and Counterfactuals." *Perspectives in Politics* 2:2, 281–93.

Selznick, Philip. 1949. *TVA and the Grass Roots: A Study in the Sociology of Formal Organization*. Berkeley, CA: University of California Press.

Shadish, William R. Thomas D. Cook, Donald T. Campbell 2002. *Experimental and Quasi-Experimental Designs for Generalized Causal Inference*. Boston, MA: Houghton Mifflin.

Shalev, Michael. 1998. "Limits of and Alternatives to Multiple Regression in Macro-Comparative Research." Paper prepared for presentation at the second conference on The Welfare State at the Crossroads, Stockholm (June 12–14).

Shaw, Clifford R. 1930. *The Jack Roller*. Chicago, IL: University of Chicago Press.

Sheffield, Ada Eliot. 1920. *The Social Case History: Its Construction and Content*. New York: Russell Sage.

Shefter, Martin. 1977. "Party and Patronage: Germany, England, and Italy." *Politics and Society* 7:4, 403–51.

Simmons, Beth A. 1994. *Who Adjusts? Domestic Sources of Foreign Economic Policy During the Interwar Years*. Princeton, NJ: Princeton University Press.

Simon, Julian L. 1969. *Basic Research Methods in Social Science*. New York: Random House.

Simons, Helen. 2009. *Case Study Research in Practice*. Thousand Oaks, CA: Sage.

Singh, Prerna. 2015. *How Solidarity Works for Welfare: Subnationalism and Social Development in India*. Cambridge: Cambridge University Press.

Skendaj, Elton. 2014. "International Insulation from Politics and the Challenge of State Building: Learning from Kosovo." *Global Governance* 20, 459–81.

Skocpol, Theda. 1973. "A Critical Review of Barrington Moore's *Social Origins of Dictatorship and Democracy.*" *Politics and Society* 4, 1–34.

1979. *States and Social Revolutions: A Comparative Analysis of France, Russia, and China.* Cambridge: Cambridge University Press.

Skocpol, Theda, Margaret Somers. 1980. "The Uses of Comparative History in Macrosocial Inquiry." *Comparative Studies in Society and History* 22:2, 147–97.

Slater, Dan, Daniel Ziblatt. 2013. "The Enduring Indispensability of the Controlled Comparison." *Comparative Political Studies* 46:10, 1301–27.

Small, Mario Louis. 2009. "How Many Cases Do I Need? On Science and the Logic of Case Selection in Field-Based Research." *Ethnography* 10, 5–38.

Smelser, Neil J. 1973. "The Methodology of Comparative Analysis." In D.P. Warwick, S. Osherson (eds.), *Comparative Research Methods.* Englewood Cliffs, NJ: Prentice Hall, 42–86.

1976. *Comparative Methods in the Social Sciences.* Englewood Cliffs, NJ: Prentice Hall.

Smith, T.V., L.D. White (eds.). 1921. *Chicago: An Experiment in Social Science Research.* Chicago, IL: University of Chicago Press.

Snow, John. 1849. *On the Mode of Communication of Cholera.* London: Churchill.

1855. *On the Mode of Communication of Cholera,* 2nd edn. London: Churchill.

Snyder, Jack, Erica D. Borghard. 2011. "The Cost of Empty Threats: A Penny, Not a Pound." *American Political Science Review* 105, 437–55.

Soifer, Hillel David. 2015. "Shadow Cases in Comparative Research." Unpublished manuscript, Department of Political Science, Temple University.

Sombart, Werner. 1906/1976. *Why Is There No Socialism in the United States?* White Plains, NY: International Arts and Sciences.

Somekh, Bridget, Cathy Lewin, eds. 2005. *Research Methods in the Social Sciences.* Thousand Oaks, CA: Sage.

Sprinz, Detlef F., Yael Wolinsky-Nahmias (eds.). 2004. *Models, Numbers and Cases: Methods for Studying International Relations.* Ann Arbor, MI: University of Michigan.

Srinivasan, T.N., Jagdish Bhagwati. 1999. "Outward-Orientation and Development: Are Revisionists Right?" Discussion Paper no. 806, Economic Growth Center, Yale University.

Stake, Robert E. 1995. *The Art of Case Study Research*. Thousand Oaks, CA: Sage.

2006. *Multiple Case Study Analysis*. New York: Guilford Press.

Stall-Meadows, Celia, Adrienne Hyle. 2010. "Procedural Methodology for a Grounded Meta-Analysis of Qualitative Case Studies." *International Journal of Consumer Studies* 34, 412–18.

Steadman, Dawnie Wolfe. 2002. *Hard Evidence: Case Studies in Forensic Anthropology*. Englewood Cliffs, NJ: Prentice Hall.

Stephens, John. 1979. *The Transition from Capitalism to Socialism*. Urbana, IL: University of Illinois Press.

Stiglitz, Joseph E. 2002. *Globalization and Its Discontents*. New York: Norton.

2005. "The Overselling of Globalization." In Michael M. Weinstein (ed.), *Globalization: What's New?* New York: Columbia University Press, 228–61.

Stoecker, Randy. 1991. "Evaluating and Rethinking the Case Study." *The Sociological Review* 39, 88–112.

Stoker, Laura. 2003. "Is It Possible to Do Quantitative Survey Research in an Interpretive Way?" *Qualitative Methods: Newsletter of the American Political Science Associations Organized Section on Qualitative Methods* 1:2, 13–16.

Stouffer, Samuel A. 1941. "Notes on the Case-Study and the Unique Case." *Sociometry* 4, 349–57.

Stuart, Alan. 1984. *The Ideas of Sampling*. New York: Oxford University Press.

Swanborn, Peter. 2010. *Case Study Research: What, Why, How*. Thousand Oaks, CA: Sage.

"Symposium: Discourse and Content Analysis." 2004. *Qualitative Methods: Newsletter of the American Political Science Association Organized Section on Qualitative Methods* 2:1, 15–39.

"Symposium: Qualitative Comparative Analysis (QCA)." 2004. *Qualitative Methods: Newsletter of the American Political Science Association Organized Section on Qualitative Methods* 1:2.

Tannenwald, Nina. 1999. "The Nuclear Taboo: The United States and the Normative Basis of Nuclear Non-Use." *International Organization* 53:3, 433–68.

2007. *The Nuclear Taboo: The United States and the Non-Use of Nuclear Weapons Since 1945*. Cambridge: Cambridge University Press.

Tarrow, Sidney. 2010. "The Strategy of Paired Comparison: Toward a Theory of Practice." *Comparative Political Studies* 43:2, 230–59.

Taylor, Charles. 1970. "The Explanation of Purposive Behavior." In Robert Borger, Frank Cioffi (eds.), *Explanation in the Behavioral Sciences*. Cambridge: Cambridge University Press.

Taylor, Frederick Winslow. 1911. *The Principles of Scientific Management*. New York: Harper & Brothers.

Teele, Dawn Langan (ed.). 2014. *Field Experiments and Their Critics: Essays on the Uses and Abuses of Experimentation in the Social Sciences*. New Haven: Yale University Press.

Temple, Jonathan. 1999. "The New Growth Evidence." *Journal of Economic Literature* 37, 112–56.

Teorell, Jan. 2010. *Determinants of Democratization: Explaining Regime Change in the World, 1972–2006*. Cambridge: Cambridge University Press.

Tetlock, Philip E., Aaron Belkin (eds.). 1996. *Counterfactual Thought Experiments in World Politics*. Princeton, NJ: Princeton University Press.

Thelen, Kathleen. 2000. "Timing and Temporality in the Analysis of Institutional Evolution and Change." *Studies in American Political Development* 14, 101–8.

Thies, Cameron G. 2002. "A Pragmatic Guide to Qualitative Historical Analysis in the Study of International Relations." *International Studies Perspectives* 3:4, 351–72.

Thies, Michael F. 2001. "Keeping Tabs on Partners: The Logic of Delegation in Coalition Governments." *American Journal of Political Science* 45:3, 580–98.

Thomas, Gary. 2011. *How to Do Your Case Study: A Guide for Students and Researchers*. Thousand Oaks, CA: Sage.

Thomas, Gary, Kevin Myers. 2015. *The Anatomy of the Case Study*. Thousand Oaks, CA: Sage.

Thomas, William Isaac, Florian Znaniecki. 1918. *The Polish Peasant in Europe and America*. Boston: G. Badger.

Thompson, Edward P. 1963. *The Making of the English Working Class*. New York: Vintage Books.

Tilly, Charles. 1964. *The Vendée*. Cambridge, MA: Harvard University Press.
  1984. *Big Structures, Large Processes, Huge Comparisons*. New York: Russell
  Sage Foundation.

Tocqueville, Alexis de. 1997. *Recollections: The French Revolution of 1848*, eds.
  J.P. Mayer and A.P. Kerr. New Brunswick, NJ: Transaction.

Trachtenberg, Marc. 2006. *The Craft of International History: A Guide to
  Method*. Princeton, NJ: Princeton University Press.

Trampusch, Christine, Bruno Palier. 2016. "Between *X* and *Y*: How Process
  Tracing Contributes to Opening the Black Box of Causality." *New
  Political Economy* (forthcoming).

Trochim, W.M.K. 1989. "Outcome Pattern Matching and Program Theory."
  Evaluation and Program Planning, 12, 355–66.

Tsai, Lily. 2007. *Accountability without Democracy: Solidarity Groups and
  Public Goods Provision in Rural China*, Cambridge: Cambridge
  University Press.

Uphoff, Norman. 1992. *Learning from Gal Oya: Possibilities for Participatory
  Development and Post-Newtonian Social Science*. Ithaca: Cornell
  University Press.

Useem, Bert, Jack A. Goldstone. 2002. "Forging Social Order and Its
  Breakdown: Riot and Reform in US Prisons." *American Sociological
  Review* 67:4, 499–525.

Van Evera, Stephen. 1997. *Guide to Methods for Students of Political Science*.
  Ithaca: Cornell University Press.

Vandenbroucke, Jan P. 2001. "In Defense of Case Reports and Case Series."
  Annals of Internal Medicine 134:4, 330–4.

Vaughan, Diane. 1996. *The Challenger Launch Decision: Risky Technology,
  Culture, and Deviance at NASA*. Chicago, IL: University of Chicago
  Press.

Veenendaal, Wouter. 2015. *Politics and Democracy in Microstates*. London:
  Routledge.

Verschuren, Piet J.M. 2001. "Case Study as a Research Strategy: Some
  Ambiguities and Opportunities." *Social Research Methodology* 6:2,
  121–39.

Vinten-Johansen, Peter, Howard Brody, Nigel Paneth, Stephen Rachman,
  Michael Rip. 2003. *Cholera, Chloroform, and the Science of Medicine:
  A Life of John Snow*. Oxford: Oxford University Press.

Vreeland, James Raymond. 2003. *The IMF and Economic Development.* Cambridge: Cambridge University Press.

Wachter, K.W. 1988. "Disturbed about Meta-Analysis?" *Science* 241: 1407–8.

Wade, Robert. 1997. "How Infrastructure Agencies Motivate Staff: Canal Irrigation in India and the Republic of Korea." In A. Mody (ed.), *Infrastructure Strategies in East Asia.* Washington, DC: World Bank, 109–30.

Wahlke, John C. 1979. "Pre-Behavioralism in Political Science." *American Political Science Review* 73:1, 9–31.

Waldner, David. 2012. "Process Tracing and Causal Mechanisms." In Harold Kincaid (ed.), *Oxford Handbook of Philosophy of Social Science.* Oxford: Oxford University Press, 65–84.

  2015a. "Process Tracing and Qualitative Causal Inference." *Security Studies* 24:2, 239–50.

  2015b. "What Makes Process Tracing Good? Causal Mechanisms, Causal Inference, and the Completeness Standard in Comparative Politics." In Andrew Bennett, Jeffrey T. Checkel (eds.), *Process Tracing: From Metaphor to Analytic Tool.* Cambridge: Cambridge University Press, 126–52.

  2016. "Aspirin, Aeschylus, and the Foundations of Qualitative Causal Inference." Unpublished manuscript, Department of Politics, University of Virginia.

Waller, Willard. 1934. "Insight and Scientific Method." *American Journal of Sociology* 40:3, 285–97.

Wallerstein, Immanuel. 1974. *The Modern World-System. Capitalist Agriculture and the Origins of the European World Economy in the Sixteenth Century.* New York: Academic Press.

Walter, Barbara. 2002. *Committing to Peace: The Successful Settlement of Civil Wars.* Princeton, NJ: Princeton University Press.

Ward, Michael D., Kristin Bakke. 2005. "Predicting Civil Conflicts: On the Utility of Empirical Research." Presented at the Conference on Disaggregating the Study of Civil War and Transnational Violence, University of California Institute of Global Conflict and Cooperation, San Diego, CA (March 7–8).

Warner, W. Lloyd, Paul S. Lunt. 1941. *Yankee City*, vols. I–V. New Haven: Yale University Press.

Weber, Eugen. 1979. *Peasants into Frenchmen: The Modernization of Rural France.* Stanford, CA: Stanford University Press.

Weber, Max. 1904–5/1958. *The Protestant Ethic and the Spirit of Capitalism*. New York: Charles Scribner's.

1968. *Economy and Society*, Guenther Roth, Claus Wittich (trans). Berkeley, CA: University of California Press.

Wedding, Danny, Raymond J. Corsini. 2013. *Case Studies in Psychotherapy*, 7th edn. Brooks/Cole.

Wedeen, Lisa. 2003. "Seeing Like a Citizen, Acting Like a State: Exemplary Events in Unified Yemen." *Society for Comparative Study of Society and History* 45, 680–713.

Weinstein, Jeremy. 2007. *Inside Rebellion: The Politics of Insurgent Violence*. Cambridge: Cambridge University Press.

Weller, Nicholas, Jeb Barnes. 2014. *Finding Pathways: Mixed-Method Research for Studying Causal Mechanisms*. Cambridge: Cambridge University Press.

Whyte, William Foote. 1943/1955. *Street Corner Society: The Social Structure of an Italian Slum*. Chicago, IL: University of Chicago Press.

Wiley, Norbert. 1988. "The Micro-Macro Problem in Social Theory." *Sociological Theory* 6:2, 254–61.

Wilson, Woodrow. 1889. *The State: Elements of Historical and Practical Politics*. Boston, MA: D.C. Heath & Co.

Winks, Robin W. (ed.). 1969. *The Historian as Detective: Essays on Evidence*. New York: Harper & Row.

Wirth, Louis. 1928. *The Ghetto*. Chicago: Phoenix.

Wolin, Sheldon S. 1968. "Paradigms and Political Theories." In Preston King, B.C. Parekh (eds.), *Politics and Experience*. Cambridge: Cambridge University Press.

Wood, Elisabeth Jean. 2000. *Forging Democracy from Below: Insurgent Transitions in South Africa and El Salvador*. Cambridge: Cambridge University Press.

Woodside, Arch G. 2010. *Case Study Research: Theory, Methods and Practice*. Bingley, UK: Emerald.

Woodside, Arch G., Elizabeth J. Wilson. 2003. "Case Study Research Methods for Theory Building." *Journal of Business and Industrial Marketing* 18:6/7, 493–508.

Woodward, James. 2005. *Making Things Happen: A Theory of Causal Explanation*. Oxford: Oxford University Press.

World Bank. 2003. *World Development Indicators 2003*. Washington, DC: World Bank.

Yashar, Deborah J. 2005. *Contesting Citizenship in Latin America: The Rise of Indigenous Movements and the Postliberal Challenge.* Cambridge: Cambridge University Press.

Yin, Robert K. 2004. *Case Study Anthology.* Thousand Oaks, CA: Sage.

2009. *Case Study Research: Design and Methods*, 4th edn. Thousand Oaks, CA: Sage.

Young, Oran R. (ed.). 1999. *The Effectiveness of International Environmental Regimes: Causal Connections and Behavioral Mechanisms.* Cambridge, MA: MIT Press.

Zeldin, Theodore. 1973–1977. *History of French Passions (5 volumes: Ambition and Love, Intellect and Pride, Taste and Corruption, Politics and Anger, Anxiety and Hypocrisy).* Oxford: Clarendon Press.

Ziblatt, Daniel. 2004. "Rethinking the Origins of Federalism: Puzzle, Theory, and Evidence from Nineteenth-Century Europe." *World Politics* 57, 70–98.

2008. *Structuring the State: The Formation of Italy and Germany and the Puzzle of Federalism.* Cambridge: Cambridge University Press.

Zimmer, Shanta M., Donald S. Burke. 2009. "Historical Perspective – Emergence of Influenza A (H1N1) Viruses." *New England Journal of Medicine* 361, 279–85.

Znaniecki, Florian. 1934. *The Method of Sociology.* New York: Rinehart.

Index